WITHDRAWN

PLANNING FOR DIVERSITY
AND CHOICE

Possible Futures and Their Relations to the Man-Controlled Environment

Documentation of a conference held at Endicott House, Dedham, Massachusetts, October 13–16, 1966, under the sponsorship of The Graham Foundation for Advanced Studies in the Fine Arts, the American Institute of Architects–Princeton Educational Research Project, and the Department of Architecture, Massachusetts Institute of Technology.

301.34
P693

PLANNING FOR DIVERSITY AND CHOICE

Possible Futures and Their Relations to the Man-Controlled Environment

edited by
Stanford Anderson

THE M.I.T. PRESS
Massachusetts Institute of Technology
Cambridge, Massachusetts

Copyright © 1968 by
The Massachusetts Institute of Technology

Set in Linotype Caledonia
and printed by The Heffernan Press.
Bound in the United States of America by The Colonial Press, Inc.

All rights reserved. No part of this book may be
reproduced or utilized in any form or by any means,
electronic or mechanical, including photocopying,
recording, or by any information storage and retrieval
system, without permission in writing from the publisher.

Library of Congress catalog card number: 68-14458

Acknowledgments

Many friends and new acquaintances gave generously of their time during the planning stages of this conference; only a few can be singled out for special mention. Professor Bruce Mazlish was a constant source of good advice. M. Bernard Cazes brought to my attention several persons and groups who made significant contributions. Professor Joseph Agassi was also generous in his consultation; it was regrettable that his absence from the country precluded his participation at the conference. Dean Lawrence B. Anderson has been constant in his support of the conference.

It is especially important to acknowledge the contributions of those who took part in the conference. Not only did their intellect, time, and energy provide the substance of the meetings, but many of them contributed their travel expenses as well.

The secretaries of the Department of Architecture of the Massachusetts Institute of Technology have been unfailing in their aid. These include the secretary to Dean Lawrence B. Anderson, Miss Anne Shepley, and the departmental secretary, Mrs. Nancy Jones. Miss Lawrie Ryerson not only carried most of the burdens prior to the conference but also contributed her unfailing charm and helpfulness to the sessions at the conference.

Endicott House provided a sustaining, yet relaxed atmosphere under the direction of Mrs. Gertrude Winquist. Mr. Harold T. Mc-Neil and his associates produced the first transcript.

I owe thanks to two people in the preparation of the final manuscript. Mrs. Benita Eisler kindly translated the paper of Bernard Cazes. My secretary, Miss Katherine Stillman, has dauntlessly carried out editorial work and the innumerable other operations involved in the completion of a manuscript.

We are grateful for the generous support of the Graham Foundation for Advanced Studies in the Fine Arts, the American Institute of Architects–Princeton University Educational Research Project, and the Department of Architecture of the Massachusetts Institute of Technology.

STANFORD ANDERSON

Cambridge, Massachusetts
August 1967

CAT Mar 26 '73

Feb 27 '73   Gift

198090

v

List of Contributors

STANFORD ANDERSON, Assistant Professor in the Department of Architecture, Massachusetts Institute of Technology, Cambridge, Massachusetts. His professional degree is from the University of California at Berkeley, and he is currently a doctoral candidate at Columbia University. With Henry A. Millon, he is writing a book on architecture in the United States since the Second World War.

HAROLD J. BARNETT, Chairman of the Department of Economics, Washington University, St. Louis, Missouri. He holds the degree of Ph.D. from Harvard University. His most recent publication, in collaboration with Chandler Morse, is *Scarcity and Growth: The Economics of Natural Resource Availability.*

RAYMOND A. BAUER, a social psychologist and Professor in the Harvard Graduate School of Business Administration, Allston, Massachusetts. He holds the degree of Ph.D. from Harvard University. His most recent publication, written with Albert D. Biderman, Bertram M. Gross, Robert S. Weiss, and Robert A. Rosenthal, is *Social Indicators.*

BERNARD CAZES, a long-range planner in the 1985 Group of the Commissariat Général du Plan d'Équipment et de la Productivité, Paris. He has studied at Bordeaux and at the École Nationale d'Administration. He has recently published *La Planification en France et le IVe Plan.*

MELVIN CHARNEY, Associate Professor at the École d'Architecture, Université de Montréal, Montreal, Quebec, Canada. He holds the degrees of B.Arch. from McGill University,

Montreal, and M.Arch. from Yale University, New Haven. He has recently edited a special issue of *Parallel* (Montreal, February–March 1967) on the theme "Urbland 2000."

PAUL DAVIDOFF, Professor of Urban Planning, Director of Urban Planning Program, and Director of Urban Research Center of Hunter College of the City University of New York. He holds the degrees of LL.B. and M.C.P. from the University of Pennsylvania, Philadelphia. He has recently published "Advocacy and Pluralism in Planning" in the *Journal of the American Institute of Planners* (November 1965).

LEONARD J. DUHL, Special Assistant to the Secretary, Department of Housing and Urban Development, Washington, D.C. He holds an A.B. from Columbia University and an M.D. from Albany Medical College. His book *The Urban Condition: People and Policy in the Metropolis* was published in 1963.

LEONARD J. FEIN, Assistant Professor, Department of Political Science, Massachusetts Institute of Technology, Cambridge, Massachusetts. He holds the degrees of M.A. from the University of Chicago and Ph.D. from Michigan State University. He is the editor of *American Democracy: Essays on Image and Realities.*

PAUL K. FEYERABEND, Professor of Philosophy, University of California, Berkeley. He has a doctoral degree from the University of Vienna, Austria. Among numerous publications is his *Knowledge without Foundations.*

I. C. JARVIE, Associate Professor of Philosophy, York University, Toronto, Ontario. He holds the degrees of B.Sc. and Ph.D. from the London School of Economics, England. He has recently published *The Revolution in Anthropology.*

ROBERT JUNGK, Codirector of the *Institut für Zukunftsfragen,* Vienna, Austria. He has studied in Paris, London, and Zurich and holds the Ph.D. degree. He has written *Brighter than a Thousand Suns* and *Die Grosse Maschine.*

BRUCE MAZLISH, Professor of History, Massachusetts Institute of Technology, Cambridge, Massachusetts. He received the M.A. and Ph.D. degrees from Columbia University. He recently published *The Riddle of History: Studies in the Philosophy of History from Descartes to Freud.*

HERBERT MOLLER, Professor of History, Boston University. He studied history and sociology at the universities of Heidelberg, Berlin, and Frankfurt. He received his Ph.D. from Boston University. He is editor and coauthor of *Population Movements in Modern European History.*

HASAN OZBEKHAN, Director of Planning at System Development Corporation, Santa Monica, California. He received his B.Sc. degree from the London School of Economics, England. He has studied law and political science at the University of Paris, France. A recent publication is his SDC report *Technology and Man's Future.*

CEDRIC PRICE, architect in London. He holds an M.A. from Cambridge University and an architectural degree from the Architectural Association in London. His work and his thought have been regularly presented in *Archigram.*

PARDON E. TILLINGHAST, Chairman of the Department of History, Middlebury College, Middlebury, Vermont. He holds the degrees of M.A. and Ph.D. from Harvard University. He has recently published *Approaches to History: Selections in the Philosophy of History from the Greeks to Hegel.*

MARX W. WARTOFSKY, Professor of Philosophy, Boston University; Director, Boston Colloquium for the Philosophy of Science. He holds the B.A., A.M., and Ph.D. degrees from Columbia University. He is the author of *Conceptual Foundations of Scientific Thought.*

Chairmen for Conference Sessions

All chairmen are members of the faculty of the Massachusetts Institute of Technology

LAWRENCE B. ANDERSON, Professor of Architecture; Acting Head of the Department; Dean of the School of Architecture and Planning

GERALD B. DWORKIN, Assistant Professor of Philosophy

CHARLES P. KINDLEBERGER, Professor of Economics; Chairman of the Faculty

HENRY A. MILLON, Associate Professor of the History of Architecture

JOHN R. MYER, Associate Professor of Architecture

Participants in Conference Discussions

MYRON B. BLOY, JR., Director of the Church Society for College Work, Cambridge, Massachusetts

CARROLL G. BOWEN, Director of The M.I.T. Press, Cambridge, Massachusetts

DAVID B. CHASE, Department of Civil History, Smithsonian Institution, Washington, D.C.

JOHN W. DYCKMAN, Professor in the Department of City and Regional Planning, University of California, Berkeley

AARON FLEISHER, Associate Professor of Urban and Regional Planning, M.I.T.

BERNARD J. FRIEDEN, Associate Professor of City Planning, M.I.T.

ROBERT L. GEDDES, Dean of the School of Architecture, Princeton University

ROBERT GOODMAN, Assistant Professor of Architecture, M.I.T.

SAMUEL T. HURST, Dean of the School of Architecture and Fine Arts, University of Southern California, Los Angeles

EUGENE J. MACKEY, Murphy and Mackey, Architects, St. Louis, Missouri

OSCAR NEWMAN, Associate Professor of Architecture, Washington University, St. Louis, Missouri

WILLIAM W. SEIFERT, Assistant Dean, School of Engineering, Massachusetts Institute of Technology

BERNARD SPRING, Senior Research Architect, Princeton University

JOHN VOSS, American Academy of Arts and Sciences, Brookline, Massachusetts

JAMES WELLESLEY-WESLEY, Corresponding Secretary, Mankind 2000 Preparatory International Secretariat, London, England

RICHARD WHITAKER, Director of Committee on Education, American Institute of Architects, Washington, D.C.

Contents

x

xi

CONTENTS

PLANNING FOR DIVERSITY
AND CHOICE

Possible Futures and Their Relations
to the Man-Controlled Environment

Introduction

STANFORD ANDERSON

In this book, the changing patterns of man's control of his environment are examined by government planners of different professional backgrounds, by "futurists," economists, historians, city planners, political scientists, planning theorists, philosophers, and architects. The broad relevance of their thought contributes to, but also transcends, the narrower disciplinary intent of this work.

The original intent of these studies, which were presented at a conference held at the Massachusetts Institute of Technology in October 1966,[1] was to provide information and opinion for an American Institute of Architects–Princeton University research project concerned with the improvement of architectural education in the United States. A parallel conference on the impact of emerging technologies on man's control of his environment was held at Washington University, St. Louis. This explains the absence of technologists from the present volume. It will be clear from the papers that none of the contributors considers technology separable from his concerns; however, the very wealth of technological alternatives may support, as something more than an arbitrary division of energies, the separate examination of methodological and normative questions.

[1] The conference title was "Inventing the Future Environment." This publication varies from the conference program in the following respects: the paper of one contributor has been omitted; Professor Feyerabend's essay, my "Summary," and Charney's Postscript have been added; all papers and discussions have been edited; section headings and the arrangement of parts have been changed in the interest of better conformity with the content.

By "introduction," one might mean either the original charge to the conference participants or a summary and interpretation of the content of the meetings. In the temporal manner of the conference, I have chosen to place a summary of the proceedings toward the end of the book. What follows here is the introduction that was offered at the beginning of the conference sessions.

The wide diversity of participants in this conference is assurance that we shall take a direction different from any that was anticipated; however, it is only fair that we put forward some of the thoughts that guided our planning.

The conference is frankly weighted toward those people who are concerned with the multiple possibilities before man — not toward those who would prophesy the future nor even toward those who find satisfaction in projecting the most probable future. I shall briefly consider this orientation as it relates to architecture and to this conference. As one part of a study of architectural education, we have been charged to explore "the societal context within which architects will work in the near future."

On the face of it, this is a doubly impossible task. To elucidate the societal context of the present or past is already more than scientists and scholars can achieve satisfactorily. To attempt this for the future may well sound like folly.

Nevertheless, the work of even those architects and planners who are most concerned with designing for change sets certain constraints on the near future. Even the creation of a physical structure that was self-adapting and always in perfect harmony with rapidly changing needs would be to participate in an attitude about the future. This would be the attitude that there is nothing in society that deserves any degree of permanence — nothing that should control or brake or test possible changes.

Furthermore, any of the more radical proposals for architecture or planning are prefaced by, or embody, certain fragments of theories about the future condition of society. These fragments may include such concepts as population explosion, increase in scarcity of materials, obsolescence and conspicuous consumption, changing patterns of transportation and communication, or the appearance of a leisure class that has a democratic majority.

To state the problem more briefly, architects and planners have been frustrated by the recognition that their work does have an effect on the future, by a consequent feeling that they must be responsible to the future, and by the disconcerting admission that they do not know the future.

Planners, and perhaps architects especially, have not responded well to this problem of having to act in an incompletely defined situation. Worried by the uncertainties of that problem, they have sought to find some way to justify themselves. This could be done by assuming that the physical environment shaped by the architect is the independent variable; the architect could then propose the ideal city that would replace cities as we have known them. Once established, these ideal cities would naturally channel mankind into the good life. For this the architect had to assume a knowledge of both the good life and how this good life is formed by the physical environment. Though never fully carried through, these ideal cities have provided a justificational image for architectural and planning acts that have contributed to the shape of the environment in which we live.

This prophetic and then authoritarian stance of the architect-planner was easy to comprehend and therefore easy to teach. The student was to accept the word of an elder prophet or else to make his own prophecy. Then, if the state, the city, or the client would only grant the architect the authority he so obviously deserved, the systematic deductions from the prophecy could be thrust upon the chaos of the existing environment.

However, the architect has slowly been forced to acknowledge that in most cases he does not act upon the environment unilaterally and that when he has approximated total control of the environment, the life of the community has far too often been as bad or worse than before. The image of the architect as the great social prophet has lost whatever credibility it may once have had.

Since that presumptive role has not been thrust upon any other group either, and since the results of the prophetic method have been highly questionable, the present conference does not attempt to achieve a new and better prophecy of a future society or a future architecture. Rather, we seek a more viable methodology for achitecture.

The more modest architects and planners — including, among others, those who are modest owing to lack of imagination — have felt that one could know only the immediate problem at hand and that consequently the only justifiable position was to be pragmatic about each problem as it arose.

Other architects have taken various nihilistic attitudes toward the problem. Recognizing that one cannot know the future, or how to make the future through architecture, or even all of the aspects and implications of a very limited and specific problem, some architects have concluded that everything is relative and therefore anything goes. Still other architects have agreed about this inability to know but have argued from this that one must therefore achieve the universally flexible, ever efficient, and never abrasive physical environment. This sounds much more socially responsible and, as an ideal behind action, might have its benefits. However, even if the ideal of total efficiency could be achieved, the concept does suggest a bland, rather than a complementary, experience of our environment.

With regard to the changing context of architecture, those attitudes that emphasize pragmatism, relativism, or universalism are either indifferent to or, at most, rely upon the continuation of trends, extrapolations from "hard" data, or probability studies. Such reliance upon the situation of the moment or on the situation of the moment viewed as a point in a continuation from the past into the future has also come to appear as an inadequate basis for architectural thought and practice. There are aspects of situations which are discontinuous or changes of scale and rates of change which cannot be accounted for in the immediate situation alone, nor even in projections or extrapolations. Consequently, the present conference engages people and ideas that go beyond trending.

I claim that the architect's problem is not how to found his knowledge positively but how to make his knowledge grow. Happily, such growth is best fostered by attending to both the general and the specific, by thinking about and adjusting one's understanding of both the context and the specific architectural act.

To grow in such knowledge requires the invention of possibilities and of possible futures. This need for a multiplicity of invention can be met only by imagination beyond that of the prophet; it calls for the creativity of a brilliant utopian. But to test such images or insights, there must also be a strong evaluative and critical faculty.

Critical utopianism, which I. C. Jarvie discusses in his essay, requires the invention and testing of multiple possible futures for an evolving, pluralistic society. This would be an intellectual and operational adventure of the first rank. Both idealist and inductivist theories are inadequate bases for the requisite adventurous confrontation of imagination and criticism. Not only the traditional theories behind architectural practice but also the traditional views of science and technology have tended to deny this spirit of creative adventure.

In the present conference, we have taken several approaches to the future and to ways of looking at the future. However, an underlying question of the entire conference would be: Is there an emerging theory of knowledge, and perhaps also an emerging technique of information handling, that will encourage a critical utopianism within a pluralistic society? In other words, is there a critical utopianism that would involve the creative imagining of possible futures, their critical evaluation, and an open-ended and flexible implementation of those possibilities which are most resistant to criticism?

Utopian Thinking and the Architect*

I. C. JARVIE

I

The problem I want to discuss might be put, first of all, like this: How can architects and planners build for the future when they happen to be imprisoned — for lack of what H. G. Wells would call a "time machine" — in the present? The future is open; we do not know what it will bring. Yet, "planners have to imagine the future as a matter of routine. Whether you are building a motorway, a chemical works or a school, you are making a forecast of the continuing need for such a thing over its economic life."[1]

What planners and builders do now will frame the future. How *can* they plan and build rationally and responsibly in the face of a total ignorance about what is to come? The answer I shall try to develop is that we can explore the future in our creative imaginations and subject our ideas to severe criticism and evaluation. Pentagon officials call it "contingency planning." They try to conceive of every possible situation that could arise and plan what they would do. The plans are not really there to be acted upon but constitute a library of ideas some of which may be useful. Also it is felt that we can better face situations that we have, in part, anticipated and thought through or, at least, trained ourselves to think about.

* Professor Jarvie's lecture was preceded by a showing of H. G. Wells's movie *Things to Come* (1966 was the centenary of Wells's birth and the thirtieth anniversary of this film).

[1] Nigel Calder, "Wells and the Future," *New Statesman*, Vol. 72, No. 1854, p. 427.

8

It follows from my thesis that it would be both irrational and irresponsible for planners and architects to avoid such critical dreaming about the future and its possibilities.

It is a corollary of my thesis that such speculative thinking should be as bold and extreme as possible, that tentativity in this part of the endeavor will defeat its object. Similarly, timidity in criticism will render it useless.

My strategy in arguing these points will be first to consider the question of ignorance, mistakes, and responsibilities and then to tackle some possible objections to the program of critical speculation. This will bring me to Wells's film, from which I shall try to draw some material to illustrate the argument.

II

When a philosopher of science finds himself invited to give the opening address at a conference organized by planners and architects, it is not unreasonable for him to suspect that what is expected of him is a sermon. Philosophy is often conceived of by nonphilosophers (not to mention some philosophers) as a rather vague and general subject, and philosophers consequently are thought to be good at giving vague and rather general advice. If you are a philosopher of science, the only difference is that the sermon is supposed to be about methodology. It doesn't take a philosophical training to know that it is best to get sermons over first. Since I see sermonizing as what sociologists call my "ascribed role," and since I have decided to play the role to the full, I need two things. The first is a text; the second, a salutary example.

For my example I shall take H. G. Wells's ideas as realized in William Cameron Manzies' film *Things to Come*, 1936. This is perhaps especially appropriate in the year of Wells's centenary, Wells being an author who constantly tried to get us to take the problem of the future seriously. As my text I shall take — not something biblical, although perhaps almost as well-worn — a corny joke:

Question: What is the difference between a doctor and an architect?
Answer: The doctor can bury his mistakes, but the architect has to live with his.

9

The first thing to do with a text is to analyze it; analysis will ruin any joke, but that hardly matters if the joke wasn't much good to start with.[2] However, the joke may be instructive. What interpretations can be put on a joke that says doctors can bury their mistakes but architects cannot?

It is undoubtedly a cynical joke, whichever way you look at it. One implication is clear: we all make mistakes — doctors, architects, everybody; the problem is that of getting away with them. There is also a hint that these mistakes will be painful or damaging. They may cause us embarrassment. The doctor can try to forget — "out of sight, out of mind"; the architect is not allowed to forget, and he must suffer.

The joke could be read as congratulating the doctors, who, because they can hide their mistakes, need not worry about them. Those responsible can forget, for the public has no means of discovering who is responsible. If the public did know, of course, they would hold doctors responsible, just as doctors hold themselves responsible. Why else, after all, do they try to forget, to bury, to repress unpleasant thoughts?

But does not the joke conceal an even more cynical message: that you need not take responsibility for your mistakes if you can conceal your connection with them and the damage they do? Does not the joke hint that architects must be especially circumspect merely because their responsibility is clear for all to see? And is not this view cynical? Responsibility for damage is being equated with identifiable responsibility.

Even the meagerest text can bear a great amount of interpretation, some of it not altogether consistent. There is one other idea concealed in the use in my text of the word "mistake" which I would like to analyze, and this is that we are in some sense responsible for our mistakes. Yet at the same time the joke says we all, doctors and architects, do make mistakes. This strikes me as very peculiar. One would agree that we can have the responsibility

[2] For examples of corny jokes and of good jokes ruined by analysis see Sigmund Freud, *The Psychopathology of Everyday Life*, Standard Edition of the Complete Works (London: Hogarth Press, 1960), Vol. 6, pp. 77 ff., and *Jokes and Their Relation to the Unconscious*, Standard Edition, Vol. 8, pp. 16 ff.; see also A. Koestler, *The Act of Creation* (London and New York: Macmillan, 1964), especially pp. 32 ff.

not to make mistakes, but to say we shall inevitably make them *and* that we should feel responsible for them is harsh doctrine, indeed. In going wrong we show our imperfections, our inability to meet our ideals; and even before we say anything or have any ideals, we are tainted by this proneness to be mistaken. The view is a variant, perhaps, of the doctrine of original sin.[3]

Leaving the joke aside, can we make sense of the problem of mistakes and responsibility? It is true that we are fallible creatures and shall make mistakes. Perhaps even more discouraging, Xenophanes was probably right when he said that even if we were in possession of the truth, there is no reason to believe we should be aware of it.[4] Consequently, we might expect all our endeavors, including our attempts to look into the future, to go awry. But if whatever we do will turn out to be mistaken, where does our responsibility lie? It can't lie in the responsibility not to be mistaken. Sir Karl Popper, in *The Open Society and Its Enemies* and elsewhere, has suggested that our responsibility is to minimize our mistakes by being severely critical of our ideas.[5] That is our responsibility. It is this suggestion of Popper's that I wish to ponder and develop in the rest of this essay.

I shall proceed by examining four critical arguments which are directed against utopian thinking in general and which I can also use to expand on what I mean by critical utopianism. These criticisms are, first, that the future is unknown, so thinking about it is futile; second, that utopias are remote possibilities, and we might do better to concentrate on the available data and the trends they reveal; third, that utopias will trap us, morally and

[3] Cf. Ernest Gellner, "On Being Wrong," *The Rationalist Annual* (London, 1957).

[4] The fragment is translated in G. S. Kirk and J. E. Raven, *The Presocratic Philosophers* (Cambridge, England: Cambridge University Press, 1957), Fragment 189 at p. 179. Compare the translations of the same fragment by J. Burnet, *Early Greek Philosophy*, 4th ed. (London: A. & C. Black, 1930), Fragment 34 at p. 121, and W. C. Guthrie, *A History of Greek Philosophy*, Vol. 1 (Cambridge, England: Cambridge University Press, 1962), Fragment 34 at p. 395.

[5] See K. R. Popper, *The Open Society and Its Enemies*, 4th ed. (London: Routledge & Kegan Paul, 1962), *passim*, and *Conjectures and Refutations* (London: Routledge & Kegan Paul, 1963), especially the introductory chapter and Chapter 1.

imaginatively, so they are to be avoided; and fourth, that utopias are produced by a selective and dogmatic imagination, and one could as easily show them to be antiutopian hells.

III

There can be no doubt that the future is open. Popper again has constructed a decisive argument to show that since what happens next is dependent on our future state of knowledge, and since our future state of knowledge is, in principle, unpredictable,[6] the future is, in principle, unpredictable.[7] Does it follow from this argument that all utopian thinking is useless and futile? This depends, I think, very much on the aim of the utopian thinking. If the aim of the utopian is to know the future, then I think Popper's argument is a knockdown winner. He constructed it to attack doctrines of historical inevitability which claimed to predict the future. But what if the aim of writing about or designing utopia is to tax our imaginations to their limit in order to maximize the choices available to planners, increase our creative freedom, anticipate, however imperfectly, some of our coming problems? Then I think Popper's argument is salutary but not destructive.

Take as an example Plato's *Republic*. There is some doubt about his aim in writing it. It may[8] or may not[9] have described a state of affairs Plato wanted to see actualized. Whatever his intentions, however, he threw into focus some very interesting

6 Perhaps it is worth making a distinction here. Of course, there is a sense in which we can say that when a successful soft landing on the moon is achieved, we shall know what the composition of its surface is. We can predict that we shall then know a certain fact. We cannot know the content of this prediction; we can only guess. If we could predict what theory will come to replace relativity in due course, we should not need to wait for due course but could move on to it now.

7 K. R. Popper, *The Poverty of Historicism* (Boston: Beacon, 1957), pp. ix-xi.

8 For the view that *The Republic* is a utopia see Vol. 1 of Popper, *The Open Society, op. cit.*

9 Northrop Frye argues that *The Republic* "is not a dream to be realized in practice; it is an informing power of the mind." See his "Varieties of Literary Utopias" in F. E. Manuel, ed., *Utopias and Utopian Thought* (Boston: Houghton Mifflin, 1966), p. 34.

sociopolitical problems: for example, that the main problem of a stratified society is strictly to control mobility, or otherwise its structure will be undermined; or that the main problem of politics is "who rules the rulers?" These by-products of Plato's dream of a utopia have been of the greatest value to all later discussions. One of the disappointing aspects of the H. G. Wells film on utopia, which I shall come to presently, is that he raises almost no problems with which the future will have to grapple. There is very little by-product from his exercise. This is a general fault of uncritical utopianism, although the film is not entirely uncritical.

Northrop Frye[10] has drawn attention to a passage in which the utopian John MacNie[11] in 1883 foresaw not only that travel would be by horseless carriage but also that traffic problems would arise, and he suggested in 1883 that these be resolved by drawing a white line down the center of the road and making it a rule that traffic stays on the left except when overtaking. That sort of thinking-through as a by-product of utopianism is very impressive. It takes relatively little imagination to see that the problems of sprawling urban areas or of population increase could become quite serious in the near future. It takes only a little more imagination to pursue some possible solutions and find out the sort of further problems which will be generated. Indeed, it would seem to be the duty of any planner or reformer to do this and to try to think out all the consequences of any change. Unless we try to do this, it seems to me that we are acting irresponsibly in seriously proposing that such solutions be adopted.

A solution to the size problems of urban sprawl might be rapid transit. I hear that at M.I.T. they have gone so far in such studies that in some systems passengers would have to be anesthetized. Another solution might be higher and higher buildings, allowing existing urban areas to be frozen at their present size, thus halting the sprawl. But this again would depend on improving and expanding transit systems and on people finding high-rise living congenial. Much thinking along these lines has contemplated community centers among the high-rise buildings to take pres-

[10] Frye, *op. cit.*, pp. 30–31.
[11] John MacNie, *The Diothas* (London, 1883).

sure off the transportation system. But, of course, the magic of London and New York and Paris is the amenities of their centers, which disappear with decentralization. These amenities are economical only because of the massive support they suck into the city, and they are supported massively only because they are so conveniently close to each other — many choices are available in a small area. As education advances, more and more people want to be near these amenities, and the cost of expanding them increases. So community centers are no solution, and at this point I break down, because I don't see any solution to this particular problem.

Now, to come directly to architecture. When British planners are given, as they just have been, the prospect of creating three new towns for perhaps a million people each, they cannot really be allowed to get away with such slogans as trying to merge "the visual delights of the village with the economic and social benefits of largeness."[12]

The same author goes on to say, in self-contradiction, "it is impossible to build a city without a clear view of the society that will live in it." A community of farmers will center on a market, whereas seamen will live where ships can dock. According to this same writer, two main suggestions to be taken into account in building such a future community have been put forward. One suggestion is that you start with transport and work outward in the planning; the other is that you start with buildings and a balance of concrete and green. Are these really premises from which to build "cities for the next millennium"? Consider the following questions: Who can predict that the separation of work and home will go on into the next millennium? Who can say whether permanently located cities will continue to be the only way to house large numbers of people? Are planners really planning for choice, or do they intend simply to offer people much the same in these new towns as they have already — with a few improvements in the way of essentials of life? I am making a very general point: not simply that portable or disposable buildings ought to be considered, but that the planner is being forced to

12 Terence Bendixson, "Cities for the Next Millennium," *The Spectator*, Vol. 217, No. 7201 (July 1, 1966), p. 15.

arrogate to himself the role of creative — or uncreative — anthropologist.

The plans of the planners will mold the lives of men. Towns and buildings are, above all, places where people live and have their being. A new city will both positively and negatively constrain the lives of its citizens, just as unplanned New York and London force large numbers of their work force to commute. If a planner does not think about the limitations he is placing on the choices open to the future society that his plans will create, then he is not doing his job in a critical manner. He is becoming that most dreadful of things, a utopian planner remaking the world to his blueprint; he is not building cities fit to live in, but challenging people to be fit to live in his cities.

Yet of a creative anthropologist we should demand at least, it seems to me, a profound understanding of his own society, as well as a respect for it and its members and their way of life. Then he will not tamper with it lightly and certainly not undemocratically. Simultaneously, I plead for architects and planners to be bolder and freer in thinking through their ideas yet more constrained in carrying them out — for them not to be allowed to influence our lives by fiat, without letting us have any say in the decision. Planners' plans are, it seems to me, far too conservative — from Nikita Khrushchev's drab dream of Russia in 1980 to the rather dreary so-called "new towns" scattered around the British Isles. This is a reason why we should not allow any more of them to be imposed upon us, for they reduce our choice and are in that way a form of dictatorship. Certainly, then, thinking about utopia is not futile.

IV

This brings me to the second criticism of utopianism that might be put forward: namely, that it is far too fanciful, too up-in-the-air. Neither the feasibility nor the likelihood of the plans is known. But one thing surely *is* known: utopia will cost a lot, take a long time, and cause much social upheaval. The only rational course for those burdened with the responsibility for planning is to focus on present trends and tendencies, collect data, and from them estimate the probabilities of this or that happening (on computers perhaps), and plan accordingly.

In fact, once we have isolated the data and sorted out the trends, the environment will, so to speak, design itself — rationalization and cost analysis will point to a definite solution.

It is not possible to challenge the contentions that utopias are fanciful, possibly not feasible, possibly expensive, time-consuming, and disturbing. It does not follow from this that hardheaded data collection or trend projection is the only rational course of action. It is neither rational in and of itself, nor is it in any way realistic. Indeed, it is another form of speculation.

Take the *non sequitur* first. However fanciful and incredible utopian thinking has been, later generations have laughed at ideas they find prosaic. Many, many things that are part and parcel of our daily lives now — like electricity, jet travel, and, of course, moon travel — were once incredibly fanciful speculations, thought to be impossibly expensive, disruptive, and not very likely. Thus what we now regard as fanciful may tomorrow be ordinary, and therefore fancifulness is no criticism of thinking about the future.

Moreover, the hardheaded approach contrives to substitute something equally fanciful: namely, the hypothesis that things will go as they now seem likely to go. The *hubris*, not to say the historicism, of this assumption is considerable. Are we now such gods that we can tell which of the many possibilities in our society will be the ones that are going to grow stronger? No, but don't data and computers surely help us? This reply is nothing but mystification with science. Data must be selected and collected and computers programmed to produce the results wanted. The whole exercise is only an elaborate way of dressing up what you already believe. There isn't a trend or tendency that can't be reversed, and there is no reason whatever for believing it won't be. There is no way of estimating probabilities in this matter.[13]

As to the environment doing anything even remotely like "designing itself," I find it difficult to settle on an argument to contest

---

13 This is a "controversial" issue, of course, but I think the arguments are decisive. See K. R. Popper, *The Logic of Scientific Discovery* (London: Hutchinson, 1959), and the various discussions of probability therein.

it. It is not necessary to argue that there is an enormous area of choice in architecture and planning at any stage — that decisions will never make themselves. If efficiency is proposed as a guide in making a choice, it would not be hard to show that efficiency itself is a very problematic idea and that even such a highly sophisticated treatment as *The Statistics of Extremes,* by Emil J. Gumbel, shows clearly that although you can make certain efficient decisions with the help of statistics, there is still a very large and quite unavoidable area of free choice. This crushes the idea that the environment can plan itself, even in terms of efficiency. Anyway, planning is not really about efficiency or solely about efficiency; it is about freedom, and it is about flexibility and the maximization of both. There are no "data," no clear-cut choices. There are people who have different ways of life. There are the decisions they are prepared to make.

If the hardheaded critic is merely saying that we should beware of fanciful solutions to our problems and proceed piecemeal in our actual building rather than our thinking, then, of course, he has a point. But since the future is unknown, each step is taken at hazard, and its consequences and ramifications are unforeseeable. Given a plan, we should proceed piecemeal because the possibility exists that the ramifications of any particular part of the plan could obstruct or prevent the rest of it from being realized. In war the good strategist phases his plan to allow time to modify and develop the plan as he goes along. Let me give some examples of how aims and plans can interfere with themselves: To expand universities may defeat the object of expanding the universities by undermining standards and thus turning them into nonuniversities. Simply to slam freeways through a city may destroy the city and turn it into something else. We can, however, dream or think wholesale rather than piecemeal in order to anticipate and think through.

I have already said that trying to impose a blueprint on society is authoritarian. The question is whether some problems are not so large that they must be attacked all at once. Thus a great problem facing American planners is the trend of migration toward California and the possibility of a continuous urban sprawl stretching from Sausalito to San Diego. The question everyone

thinks of is less whether or not this is desirable than how to ameliorate its horrors. Such planning for urban renewal and building
of superhighways is highly necessary and desirable. Why should
we think or dream or plan on a wholesale basis, considering the
urgency of such problems? One argument I shall marshal is that
trends are reversible and that there should be contingency planning in such a case; and this planning must be large-scale. The
trend to California, of course, could be reversed.

Another argument might be that advances like the total separation of motor traffic in town centers — such as Coventry —
seem to have taken their cue from wholesale dream cities like the
Wells-Korda-Moholy-Nagy vision in *Things to Come*. Only the
over-all vision allows one to see whether, for example, present
patterns of dispersing homes so that people must cluster for work
and entertainment are sustainable if cities are developed in different ways. There is no reason, then, why piecemeal planning
should not follow on and benefit from utopian dreaming.

V

This brings me to the third of the arguments directed against
utopianism in general, and one that actually contradicts directly
the previous sentence: namely, the view that we become en-
thralled by and enamored of our utopian dreams — constructed
so often in accordance with what we conceive as the highest principles. Not to desire this utopia is like not desiring the Good Life.
Utopianists are thus tempted to impose their dreams upon their
fellow creatures, even if the latter are reluctant. Sooner or later
their fellows will come around to recognizing the Good Life for
what it is; and in the meantime, for their sake, a little persuasion
may be justified.

Even dreaming is dangerous, then, because it produces authoritarianism. This argument draws attention to a very serious danger
in utopian speculation. Our awareness that this danger exists and
our actual experience of the bureaucratic tyrant who would love
to make society "well ordered" and "well run" must put us on
guard. However, it seems to me that architecture and planning
are here being connected with a very general political concern:

"Beware of blueprints of society." To the planner this should be translated to read: "We want to dream of utopias in which men could better live the lives they now lead and even broaden their range of choices of life styles. We do not want you to tell man how he should live.Your dreams are for us to choose from and learn from, not for us to live up to." What we obviously cannot do, of course, is censor people's thinking. There is nothing we can do to stop dreaming. It may, therefore, be as well to encourage it in a critical spirit.

From the point of view of the planner, another reason that utopias trap us is that they involve our imaginations. This argument cannot easily be bypassed. What it says is not so much that we fall in love with our utopias as that we are so involved in them and their concepts that we cannot be critical of the concepts, categories, and terms in which they are set. For example, in our present way of life, home and play are frequently separated spatially and are put in different categories. A dreamer might conceive of a city in which this separation is calculated, built-in, and beautifully organized. But if you suggest that not thinking beyond these categories is a rather conservative approach, he might recoil, uncomprehending — what kind of life would it be without them? They are fundamental. Well, of course, the answer is simply that it is not even bold to imagine a life without the separation of work, home, and play. Such living already goes on around us: namely, by anyone who loves his work and does it at home. Most academics will probably, like me, be in this category. Most of my research and writing work is done in my home, and I go to the university only because it is a matter of convenience; the teaching and libraries are centrally organized at the moment. I can well imagine this changing, and indeed there are signs that it is already doing so. Why not imagine a city in which certain housing units for teachers included a large room in which students could foregather? Why not? Because the transport problems, administrative problems, and library problems created would be insufferable. But in the age of conference television telephones and such things, do administrators need to be housed together? Librarians already are thinking beyond readers having to go to libraries. Could we not imagine dialing a number for the catalogue, turning a knob till we found the entry, dialing another number, and having a microfilm of the book appear on our screens, or even having a Xerox copy of its pages made?

So far are we from a utopian university of this kind being worked out in detail and explored that we hardly conceive of it — as shown by the deplorable conservatism of the new British universities, none of which has, as far as I know, a single innovation of this kind.

Yet this dream is, in fact, rather prosaic. Most of the technology required has already been invented.[14] By contemplating problems it might create, it certainly opens up multiple choices to us.

In advocating utopianism I am going much further, however, since we should try to dream critically of situations which are yet beyond the technologically possible. If we are uncritical of dreams, then such dreams become a rather aimless kind of science fiction; but if we are critical and proceed only with particular problems and discipline ourselves, then it could be, I think, very fruitful; and the more disciplined by criticism, the more fruitful.

To reinforce my case — perhaps some of you are impressed by our new universities — I shall refer to two British planners' works: Gordon Cullen's *Townscape*[15] and G. A. Jellicoe's *Motopia*.[16]

Cullen's book is one that I found almost as depressing as some of the townscapes he praises. It is a book in which design and function are somehow being pushed so that one can imagine life going on much as before in the suburbs, with a little tidying up. One gets a picture of endless vistas of suburbia, slightly prettified, but not requiring any major changes. This will be his ideal townscape. Not only does he ignore the aesthetic core of much that he discusses, but he doesn't go behind the buildings to the way of life that is being produced by them and discuss whether it is in any way satisfactory.

[14] That it is not so startling is perhaps evidenced by the appearance of these ideas in "2000," a series of articles in the British popular magazine *Woman's Mirror*, October 1966.

[15] G. Cullen, *Townscape* (New York: Reinhold, 1961).

[16] G. A. Jellicoe, *Motopia* (New York: Praeger, 1961). Motopia is only the latest neologism in a long chain. Besides "utopia" itself, which is a synthesis of "outopia" and "eutopia," we have had "antiutopia," "dystopia," "kakotopia," and even "pornotopia."

The same is true, to a less extent though, of the more critical look at the future possibilities to be found in *Motopia.* Jellicoe's explicit premise is that the motorcar will be with us for the foreseeable future. We have, therefore, to design dwellings working outward from the motorcar. Jellicoe takes the simple ideas of rooftop roads and buildings in grids and produces an efficient way of fitting the motorcar and its owner into the suburban landscape. But Jellicoe is too critical in many ways, or uncritical of his criticism. For example, he rules out putting roads underground because of cost. If anything changes over time, it is relative cost. That is obvious. Then, after seeing his monotonous apartments my first thought was, "Why aren't they underground, too?" Because, after all, at least Wells went that far in the film we have seen. And again, Jellicoe's plans are bedeviled by his uncritical attitude toward the way of life in motopia. All he does, in fact, is assume that life patterns will be exactly like today's in suburbia, and his aim is to organize the town a little more efficiently around them. He assumes, for example, that regular shopping will continue to be a part of life and that every block will have to have a certain amount of shop space.

In Hong Kong, where I have been living for almost five years, and which is generally regarded as rather old-fashioned, much shopping is done by telephone and order book because delivery is cheap. Again, it is a question of the relative cost. It is not hard to imagine the relative cost of delivery coming down perhaps because of some mechanical means, and this kind of regular avenue of shops for household goods would then be quite out of date. In a decade or two it would already be wasted space. This is not even considered in the course of the argument. He could have considered the possibility of such patterns of shopping more or less being abolished — at least regular shopping, as opposed to specialized shopping, for which we might continue to go a long distance.

Jellicoe might reply that shopping is not just an economic necessity, that it has a certain social function in a community, especially for unoccupied married women. The answer to this, after one thinks it through, would be: (1) to find ways to occupy the women and (2) to dream up alternative social activities for those still unoccupied. Shopping is only a substitute. These women want to socialize together, but why do they *have* to do it through shopping?

Apart from Jellicoe, the problem is that while architects have no business moralizing about our present ways — none of us have — they should also avoid being too conservative in accepting patterns that exist now as though they were essential to our way of life. When they do this, they limit our choices. Some of our present social institutions are already very abstract and could become much more so — like the university I have envisaged. Others, like the family, are not, and the architect could offer to make them still less abstract by, for example, constructing a city in which separations within families are minimized. We have a regular separation now. The worker or provider goes away from the home, comes back, and so on. Maybe he doesn't want to stay at home. That is another social problem which one has to consider, but why not give him the choice? We can dream of a community in which the organization is different and see what the consequences are.

The architect, then, has scope for being a social force. He can point out possibilities. The London County Council planners were presented with the problem of transferring the Bethnal Green community to Roehampton. The main specification they were given was that Bethnal Green as a community was to be preserved as much as possible. They did not interpret this as meaning that the working-class terrace houses should be reproduced in the countryside. They tried instead to create an environment which would not kill any valuable aspects of the community as it was but which might create opportunities for the community to develop and change if it so wished. The unfortunate part about this was that the community wasn't really brought in on the planning; it was done by government fiat.

In suggesting the architect is a "creative anthropologist," I mean that his buildings are frameworks around man's activities, and the activities that men want should be the basic decree for the planner, for the architect; it is a mistake to take our present life patterns as fixed and unchanging. An argument to underline this last point is that technological progress is accelerating and there are consequent changes in the patterns of our activities; the frameworks are going to have to accommodate stranger and stranger social patterns. What thinking critically about the future can do for us is partially to ameliorate that strangeness or to prepare us for it and thus to help us adapt to it, to think in terms of it more quickly and effectively than otherwise.

So much, then, for the first three criticisms of utopianism. I seem to have refuted them all, at least to my own satisfaction, but not without conceding and learning a great deal. My position at this point can be summed up by saying that our proneness to error, the openness of the future, the blindness of present trends, our self-set moral and imaginative traps — all of these should make us hypercritical of any utopian exercise; but we blind ourselves if we give up altogether.

VI

From the very first dream of utopia it has been distrusted and disliked. There has been a flourishing tradition of antiutopias beginning with the horror stories of Jonathan Swift and proceeding through Butler's *Erewhon* to the gloom of Orwell, Huxley, and Michael Young. The criticism which these authors direct again and again at utopianism is that it is naïve and optimistic, and this is also my fourth criticism. These authors adopt the reverse stance — pessimism. Then selected tendencies in the present are extrapolated, and the result is a monstrosity. This technique yields a very powerful argument against those who simply extrapolate from the so-called "hard data" of the present situation. We can see that the selection is everything, and whether the result will be hell or paradise depends on whether the governing vision is optimistic or pessimistic.

Between these two poles of optimism and pessimism there has hitherto been virtually no middle ground. To present this schematically, the future could be confronted or thought about in three ways:

1. Things will go on as they have — with a few small changes. This is a rather conservative prediction about the future.

2. Certain present tendencies will become dominant. This is inductive prediction.

3. Wild speculation about the future; or we have no idea, but maybe such and such will happen.

My contention about these three possibilities is that they are all on the same level of likelihood. There is absolutely no way of telling whether we are in for a period of quiescence (1), whether certain present trends will grow stronger and become dominant (2), or whether drastic wholesale change will occur without warning (3). The advocates of 1 and 2 are simply conservative and inductive in their refusal to face this fact, that we really don't know.[17] However, those who approach wild speculation and prophecy in a critical way might at least learn something unexpected and conceivably useful.

This plea for a critical utopianism can, of course, be easily argued with hindsight. One can make a case for saying that the planners of the Los Angeles freeways did not make it clear that their ideas might create a noncity like nothing else known previously. I don't say this in any moralizing spirit. Some people, and I would number myself among them, appreciate very much the special way of life possible in Los Angeles. But I also say that the flood of criticism of Los Angeles suggests that it was not created with foresight.

Any action we take, like building freeways, will have countless social and other repercussions, many of which we cannot foresee.[18] Some, however, might have been foreseen. Since city planning goes back to the Greeks, does it not shame us when we contemplate the hideous suburban sprawl which surrounds our major cities? Not only is it horrible to look at, but it stultifies and limits whole ways of life. Apart from making people commute and imprisoning housewives in home and garden, it has also ruined the cities socially. Increasingly, only the very rich and the very poor live in the cities themselves — the poor because they can't afford to get out, the rich because they can purchase the en-

[17] See K. R. Popper, "Probability Magic, or Knowledge Out of Ignorance," *Dialectica*, Vol. 11 (1957), pp. 354–374.

[18] See my *Revolution in Anthropology* (London: Routledge & Kegan Paul, 1964), pp. 216 ff.

vironment they want there. It is difficult to know if this is inevitable — whether, for example, if we tried to diversify the cities, having houses at all prices available, the natural forces of the city environment wouldn't drive house prices up or "slum" them all down. But certainly the sprawl seems to me a product of diffidence by authorities and planners. What happened could have been foreseen and fought against. Why it wasn't or, if it was, why resistance failed, I don't know.

The only way to avoid such things in the future is to put before the public, through the elected government, or whatever, in the boldest possible terms all the choices and all the consequences we can see at this time. As we implement whatever choice is made, we must then constantly reappraise the whole set of choices we adopted at the beginning. Perhaps in order to dramatize matters we should resort more seriously to the world of science fiction. This brings me to the film *Things to Come*, because all science fiction writers from Jules Verne and H. G. Wells through to Isaac Asimov have from time to time looked at social design and other problems in the futures they envisage. Asimov conceives of the entire "rise and fall of civilization" in one of his works.[19] In the movie we can see all the elements of looking into the future that I have discussed and some others. We have there utopia, anti-utopia, prophecy, shrewd projections of trends of 1936, wild miscalculations, and other conservative miscalculations; and we also have critical utopianism.

We have in addition, and I had better get this out of the way now, a rather bad film. As Alistair Cooke remarked, "It is just a fancy dress ball, here and now, at the R.I.B.A."[20] A critic in *Era* said that it was "based on what is possibly . . . the worst scenario that has ever been written."[21] The tale it tells after the portentous caption "Whither Mankind?" is of how the world plunges in 1940 into a war that devastates Europe. But somehow, somewhere,[22]

[19] See Isaac Asimov, *Foundation* (New York: Gnome Press, 1951); *Foundation and Empire* (New York: Gnome Press, 1952); and *Second Foundation* (New York: Gnome Press, 1953).

[20] Alistair Cooke in a review of the film in *The Listener*, March 18, 1936, p. 545.

[21] G. A. Atkinson in *Era*, February 26, 1936.

[22] *The Times* film critic commented that the world will be saved by

25

civilization is rebuilt by the scientists and engineers. They proceed to subdue the war lords and deal firmly with reactionaries before shooting off two of their *Herrenvolk* on a journey to the moon. Will mankind, Wells asks, listen to the reactionaries or to the forces of science, reason, and light?

Let me isolate from this film some of the different strands as they relate to the critical exploration of the future. First, there are the conservative elements: In the film there is something irresistibly of the thirties and Wellsian about the furniture on the one hand and the personal relationships in the film on the other. A writer in the journal *Design for Today* commented in 1936 that "The glass couch is somehow reminiscent of Burlington House."[23] And several writers have noted the pseudo-Grecian garb adopted especially by the female characters. But, above all, the posturing, speechifying, and the self-righteousness of the scientists make one feel very uncomfortable if this is the world of the future.

Second, there are projections of current tendencies: Here we note the prediction that the airplane is becoming an important weapon and will fight the next war. The tendency to high-rise apartments and to artificially controlled lighting and air-circulation systems is also carried through. The increased use of glass and plastic was also what looked like a reasonable guess. So much for projections.

Third, there are elements of prophecy: The amazing one, of course, was the prediction of the war in 1940. Nobody knows how Wells came on that idea. The other was the journey to the moon. We are apt to be impressed by these superb guesses. But they were only that and cannot be systematically repeated by even, I think, a critical utopianism.

What about the strictly utopian aspects of the film? Utopia is the paradise on earth, simultaneously here and nowhere. For Wells it comes after the holocaust. Antiutopia in the conscious sense is portrayed in the scenes of war, destruction, disease, and

---

mechanics, research students, and airmen. The latter emerge from the war ruins they made, mysteriously endowed with wisdom, detachment, and nobility. What happened to make them like this is a moot point — a mystic communion with machinery, perhaps?

[23] A. Vesselo, "Design for Tomorrow," *Design for Today*, April 1936.

dictatorship. This is when the antiscientific forces get the upper hand, when men try to run their affairs in the same old muddling way. They almost succeed in destroying civilization on earth.

Wells is an optimist, however, and so we get a fourth element of utopia: the scientific civilization of pure air and light, the benign reign of the scientist-airman. Wells is so optimistic that he fails to realize that his picture of the airman's civilization is in many ways repugnant. The all-knowingness of the new leaders, their self-righteousness, and the artificiality of their perfect environment are very depressing. He seems to take it for granted that people would be happy to be dressed and housed more or less homogeneously.[24] It didn't occur to him that our present diversity is not solely the result of our society having grown up piecemeal but also something we have chosen.

As Colin Welch wrote apropos of Wells in general, and it applies beautifully to Wells's caricature of the reactionaries in the film, "The idea that people should be taught to think; the idea that, thus taught, they might reach conclusions different from each others', even from his own: these were . . . repugnant to him [Wells]."[25] This is where Wells's utopianism is uncritical and, I think, authoritarian.

Finally we come to his critical utopianism. Despite his naïve optimism and trust in science, scientists, and engineers, Wells put into the mouth of the reactionary sculptor some critical remarks about his monstrously dehumanized vision; there is the suggestion

[24] "I would say to *our designers*: 'For God's Sake let yourselves go'. . . . Being inventive and original is not being extravagant and silly." Wells said this in a memorandum to everyone concerned with designing *Things to Come*; reprinted in *Two Film Stories* (London, 1940), p. 16. How, then, did the following come to be Alistair Cooke's judgment? "It must be heartbreaking for Mr. Wells to be told that the costumes he predicted they'd be wearing in 2030 are to be the very thing in beach-wear this summer. But there is a category of less inevitable error: the aeroplanes drone away from exhaust trouble. The chairs are any modern chair done in glass: they have glass elevators but, the point is — they still have elevators. . . . "Things to Come" shares with most Utopias the primary error of making today the premise, of pretending that new civilizations do not differ in kind but only in degree of decoration, luxury, leisure, and so on." Cooke, *op. cit.*

[25] Colin Welch, "Father of Little Superman," *Daily Telegraph*, September 21, 1966.

that a society with a surfeit of comfort, leisure, and beauty might suffer serious and disruptive tensions. The fundamental objection is that the whole civilization has lost the human scale, and the scrambling after progress has become completely pointless and cannibalistic, feeding on itself. Now, certainly this is a serious architectural and planning problem, the human scale; interestingly enough, Jellicoe in his *Motopia* harped quite a bit on the necessity of considering it.

These are some of the ideas of the future to be found in the film. But where, for instance, do we place the speech in which the airman tells the war lord his way of life will not be permitted to go on? Is that utopian or antiutopian? What, too, of Wells's theme that the reactionaries would be the artists?[26] Is that a prophecy that the present two cultures of the sciences and the humanities will be increasingly separated? I confess ignorance.

VII

What are the implications of my argument for architects and planners? Most of them were spelled out as I went along. The main one is that looking into the future is almost impossible, and our only hope is to pool our ideas and criticisms. None of us, by magical prophecy or cryptomagical induction from data, can know what is to come. But if we explore critically and creatively, we may be able to do a better job than the urban sprawl which spoliates our countryside, the dull grid patterns of Manhattan and motopia, or the hygienic inhuman and synthetic world of *Things to Come.*

If the problem of expense is raised, then I am tempted to answer with the following cheap argument: If we can afford to fill the archives of the Pentagon with libraries of so-called "contingency plans" for wars that may never take place, why can't we afford to do the same for civilian life in peacetime?

---

26 "Mr. Wells as applied scientist probably gave a lot of help with the detail of the sets. But Mr. Wells as sociologist should surely have called in Mr. Lewis Mumford, who would have told him, what Korda's settings visibly demonstrate, that the artist as beauty specialist will be a vulgar survival." Cooke, *op. cit.*

One of the main problems is to see that the attack — that is, the criticism of the utopian — reaches even the most deeply entrenched categories and institutions to see if they are essential. I have touched on the idea that the termination of the rigid work-play separation is not very utopian. Wells imagined an environment controlled so that night and day and the seasons were eliminated. Further lines of thought are that the tables might be turned on my opening joke and that buildings might become much less monuments of indestructibility and immobility. The town-country dichotomy might disappear. The whole idea of separate buildings might give way to continuous ones. And on the moon we may get the situation where the outside appearance of buildings is of little concern and all the emphasis is on the interiors.

Concerning architectural education, I have only one suggestion as to how we can teach students to be less imprisoned by their received categories and concepts — and that is to teach them comparative sociology and anthropology. This follows directly on my suggestion that in an important way an architect or planner is a creative anthropologist. This would require, for me, that when he is planning a scheme, he should do what is called "field work." That is, he should live as a participant observer in the firm or institution he is going to build for, get to know its way of life, its aspirations, and so on, while he starts designing. But at each stage he should try to expose his ideas to criticism by those who may have to or may choose to live in what he is designing. All this will be anathema to those imprisoned by the romantic idea of art as self-expression; I can't help that.[27]

Acquaintance with different ways of life through the study of comparative social institutions has of itself a liberating effect. But some deeper study of sociology would also be of value. The nature and persistence of social institutions are very peculiar, and their intractability has to be studied. In some ways an institution is like a rule of the road, which is more effective in getting drivers to drive on one side than is a physical thing like a big sign saying

[27] I have tried to criticize the idea in my article "The Objectivity of Criticism of the Arts," Ratio, Vol. 9 (1967), pp. 67–83; see also E. H. Gombrich, Art and Illusion (London and New York: Phaidon, 1966), passim.

"drive on the right." This applies to planning and architecture. For example, it is not good enough to clear the slums and build nice new buildings if the society which produces slums will turn the new buildings into slums — this is what has happened in England again and again. It seems to me that the planners are trying to treat this problem purely architecturally. The old houses are ugly, so they build beautiful new houses, and they become slums.

Finally, consider critical utopianism itself. Utopia is the perfect place, the perfectly good place. Utopian thinking is probably most fruitful if it narrows its focus and takes only one aspect of this perfect life at a time. In methodology we stress the importance of concentrating on a single problem and its ramifications; otherwise, it can't really be followed through. I have mentioned contingency planning; Herman Kahn, who has explored the methodology of war games, contingency planning, and scenarios very extensively, also has come to exactly the same conclusion: that the main technique is to decide what problems you are talking about and then to break them down into as many manageable subproblems as you possibly can. In this way, you find that a large number of them have obvious solutions and that others are very difficult; but you have at least narrowed the points of concentration. This seems to me one of the easiest ways to break down existing categories and preconceptions.

I end with some direct ways in which I think the utopian dream can be strongly criticized without being put into practice. The first is to follow the ramifications as far as you can and to find out whether the utopia is self-defeating. This is like looking for internal consistency in the dream. A second check or criticism would be to see whether the dream would be destructive of certain things you value, whether there is some conflict with other things you consider important. The third and very important mode of criticism would be to see whether the utopia actually solves whatever problem you began with. Let's say it is suburban sprawl. You may find that the solution does other things but doesn't solve the exact problem. The fourth and final kind of criticism you could make is to ask whether the utopia accords with present facts.

When I began, I said that I would play my ascribed role to the full. So, as promised, I have preached a sermon in which I have reasoned my way to vague and rather general conclusions. Not *so* vague and *so* general, I hope, that they are without consequences which you find of interest.

DISCUSSION

Professor ROBERT GOODMAN: You warned us about continuing to impose designs, planning by fiat. You said that there should be some method whereby choice could be made. Have you thought at all about how this choice would be made? How do you get participation by the community, by the design makers, and others affected by the plan?

JARVIE: I am not a populist. It is no good just putting it to a referendum. Yet there are other means. Presumably, it would depend on the specific problem.

Let's say you have a slum like Bethnal Green that you want to pull down, and you have several alternative sites where the people could be relocated. You could start on that basis and with that community. You could set up an office of the planners on the site and let people come in and out to look at the plans and participate; but, of course, the bigger the scale, the sooner this becomes impossible.

However, from what I know of the governmental process in England, even responsible government committees proceed much more like this: They have a problem to deal with — a new town perhaps. They say, "First of all, we want consultants and designers and planners," and they appoint firms. These commissions at least give you some choice. But, of course, the commissions may have been dreamed up in Japan or New York and may have nothing to do with the particular needs of that place or anything else — apart from what is given in the program.

It would seem to me that even in the present planning structure, for example, in government, there is room for more participation. Elected representatives would actually be in a position to act as (inefficient) transmitting instruments. They could meet with planners and explain to them the society that is being planned for, and its nature, and see whether they get a response.

If they get a response that they like from a particularly creative planning team, they can then figure out ways and means of making the transmission between the planners and the community better.

Again, it might be a question of setting up the office in the community itself. It might be much more like anthropological field work, where the planners themselves would go and attempt for a time to live the life of those for whom they are planning. Anthropologists go to the Hottentots and try to live with them. It is very difficult. On the other hand, it is extremely valuable personally, and it gives a great deal of knowledge. That is not too much to ask of someone to whom you are giving the tremendous power to build a city. He should live among existing city dwellers and also discuss with them the question of what is wrong in this city. What do they like? What do they feel should be available in this city? Why would they move to a new city; why not? What are the factors involved?

What you can't do is go into the future; you can't go to the new-town inhabitants before they exist and say "What do you want?" But we are talking about a way of life which has a certain continuity, and the best you can do is to look at it as it is and then try to imagine whether it will go on like this. If presented with such and such a kind of plan when they moved in, would people adapt their way of life, or would they find ways around our plan that wouldn't blot out their present way of life?

GOODMAN: You seem to put a lot of emphasis on training the expert — in this case the planner-designer — to respond more sympathetically to the people for whom he is planning. Paul Davidoff once suggested that we should try to inject this kind of thinking into the political process, so that we get a number of views of what the good life would be. Just as we get a number of economic theories of how society should be run, each political party might have its own view of the best physical environment. In determining who should represent them, choices would be extended to include a much broader aspect of what our lives should be like.

Professor STANFORD ANDERSON: Bob [Goodman], there is a point in Jarvie's talk that interested me with relation to your attitudes. Both of you put a great deal of emphasis on the amount of choice that should be open to man. Perhaps Jarvie was going further in emphasizing the degree to which the architect should generate choices that man didn't know he had before. Did you feel anything about the degree to which the architect should assume this responsibility?

GOODMAN: I think the architect should take that responsibility, but what is important is the mechanism by which people make their choice. There is a real difficulty in creating many views of what society could be like. There is always the problem of what is called "educating the public." We do have a number of theoretical views of different environments; perhaps we don't have enough, but still we just don't seem to have the mechanism of telling people what life would be like in those communities.

JARVIE: I don't think it is a question of educating the public. Apart from being almost impossible, the people already at certain levels are able to make choices. They go to California. When I saw California, I didn't understand why everyone didn't move there. As long as people are not enslaved in their society, they can go to other places; but even when they move, the ranges of their choice are at the moment very limited. This is true of both those living in the Harlem ghettos and those living in Los Angeles. It is not so much a question of educating them as of having choices which they can take or leave. The responsible planning authorities should not be afraid of innovation: it is unlikely that they are going to build something that people won't live in; but if they do, too bad. That is the social cost of providing choices.

I don't see much point in trying to generate ideas so that they come up from below. I don't see exactly how that could work. I mean, an architect is an architect, and a nonarchitect is a nonarchitect; one shouldn't dictate to the other.

Insofar as the architect or planner has command of the resources, his responsibility is to be even more critical of the social dimension of his work than he now is. This would involve more knowledge of society and of the effect of his work on society.

GOODMAN: You hit upon one point just now in terms of providing the choice and the mechanism for making the choice. You said that if you do have some kind of utopiar view, you ought to build it; perhaps you ought to build a lot of them. We do have different kinds of cities; but perhaps the range is not great enough. Of course, this is a very expensive way to allow people to have real choice; but it may be all we can do with the tools at hand.

From the Floor: What I am worried about is that it may not be the question of providing a whole series or an infinite number of choices at all when you are not really providing the type of choices these people are after. You [Jarvie] made a point, when you were talking about building new areas of cities and watching them become slums again, which made me think that you are on the right track. The problem there was not providing people with a better physical environment at all. It wasn't a question of studying what type of dwelling they wanted either; the problem wasn't that of dwelling at all.

JARVIE: But it was. I am pretty sure that the assumption at the time was that old housing, rotten housing, was producing this slum mentality. Then, of course, they found it wasn't true; but they still haven't a new theory concerning slums. I am speaking about England. These are the only slums I know. In Hong Kong, they have something like planned slums. They think they can't house everybody unless people are in slums, so they build more slums.

From the Floor: But as long as you keep thinking of the housing as slums, you may be on the wrong track. You may never find the right type of dwelling that will satisfy people or keep dwellings from becoming slums. It may be the question of raising the income level of slum dwellers.

S. ANDERSON: The question, apparently, is what kind of anthropological field studies would help the architect to learn about what people need in their environment. To build a number of possibilities and study them would be a kind of experimental anthropology; but another possibility is education, which has been generally played down. I am thinking of the "Mankind 2000" project, of which Dr. Jungk is one of the leaders. It is very definitely oriented toward education; in Dr. Jungk's presentation I think it will be interesting to hear how his group has contemplated such things as didactic exhibitions. In such exhibitions various possibilities would be put before large populaces in visual

34

and verbal terms. In this way you can both educate and get back information about people's responses to new environments before they are built.

Are there others here who are concerned about how the architect or planner discovers more about the conditions he has to satisfy?

Dr. LEONARD DUHL: At the risk of anticipating what I want to say tomorrow or antagonizing a group of architects and planners, I believe the whole process of social planning is too important to be the sole province of planners and architects. In fact, today's real issues surrounding social planning have nothing to do with the architecture and the city planning we have known.

Many architects and city planners (technicians who have grandiose notions as to the impact of their efforts upon the future) still do not realize that the real *planning* is taking place in some of society's basic political processes. Planning grows out of the confrontations between people and between those in the community and those who are making the decisions. Planning is affected by the way budgets are allocated, the way we write our governmental rules and regulations, and the like. In this particular game of political processes and planning of policy, most architects, planners, and technicians, whether they are doctors or anything else, are babes in the woods. They really don't understand this game at all.

If you really wanted to talk about the question of policy planning, I hope that you would distinguish between the two major orientations: (1) *technical planning*, which deals with specific programs, categorical activities, buildings, and what have you, and (2) *policy planning*, which concerns itself with the kind of world we want to live in — some of the values that are (or should be) built into this world.

One of the questions that was raised earlier, one that I think is really critical, was whether there is participation in this world in terms of the planning. Actually, most of the people who today confront the system can only scream and shout that something is wrong with the system. They really don't have the data or the ability to confront it effectively and authoritatively. For example, when a government bureaucracy is challenged, the amount of data available to the man inside the system is so much greater than to the man outside confronting it that it is virtually impossible for a meaningful confrontation to occur.

Thus, one of our major concerns must be that of establishing structures and a process whereby the confronter has access to the data and the ability to understand better when and where and how to confront the system. This is what makes a viable, self-renewing society or profession or institution — one in which profession confronts profession, the poor confront the establishment, and almost every segment of society confronts every other, creating those interchanges with each other which evolve into policy and determine the future.

I don't know anybody here who can honestly predict the future. My belief is that the future is predicted by acts and events occurring in the present, and that not all of those acts and events are predictable — in fact, a large percentage are irrational and idiosyncratic, and it is the combination and interaction of these forces which shape future directions.

The planner's role is that of bringing the related (or possibly related) forces into "comfortable" situations. He can do no more than set the processes of image evolvement and of interaction in motion and then just see where these processes take us.

Professor RAYMOND A. BAUER: One objection to what Len Duhl says: I think it ill behooves the psychiatrist to say that irrational behavior is unpredictable.

Professor HENRY MILLON: The statement you [Duhl] made was contradictory. You started out saying that planners and architects have the role of a technician. Another statement was that planners indeed set the image, and everybody else then tests the image.

DUHL: I was talking about another set of planners. I was dividing the planners into two kinds — the technical planners and policy planners.

S. ANDERSON: In terms of education, do these policy makers just occur, or should we be training them?

DUHL: The people who are entering the area of policy planning must be trained. They have to be trained very differently from current educational scope and techniques in each one of our professions. Our professions are still narrow craft guilds — no matter how broad they seem to be getting — in a world that is much more complex and ecological.

From the Floor: I tend to agree with the assessment of the present situation, but are we to consider the continued separation between the policy makers and the technicians a desired situation for the future?

DUHL: I love to see technncians concern themselves with policy; however, on the basis of my experiences, I believe very few of them do.

From the Floor: When you come to participatory democracy on the part of the poor or of black power, the policy makers often turn out to be the technicians. Such movements for participation often ignore both policies and certain kinds of technical apparatus required by a complex urban environment. This seems to be a tremendous source of conflict, and if there is any solution, it will be at that point of conflict.

DUHL: Yes, all people affect policy by their actions — whether one is a Stokely Carmichael or somebody else. However, they are quite different from the people I would like to call "policy planners."

The "policy planner" is really concerned with the over-all direction, with setting the image for the society and offering the choices not just to top policy makers but to people all the way through the system. Through this policy process of democracy we move ahead, shape, and reshape our society.

From the Floor: How does this policy maker come to those choices? And how does he offer them?

DUHL: If I may become a psychiatrist again for a moment — if Ray Bauer will let me — one of the most intriguing aspects of psychiatric practice is that when the patient presents his problem, the role of the psychiatrist may be one of completely redefining or helping the patient to redefine the problem he must face. The very process of helping the patient redefine the problem enables him to consider and ultimately to attempt actions which are alternative solutions to those he has customarily employed. I am suggesting here that the role of the policy planner may be that of helping to reformulate the critical questions.

Someone just mentioned that the problem of poverty may have nothing to do with slum housing. If he would extend this further, he would ultimately redefine the problem of poverty as having really very little to do with slum housing, but having to do with a complex interplay of things. Once one is able to demonstrate that this complexity (the very concept of "ecology") must be considered, the solutions will find themselves — if one can start the process rolling. The role of the policy planner is to do just this with societal problems, and not to come up with the answers himself.

S. ANDERSON: Dr. Jarvie, would you like to close by taking up that challenge? The claim has been made that the policy maker is operating within society but is not offering any solution. Somehow the solution to the problem generates itself out of the analysis of the problem. This would appear to come in direct conflict with some of your statements.

JARVIE: Yes, it does. Even if I could think of a case where such a problem solves itself by the very fact that we understand it better, I still would not see that by parallel reasoning one could say that, therefore, other planning problems, including more specifically architectural ones, will solve themselves.

DUHL: May I suggest a case and ask for your reaction? I think the greatest case in the last few years has been the fact that *somebody* brought about the creation of an "antipoverty program," which has given the American public an entirely different perception of what the problems of poverty are; and that *somebody* happened to be the civil rights movement, with a few other people thrown in. By redefining the very question of poverty, suddenly a whole set of programs that have nothing specifically to do with poverty have evolved in the departments of the federal government. There are programs which are starting to deal with a wide variety of issues — programs which, in the long run, will affect that poverty.

What is happening in HUD [Department of Housing and Urban Development] — in fact, the creation of HUD — would never have occurred without the issues and events surrounding the civil rights movement and the "antipoverty program." The concept that evolved through the civil rights movement and the "antipoverty program" has really started this country toward a major shift in social policy.

From the Floor: Who, in this case, was the policy maker?

DUHL: In this instance, it was that group running the school, involved in the civil rights movement, and a group of people in government who began to switch some of the thinking in government in order to develop an "antipoverty program." But the people who made "antipoverty program" policies were not those who acted on them; they were all kicked out.

JARVIE: Your example assumes that the problem of poverty was brought to the surface by, and perhaps was better understood on account of, the civil rights movement. Then the solution was government intervention. But this solution in itself is highly questionable. Whether, in the long run, government intervention is the answer to poverty is a moot point.

DUHL: I was talking about a complete attitudinal change in the United States, where a whole host of people, including big government, big businesses, and the academia, who I would never have thought were concerned with the problems of the poor, are concerning themselves with it. The whole atmosphere has completely changed in the last five years.

From the Floor: This didn't solve the problem.

DUHL: No, but it is making a start on the problem, which is really a major step forward.

BAUER: There is a similar movement with the Watts riots. Up to that time the problem had been posed mainly as one of integration. I happen to know, because I was giving lectures on the Negro market, and this was thrown at me all the time: "This is going to change." Everyone was thinking solely in terms of segregation. There was virtually nobody who was talking about deprivation at that time. It became clear after the Watts riots and a few other events that segregation per se was not the end of the problem, that segregation had produced a residue of social effects which could be summarized as deprivation, that this was going to last even if you got complete integration, and that it posed an entirely different problem to solve.

Now, the articulation of the difference between deprivation and segregation turned people's attention to consideration of different remedies.

JARVIE: I think we are talking at cross purposes. I think by solution of the problem you mean the practical solution, that the whole attitudinal change is initiating a process that will attain the goals of the poverty program in a practical sense. By solution I meant the theoretical knowledge that leads us to act, and in both the case of poverty and the case of segregation it has been long theoretically understood what the underlying causes are. The deprivation aspect is not new to sociological and economic studies of the race situation; it has somehow just become more articulated, more clearly seen. I don't quarrel with this at all; you are quite right. In a sense, action to solve a problem depends very much on bringing it to the surface.

In my talk I was referring more to problems which at the moment we have no idea how to solve. I really don't think we know how to solve the problem of urban sprawl. One breaks one's head over it. Similarly, what can one do about enormous cities generally?

Professor OSCAR NEWMAN: We quite agree, I think, that your analysis was superb when you were talking about a process and a methodology. Where you err, perhaps, is in thinking that physical purposes have much to do with some of the problems we are involved with.

What is a problem of urban sprawl or suburban sprawl? What do you do with the slum? It is not necessarily a question of the physical product. The physical product may just be an offshoot that affects the visually concerned architect more than anybody else.

It seems to me that, as planners and architects, we should ask: What are the possibilities? What are the limitations of exploring physical alternatives? And I think we have to do this with the help of people like Mr. Duhl; we have to evolve a process very much along the lines that you are suggesting, but it has to be a total one. We cannot explore physical utopias and expect that we shall come up with an answer to our physical society since physical utopias don't exist in a vacuum. The other question that concerns and frightens me most is: Within the limits of my abilities as a technician, what is my frame of reference? What can I do? After all, I am a technician, and I am involved with building physical alternatives.

S. ANDERSON: Oscar, I am extremely sympathetic with your analysis; I also sympathize with the idea that we must learn from people who are taking the positions that Dr. Duhl has taken both in this discussion and in his work. All of this I can agree with; but after you have conceded that architects and planners have to learn and become sympathetic to all these things, one is still going to make the decisions that architects and planners have made in the past. And the way those "technical" decisions are made comes to have an effect on the sociological and psychological conditions too. It is at this point that the present very healthy shift from a purely physical concern to a social concern could be overweighted. Architects have to keep trying to find the right balance here.

Professor PAUL DAVIDOFF: I think what you mean is that when we do contribute to the things that Mr. Duhl is involved in, we realize that we are contributing a certain knowledge and perhaps the ability as utopians to predict or create utopias; but we cannot do it in the framework of creating only physical utopias. We have to explore with him and other people like him the combinations of government action and the effect of physical utopias within this framework.

Current General Studies of the Future

Future-oriented studies have become increasingly common. A summary of a few contrasting examples of such studies should provide a framework for our concern with the future environment and also objectify some of the opportunities and pitfalls inherent in long-range planning.

M. Bernard Cazes, a planner in the French government, indicates the increasing role that long-range planning has played in the successive French five-year plans. The time dimension of "long range" has constantly lengthened, and there has been a shift from the analysis of trends to an increasing concern with the recognition of discontinuities.

At the request of the conference chairman, M. Cazes also gave a short description of the significant international program *Les Futuribles*, directed by Bertrand de Jouvenel of Paris. This is a foundation-sponsored work devoted to the study and characterization of a multiplicity of possible futures.

Dr. Leonard Duhl, a special assistant to the U.S. Secretary of Housing and Urban Development, is concerned with improved social planning. But because he works within a government that has never accepted planning wholeheartedly, Duhl's discussion contrasts interestingly with that of Cazes. The American planner finds himself more intimately involved with immediate governmental action and must often develop and exercise his long-range interests through informal networks of experts most of whom are not in the government.

Dr. Robert Jungk of Vienna speaks for an independent international group called "Mankind 2000." A fundamental idea of this group is that we must make the creation and testing of possible peaceful futures as challenging and rewarding as "war games" if people are ever to imagine a peaceful world positively — as something more than the quiescent absence of war.

Even though they cannot be discussed here, it is relevant to mention a few other future-oriented research programs:

1. American Academy of Arts and Sciences, Commission on the Year 2000, Daniel Bell, chairman
2. American Academy of Political and Social Sciences, special seminars conducted by Bertram Gross
3. Center for the Study of Democratic Institutions, Santa Barbara, California.
4. Hudson Institute, Harmon-on-Hudson, New York, Herman Kahn
5. Institute for Policy Studies, Washington, D.C., Arthur Waskow
6. University of Michigan, Institute for Social Research, Center for Research on Utilization of Scientific Knowledge, Donald N. Michael
7. Rand Corporation, Santa Monica, California, Olaf Helmer and T. J. Gordon
8. Resources for the Future, Washington, D.C.
9. University of Southern Illinois, World Resources Inventory, John McHale

Long-Range Studies of the Future and Their Role in French Planning[1]

BERNARD CAZES

It may seem obvious that no middle-range development plan should be elaborated unless, in some way or other, it forms part of a longer projection, since middle-range planning itself is justified by the narrow scope of an annual framework in those areas where decision making has far-reaching consequences.

Nonetheless, although the First French Plan got under way in 1947, it was only with the Third Plan (1958–1961) that an economic projection was achieved which covered a length of time exceeding that of the Plan itself. The rationale for this exercise was formulated in these terms: "By situating the prospects of the period 1957–1961 within a longer projection, it will become possible to identify them with greater certainty, thus facilitating the definition of the objectives of the Third Plan."

With the Fourth Plan (1962–1965) a longer-range projection was also established for the period 1956–1975. The statement of objectives was expressed somewhat more precisely: "At the end of a very few years, the wide options offered by developing needs, technical progress, and evolution of foreign relations will not emerge with sufficient clarity. A longer-range view alone can make us aware of the slow structural modifications entailed or necessitated by development."

---

[1] It must be remembered that in French terminology *long terme* indicates a period of time longer than ten or fifteen years. What is frequently called "long term" in English (four or five years) would be referred to as "middle range" in French.

With the Fifth Plan (1966–1970) a somewhat new phase opens: the study of long-term prospects which both enclose and clarify the preparation of a middle-range (five-year) plan ceases to be a matter only for those who make projections, but has been entrusted to a commission composed primarily, but not exclusively, of experts. These experts were asked by the Commissaire General du Plan "to study, in the light of discrete, discontinuous sources of change, what it would be useful to know at present about France in 1985 to illuminate the general orientations of the Fifth Plan."

The present essay will bear upon this experiment and will be divided into three parts: (1) how the 1985 horizon was studied, (2) the main characteristics of the 1985 horizon, and (3) the place of long-range planning in the drafting of the Sixth Plan.

1. HOW THE 1985 HORIZON WAS STUDIED

Some Methodological Remarks about the Study of the Future

Theoretically, the domain of possible futures is unlimited. Practically, it is possible to narrow it, because of a certain number of conventions:[2]

a. Certain alternatives can be eliminated as being highly improbable (return to a predominantly agricultural economy).

b. Other alternatives will be deemed too uncertain for any useful statements concerning their probability (world conflict, social subversion).

c. Any variables that contribute toward defining the image of the future should, if they are quantifiable, obey the law of any balanced accounting (resources = expenditures, resources produced = resources used, etc.).

d. Finally — and this is the most interesting area, from the viewpoint of methodological problems — it is possible to identify structural relationships between diverse variables and evolutionary trends thereof, and then to project these

[2] This number will obviously vary according to the normative character or desire for exhaustiveness of the particular conjectural study.

relationships and these trends into the future. This method permits us to limit the scope of envisioned futures.

In order to discern these relationships and tendencies, one can make use of extrapolation or, when that is impossible, consultations with experts and specialists in this field. Both approaches were used in conjunction to explore the 1985 horizon, whereas for the two preceding plans only the first was employed.

The 1960–1985 Projection Established by Institut National de la Statistique

The goal is to identify the probable orders of magnitude that will characterize the economy in 1985 and show wherein its proportions will be modified in 25 years. This projection is based upon the extrapolation of past trends and upon international comparisons; it does not attempt to analyze in depth the role of fundamental growth factors or to explore the effects of an important transformation in the objectives of the society.

In this projection, the growth rate is not given a priori but results from hypotheses as stated at the outset and based upon the availability of manpower and progress in productivity. Several variants were elaborated; these are distinguished principally by the rates of anticipated productivity. In one case it was assumed that recent rates would be maintained, while in another case the assumption was that the growth of productivity observed since 1950 would slacken to a certain extent. The growth rate of production is obviously affected thus: 4.7 per cent a year in one case and 3.5 per cent in the other.[3] Other variants were calculated by changing the assumptions concerning the total population, length of the work week, participation rate of women, and the demand structure.

Concerning the "heuristic" value of this projection, it may be said that it had the great merit of clearly emphasizing a certain number of probable structural shifts to be expected, for example, in the working population or the distribution of household con-

[3] The principal results tabulated from this projection will be noted in Section 2 of this essay.

sumption between industrial products and services. It also showed the effects of a slack in the progress of productivity (or a marked reduction in the length of the work week) on the possibility of increasing the supply of goods and services.

However, it must be acknowledged that the results yielded are implicit in the starting assumptions, whose validity must be carefully examined (and here we confront the inherent limitations of extrapolation). This kind of exercise, moreover, lends itself poorly to the discovery of discontinuities and radical changes. It should be noted, nonetheless, that the 1960–1985 projection called the attention of the planners to the probable high increase to be expected in areas of social overhead equipment expenditures up to 1985 and its financial implications.

The Work of Group 1985

Its Practical Organization. Established by the Prime Minister at the end of 1962, Group 1985 was composed of a number of distinguished people, drawn from various disciplines: the chairman, P. Guillaumat (former Minister of Defense), Mme. Krier (economist), Professor Bernard (cancer specialist), E. Claudius-Petit (mayor, former Minister of Construction), M. Demonque (industrialist), J. Fourastie (economist), C. Gruson (at that time director of the Institut National de la Statistique), B. de Jouvenel (economist and political theorist), P. Lamour (president of a regional development corporation), G. Levard (trade-union leader), L. Estrangin (agronomist). The group was assisted in the organization of its work by a group of *rapporteurs* who were engineers and government officials.

Between January 1963 and February 1964, the group held about twenty meetings, based upon topics suggested by leading figures outside the group itself. The list of topics included: the economy in 1985 (the afore-mentioned projection); development of the Paris region; leisure; the contributions of ethnology to long-range forecasts; consumption trends; urban structures; problems of economic growth; transportation; scientific research; education; agriculture; trends in public finance.

The ideas set forth by the group were subsequently synthesized by the *rapporteurs* in a document that was made public at the end of 1964, *Reflexions pour 1985,* of which 60,000 copies have already been sold. Conversely, neither the preparatory documents nor the minutes of the meetings have been published. Moreover, certain aspects of the report were the subject of a series of television programs called "France in Twenty Years." It should be noted here that the projections for 1965 and 1975 were not published in any form.

Methodological Apparatus of the Work. In the report itself, questions of method play a very minor role. Nonetheless, we can reconstruct the intellectual process of the prediction makers. The image of the future should integrate as large a number as possible of sources of change, sources which can be classified into two categories: (*a*) long-range trends; and (*b*) discrete, discontinuous sources of change (*faits porteurs d'avenir*).

> *a.* The long-range (or durable) trends are related to the economic and social evolution of a country and are characterized by the fact that they can be expressed in terms of "plus" or "minus." As examples of these, *Reflexions pour 1985* cites "demographic expansion, growing scarcity of space and water, urban growth, increase of leisure activities, the growing reliance of France on imported raw materials, desire for motorization, and increased household medical expenditures."[4]
>
> *b.* The discrete sources of change correspond to any innovation which cannot be integrated within a trend (with the exception of the very general one toward technical progress), and these sources appear within a society in a discontinuous and dispersed way. Their importance for the future does not stem from an increase or decrease of a quantifiable variable but from the fact that innovation does or does not exist. This existence alone suffices to produce far-reaching consequences, in terms of either modifying or strengthening existing trends, or even in the creation of new ones (for instance,

[4] See *Reflexions pour 1985* (Paris, 1964), p. 11. On p. 90 it is also noted that evolution toward a mass economy in the size of units of activity constitutes a long-range trend.

one could speak of a "trend toward motorization" only after the invention of the automobile). Although we generally think of innovation in the technological sphere, there is no reason why we cannot conceive of innovations in the social order, although the latter are indeed rarer.[5]

Practical Consequences of the Report. These can be considered on several levels. At the level of public opinion, *Reflexions pour 1985* helped to popularize a concern for the long-range future without resorting to sensational journalism or pseudo philosophy, and it contributed to educating the general public in problems of necessary economic choices and impending changes.

On the level of the Fifth Plan, its principal options, as voted upon by the Parliament at the end of 1964, reflect in many places the work of Group 1985 (to which an entire chapter is devoted in the report on Options). Two recommendations emerged: first, the creation within certain ministries of a "long-range planning unit" whose function it would be to guide each administration concerned in areas affected by long-term change pertaining to its field of activity; second, the suggestion to concentrate social research on such topics as continuous education, problems of old age, and the financing of social overhead capital expenditures. Furthermore, the content of the Fifth Plan was unquestionably influenced by the work of Group 1985, especially as reflected in the cautious attitude of the Plan in regard to the shortening of the work week and the financing of some public investments by the users.

Any appraisal of the work of Group 1985 should, on the positive side, stress its breadth of outlook, the rigor and objectivity of its analyses, and the economy of means with which its work was carried out. On the negative side, it is only fair to note that some problems were rather summarily treated (education, work conditions, economic consequences of technical progress), representation of the social sciences was insufficient, and finally, a meager place was alloted to methodological problems raised by the study of the distant future.[6]

[5] Professor John R. Platt, in his book, *The Step to Man* (New York: Wiley, 1966), deplores this fact.

[6] On this subject, see the paper of Fred C. Iklé, "Can Social Predictions Be Evaluated?" in *Daedalus,* Summer, 1967.

2. THE MAIN CHARACTERISTICS OF THE 1985 HORIZON

In the interest of simplification, the image of the French economy and society as depicted by the group will be presented under a small number of headings: (1) man, (2) the economic consequences of technical progress, (3) growth prospects, (4) the results of economic growth, and (5) the international environment.

Man

Quantitative Aspects. Taking into account the uncertainties that affect both a long-term drop in the death rate and demographic behavior, we can anticipate a population of about sixty million inhabitants, which represents an annual increase of 0.9 per cent. As the working population will increase only at the rate of 0.5 per cent yearly,[7] the burden of the nonworking population upon those working will become greater (227 nonactive for 100 active in 1954, 247 in 1962, 251 in 1965, 254 in 1970, 259 in 1985).

A greater number of French people will live in cities, and especially in large cities. (See the table.) The group believes that

Year	Population of Industrial or Urban Zones	Population of Industrial or Urban Zones with More than 100,000 Inhabitants in 1954
1936	27,850,000	17,920,000
1954	30,110,000	19,430,000
1962	34,180,000	22,400,000
1970	39,310,000	26,080,000
1985	49,870,000	33,830,000

geographical segregation of generations will persist: The more mobile young "will flee to the suburbs, while older people will tend to congregate in the center of the cities; according to certain indications, this would seem to be an irresistible trend (noted

[7] This derives from a number of assumptions made about the length of compulsory education (eighteen years), the length of the work week (40 hours) and the length of paid vacations; the total rate of participation would decrease (38.3 per cent against 41.7 per cent in 1960).

in the United States and Great Britain as well as in the U.S.S.R.)."[8]

Per capita consumption will be multiplied by 2.3, and its structure will naturally continue to change (in particular, a strong increase in medical and other health expenditures, in leisure and cultural activities, and for transportation, with one car for 2.8 persons).

The length of the working life may increase, necessitating social adjustments which will allow older people to maintain a certain degree of activity after the legal retirement age. The average level of education will rise, but a significant part of this education will be distributed throughout the working life, calling into question the traditional division of life into three slices: years of schooling, work, retirement.[9]

Qualitative Aspects. With regard to man's aspirations in 1985, the report indicates at many points that, because of his higher standard of living, man in 1985 will be more demanding and, in particular, will demand a more aesthetically satisfying daily environment.

Constraints necessary to obtain a more efficient economy are mobility (to which a whole chapter is devoted), moderation in the increase of nonworking time, and discipline of personal income growth. The growing role of satisfactions obtained from nonmarket sources will require a more detailed investigation of "nonaccountable satisfactions" and of leisure time.

The report makes the following statement regarding man's frustrations in 1985: "It is no longer a question of nostalgia for the Golden Age but of the need for a careful study of these (psychic) difficulties and their causes; in particular, the individual's loss of contact with his biological rhythms, the necessity of living within a narrow and artificial man-made environment, the abusive pressures of complex and hierarchical socioeconomic structures."[10]

[8] *Reflexions pour 1985,* p. 57.

[9] In the 1960–1985 projection, it was estimated that there would be a reduction of 300,000 persons from the labor resources available in 1985 owing to adult education, retraining, etc.

[10] *Reflexions pour 1985,* p. 30.

The Economic Consequences of
Scientific and Technical Progress

These consequences could be classified according to the useful terminology of Richard Nelson,[11] who distinguishes two major types:

a. Consequences translatable in terms of productivity increases: agriculture (production to be doubled between now and 1985, with the working population reduced by half), industry (the problems of automation and its impact on employment is touched upon only briefly),[12] transportation and services (plane reservations, administration of banking services, etc.).

b. Consequences translatable in terms of improved satisfaction of needs (use of plastics in buildings) or even by satisfactions which were formerly unimagined (progress in medicine, multiplex televised meetings, air-cushion trains, etc.).

In these respects, the report notes an interesting contradiction, to the effect that the consequences of scientific and technological progress move in two antagonistic directions; as the average durability of capital goods is extended, their obsolescence is accelerated.

Prospects for Economic Growth[13]

Does economic growth constitute a desirable goal? Is it realizable? To the first question, the answer is unquestionably affirmative for obvious reasons, but at the same time it should be recognized that we are poorly equipped for a comprehensive grasp of the negative aspects entailed by the achievement of rapid economic growth (a problem already noted in the discussion of constraints).

[11] See, for example, his paper "Science, the Economy and Public Policy," presented to the Berlin symposium on *Planning, the State and Society* (Berlin, 1964).

[12] *Reflexions pour 1985*, p. 116.

[13] This point is developed at greater length in the chapter in *Options of the Fifth Plan*, devoted to prospects for 1985, than in the body of the report itself.

Concerning the second question, there seems no reason to anticipate any forcible slack in the rate of growth, since the economy "is barely emerging from a catching-up period. This means there is still a significant margin for evolution, since, if the current rate is maintained for the next twenty years, the nation will attain only a level barely above that of the United States at present, and there still remain numerous possibilities of conversion from areas of weak to those of strong productivity."[14]

The price to be paid for rapid economic growth lies in a vigorous effort in research (multiplication of expenditures by 6), modernization of public administration, the necessity of training people for greater mobility and openness to innovation, and finally, an increase in the average dimensions of production and research facilities.

The Results of Economic Growth

Sharp Rise in Government Spending. The gross domestic production would be at an index of 315 (1960 = 100), household consumption at an index of 307, gross capital formation at an index of 359. But a wide distortion appears when we look at figures showing the rise of social overhead capital and social welfare payments, with the first at an index of 700 (1960 = 100) and the second at an index of 800 (1959 = 100).[15] When we realize that these two categories of expenditures are currently financed by compulsory payments from the public (taxation and welfare contributions), we begin to see the problem created by a multiplication by 7 or 8 of these compulsory payment receipts, while, on the other hand, real income is only tripled. Thus, the Fifth Plan strongly emphasized the problem of financing by recommending

14 *Reflexions pour 1985*, p. 19.

15 For social overhead capital, a progression has been charted which presupposes the necessity of a vast catching-up effort for the beginning of the period (1970–1975; 7.8 per cent a year) and that by the end of this period, the rate of increase of this item would be close to that of the gross domestic production (1975–1985; 4.5 per cent a year). For welfare payments an increased rate has been assigned of 8.6 per cent lower than the trend observed since 1950.

that whenever it is possible to individualize taxation, public services should be paid for by those using them.

In a longer-range view, Group 1985 maintains that the growing role played by nonaccountable elements in the standard of living will lead to introducing procedures to identify individual preferences which will assure a "simulation" of the market.[16] These elements will also necessitate a personal income policy which the group does not define specifically but which provides an opportunity to explain to the public "the fact that a greater possibility for unaccountable satisfactions has been added to individual income" (a policy, moreover, which the group expects to be generally accepted in France by 1985). Finally, "those dissatisfactions, demands, and disputes, which are among the principal permanent features of our history, will become more concerned with rights of usage and distribution of collective goods and services than with monetary income."[17]

No Affluence in 1985. The group particularly warned the public against any illusions of affluence, such as the belief that the French will have no economic problems in 1985. It is true that in 1985, the gross domestic product per capita would be greater than that of the United States in 1960. If we accept a long-term growth rate on the order of 1.8 per cent in the United States, the two countries will be at almost the same level in 1985.[18] But the income figure in absolute value to be attained by 1985 (average per capita annual income of about 10,000 francs, or 2,500 francs a month for a family of three) is already considered inadequate, or at least as subject to improvement, by those who now receive it. Furthermore, this average should not allow us to forget the probability that part of the population will fall well below it; thus we run the risk of having "the other France," those left behind by

16 For instance, television discussions which would "familiarize a wide public with various patterns of living of other countries could contribute thereby to educating consumers by helping them to formulate judgments about their own environment and about the future which they envisage for their children" (*Reflexions pour 1985*, p. 63).

17 *Reflexions pour 1985*, p. 36.

18 At least if we utilize a measure based upon American prices. A measure based upon European prices would still show a marked discrepancy between the two countries in 1985, of about 25 to 30 per cent.

economic growth. Finally, new scarcities will be created; to the problem of social overhead capital expenditures whose financing, as we have already seen, is not facilitated by the rise in the standard of living, must be added raw materials, air, water, and land, that is, all of the nonreproducible natural resources. These new scarcities could lead to a reconsideration of the responsibilities of the private and public sectors, according to the urgency of particular changes.

A final reason to abandon any expectations of affluence in 1985 relates to the particular way in which economic growth unfolds. In other words, those things which are technically feasible and psychologically desirable develop more rapidly than what is economically possible. Furthermore, those areas of progress already achieved are increasingly taken for granted, thus establishing expectations among those who have not yet been affected by the tide of economic advance. And finally, the causes of "antiprogressivism" (or negative progress) are numerous in a densely populated and technologically sophisticated society, thus weakening awareness of progress already achieved.

International Environment

In its introduction, the report specified that the group had deliberately excluded from its area of investigation "the vast options of international politics, such as military power or aid to underdeveloped countries." The report emphasized, for example, that economic necessities would, at most, render it "increasingly difficult to consider a certain number of problems on a scale smaller than that of Europe."[19] It also underlined the fact that certain specifically French cultural and intellectual traditions could be maintained only through the greatest efforts of scientific and technical research.

On the purely economic level, the group examined in great detail the extent of France's dependence in terms of raw materials and the various problems which this entails.

[19] *Reflexions pour 1985*, p. 10.

3. THE PLACE OF LONG-RANGE PLANNING IN THE DRAFTING OF THE SIXTH PLAN

The following remarks, only provisory in nature (and in no way meant to prejudge the preparatory work of the Sixth Plan), envision studies relating to the long-range future within a well-defined perspective, namely, the establishment of five-year development plans. In other words, we assume, with Professor Mazlish, a relationship of cause and effect between the prediction of social phenomena and the possibility of acting upon these to good effect.[20] We also assume that prediction is a guide to action, not just a means of helping us to overcome our indecision or of contributing to our entertainment or our spiritual edification, to borrow the useful classification of Professor Iklé.

But this assumption raises the problem of limiting those subjects to be explored. In the sense that we must clarify those decisions made within the framework of the plan, everything lends itself to surmises, and the planner runs the risk of being submerged by the sheer mass of studies which, theoretically, he must launch. By way of a working hypothesis, we might use the guideline suggested by L. A. Vincent.[21] Long-range forecast should rely upon all those elements of capital which, because of their intrinsic rigidity, cannot be readily adapted to the environment into which they are introduced. Vincent proposes to retain the following four categories, in rising order of flexibility: (1) man's professional knowledge; (2) natural wealth, either permanent (land, living resources) or limited (mineral, oil); (3) economic infrastructure and its geographical distribution; and (4) durable equipment and consumption goods.

Therefore, a possible criterion for selecting or rejecting a topic for prospective study could be that this topic should have significant implications for the national capital in its various forms

[20] Bruce Mazlish, ed., *The Railroad and the Space Program: An Exploration in Historical Analogy* (Cambridge, Mass.: The M.I.T. Press, 1965), p. 15.

[21] "La prévision à long terme," *Études et Conjoncture*, September 1960. See also William Gorham's interesting reflections in "Government Planning for the Year 2000" in Daniel Bell, ed., *Commission on the Year 2000 Report* (Brookline, Mass.: American Academy of Arts and Sciences, 1966).

(skills, natural resources, "artificial" capital) and for decisions controlling the quantitative and/or qualitative growth of this capital. At the very most, this will mean ignoring any discontinuous source of change, even an important one, if it has no impact upon capital (or, to be more exact, if it has no perceptible impact, to the best of our knowledge and means of observation).

Let me add that we can correct the restrictive aspect of this concept by more or less broadening the definition of capital, by including, for example, as Group 1985 has already done, the biological and psychological aspects of man.

Once we have agreed upon the utility of replacing the preparation of a five-year plan within a longer over-all view,[22] the question then arises concerning the organization of the work. Should long-term studies be based upon the same rhythm as the development of the plan itself, that is, keyed to alternating phases of activity corresponding to the establishment of the plan and a hibernation period between two plans? Some have regretted the fact that Group 1985, explicitly created as a contribution to the preparation of the Fifth Plan, was an isolated enterprise, and not integrated within a framework of continuity. The "planning units" created within certain ministries constituted the beginning of a permanent structure, but there is still no provision for the specific needs of central planning organisms.

What can we expect from surmises about the long-range future? Ideally, they can provide us with three types of "lessons."

First, they can identify *undesirable* future situations that will engender problems of *prevention* and lead to a definition of the means necessary to prevent the emergence of such situations or, at least, their consolidation (in other words, lowering the cost of their elimination or of their reduction to a tolerable threshold). Examples are overpopulation, pollution of natural resources, or, in general terms, phenomena of overcrowding.

Second, these studies can identify *irreversible* trends (as op-

---

[22] This utility should be considered at two levels of reflection and decision: that of the main options of the plan (growth rate, length of work, programs of social investments, regional development policy) and that of the work of commissions for modernization (notably those proposing programs of social legislation).

posed to the preceding case, where the trend is considered reversible) which engender problems of adaptation. Examples in demography are the survival of 90 per cent of newborn infants to the age of ninety, the lengthening fertility period of women, the wide accessibility of contraceptive devices, easy to use and of maximum efficiency.[23]

Third, they define *desirable* objectives whose realization would be spread over a long period of time and which would be studied with a view to determining to what degree their realization is favorably or unfavorably affected by long-term changes in the environment. For example, studies might be made of ways to hasten the progress of equalizing opportunities for the material and cultural improvement of various sociovocational categories.

This typology, based upon the expected applicability of studies of the long-term future, may be related to the idea of *capital,* chosen as the criterion for determining what is relevant or irrelevant to long-range prospects with a view to planning. The real goal of prediction is either to prevent this capital from irremediable devaluation or to avoid its inadaptability to what is expected of it (or to foresee how it will be affected by a particular social factor) or, finally, to facilitate a better knowledge of the influence of a normative action on this capital.

The recourse to economic-demographic projections as a means of making surmises about the future has often been criticized by those who consider it unwise to be unduly influenced by the past when trying to discover useful images of the future. These critics feel that, conversely, one should begin with the future in order to act upon the present. Their reasoning is that either the past *might* transform itself into something radically different (or run the risk of doing so), thus providing an inadequate frame of reference, or that the past *must* change for the better, and this change could only take place precisely by breaking with the past.

It is impossible to resolve this argument in a few sentences, but we can nonetheless call attention to the fact that in certain cases

[23] Under this second category we should perhaps include what Bruce Mazlish, *op. cit.,* calls *social invention,* that is, any novelty (railroad, automobile, space explorations, etc.) which has an impact upon a great many aspects of social reality.

reference to the past is inevitable (when, for example, the biological heritage of man must be taken into account) and that in other cases a so-called detachment with regard to the past simply masks the desire to project present "modernity" into the future. It is, however, equally true that concepts utilized in a projection describe reality within a carefully determined perspective, and this perspective is not always the one most pertinent to the problem under consideration.

On the other hand, one must credit projections with the virtue of coherence, without which no study of the long-range future is entirely valid. Consequently, it would be wise to retain projection as an "anchorage point" of conclusions whose prospective content is obtained by more specific studies — by studying, for example, in a more comprehensive way the factors which influence the evolution of elements treated as exogenous variables (housing, social overhead) and by making more systematic use of international comparisons to give the future a more precise shape.

The specific studies mentioned earlier should attempt to provide raw material that the projectionists will integrate directly into their quantitative framework, or which will serve other researchers in their own needs. One could envision, for example, that a study of demographic conditions in twenty or thirty years could provide evidence directly assimilable in a long-range projection — possible changes in the birth or marriage rate or the proportion of retired persons in the total population. Other evidence, however, such as the accumulation of capital in the hands of the aged or transformation of the family due to the extended fertility period, cannot be assimilated and would have to be exploited elsewhere.

Normally, anyone in charge of a specific study should ascertain that all statements about the future manifest the double characteristic of being important and (more or less) probable. He should also ascertain, when confronting a mass of partial results to arrive at a synthetic picture (quantitative, by long-range projection, and qualitative) whether the different elements of this picture are coherent in relation to one another, a task which perhaps can be accomplished only at the central echelon, and one which will assuredly raise delicate technical problems, since future coherence is all the more difficult to determine in advance when the future is far removed and the qualitative elements numerous.

Nevertheless, a problem still more difficult than that of future likelihood remains — one of the judgment brought to bear upon the desirability of the picture (or pictures) which finally emerges. On the one hand, the criteria for judgment are multiple; a particular future technical evolution, for example, may be weighed according to criteria of improvement of material well-being, conditions of life, equalization of opportunity, importance of leisure, or international prestige of a country (always with the condition of trying to establish a link of cause and effect between the criteria of value and the thing being judged). But, on the other hand, there remains also the impossibility of placing ourselves in the position of those who in twenty or thirty years will be the actual judges of the situation that we have tried to anticipate — unless, obviously, we could determine objectively, once and for all, what is good or bad for man.

Whatever the difficulties, it is to be hoped that long-range prospects, prepared in view of middle-range development plans, will not remain the work solely of experts but that they will become the subject of an ever wider range of public discussion, so that the preoccupation with the distant future will not remain the prerogative of a minority.

DISCUSSION

Chairman MILLON: Would you give us a brief explanation of another future-oriented group in Paris — that which centers around Bertrand de Jouvenel?

CAZES: *Futuribles* is an intellectual endeavor which deals with the most difficult part of any surmising effort — that is, with trends and discontinuities in the political arrangements and institutions. *Futuribles* is primarily oriented not toward social or economic aspects of the long-range future (whatever interest its initiator, Bertrand de Jouvenel, may feel for these matters, which he has studied in a very profound and illuminating way) but toward the political field in its international and domestic aspects.

The second aspect of *Futuribles* is that it has no institutional basis, no permanent staff of its own. It is not an "institute of the future" but rather a platform where people with all kinds of intellectual and political backgrounds can express their views of the future, with only these explicit rules of the game: one must not put forward one's personal preferences, and one must avoid the identification of only one possible future. The word *futuribles* (which comes from the Spanish Jesuit Molina) implies that there are more often than not *several* possible futures, depending on the assumptions one makes.

From what I have said about Group 1985 and the *Futuribles* venture, one can see that these are really complementary endeavors without any duplication, because we don't think that our task as government planners should be the investigation of the future of democracy, of parliaments, and so forth. These are very fundamental questions; but for obvious practical reasons, we have to be very selective in the range of questions we consider as relevant for planning purposes. So one might say that between *Futuribles* and ourselves there is a division of labor: *Futuribles* is engaged in the political aspects of the future, while we are concerned with the social and economic conditions of tomorrow. But this distinction should not be pushed too far. In fact, we hope that *Futuribles* and similar studies will help us to see the social and economic facets of the future in a wider and richer context, while on the other hand our conclusions may have some relevance for political scientists who look into the future of international and domestic politics.

Professor PARDON E. TILLINGHAST: You said at one point that the projected income in 1985 is considered now to be inadequate by those who would benefit from it. It was not clear to me just what that meant.

CAZES: What I meant to say was that just now some people have the level of income which will be average in 1985. They obviously consider this level of income inadequate as compared with their needs and aspirations. Therefore you can conclude that this average for 1985 will not mean general affluence and disappearance of all frustrations coming from economic causes.

TILLINGHAST: Surely there is no level of income which will get rid of all of the frustrations, is there?

CAZES: Do you mean economic frustrations? This is an interesting point. Some years ago I read a paper that gave some hints about the possibility of an absolute saturation of economic needs.[24] It said that George Romney, president of American Motors Corporation, and John O. Ekblom, chairman of Hupp Corporation, refused in 1960 an increase in salary on the ground that their earnings were already largely adequate for their needs.

---

[24] Saul Engelbourg, "Insatiability, a Problem for Utopia?" *The American Journal of Economics and Sociology*, Vol. 22 (January 1963).

The Parameters of Urban Planning

LEONARD J. DUHL

To expand on Victor Hugo's "one can resist the invasion of armies, but not the invasion of ideas," long-range planning is perhaps an idea that has found its time. As I rewrite the original version of my speech, I cannot help remarking at the progress made by the "invasion" of long-range policy-planning advocates on the American scene — particularly since the Endicott House Conference in October.

With the passage of the Model Cities Act[1] and the mustering of seasoned troops (led by New Haven's Ralph Taylor), one can envision the advent of "planning" on the horizon: ecologically oriented planning that is comprehensive and coordinated; long-range planning that considers the implications of short-range (or "fire-fighting") decisions; integrated and coordinated planning that involves agencies in both the public and private spheres; "democratic planning" that includes and involves the total community. For those who have long advocated such planning but

[1] The Demonstration Cities and Metropolitan Development Act of 1966 (which has become popularly referred to as "Model Cities") authorizes the Department of Housing and Urban Development to make grants and give technical assistance to help cities and metropolitan areas develop *comprehensive plans* for improving the conditions of whole communities, with specific emphasis placed upon that planning (1) which includes and evolves from community-wide involvement, and (2) which demonstrates the evolution of integrated planning (health with transportation with education, etc.) within the community. This involves the coordination of the entire range of federal urban assistance — social, health, educational, and employment, rehabilitation and construction grant and loan programs — with state and local public and private resources,

have been content to settle for achieving 5 per cent of what they called for, perhaps, just perhaps, "Model Cities" is a dividend.

The Endicott House Conference is addressed to "Possible Futures and Their Relations to the Man-Controlled Environment." Because I was asked to discuss the problems surrounding long-range planning for urban social policy, I felt called upon to begin by frankly stating that (1) there really is no structure within the federal establishment basically concerned with this subject; (2) nor is there any structure within the federal establishment which pursues fundamental cognitive research in this regard; and (3) practically nowhere is there an ongoing training program for those who would so concern themselves or who would prepare themselves for the impending issues.

This in no way implies that long-range planning is not part of our American society nor that *some* people in *some* areas of this nation are not so engaged. In fact, almost every area of the United States has established some version of an "Office of Planning." However, such efforts are typically concerned with "implementation" or "program" planning (how to establish and operate *a* neighborhood center, *an* urban transport program, or *a* sewer system), not with long-range policy planning, heedful of the concomitant long-range and tangential implications of every single decision.

The categorical approach that is traditional with our craft-guild professions and institutions has not encouraged across-the-board, long-range policy planning; in fact, one might say that they have discouraged such amalgamations, even on a programmatic level. Is it fear of loss of authority, loss of prestige? Is it the very basic and real fear of "change"? Surely, it is much easier on body and mind to do one's job, day by day, and leave it at that. The oft-heard and usually valid excuse is: "Because each day brings its many crises which must be met, who can take time to 'game-out' what might happen tomorrow?"

Perhaps it is all of these excuses and all of these misconceptions of what "planning" really is and can be that have made it what it has been. Planning, in its truest sense, is not a static state; planning is not a product but a process — a veritable evolutionary continuum. It is not creating a grand or master plan that must be implemented no matter what happens. For a plan to be effective, the plan must change; for a planner to be effective, the planner must also change. I am here drawn to a personal reference that will further elucidate my conception of this phenomenon called "planning."

In a sense my own personal odyssey as a psychiatrist runs parallel to that of others in a variety of professions. We who have found the craft-guild boundaries of our own individual professions to be too restrictive as we worked in our particular calling have broken out — moved into the "para" areas. I really didn't move "out" of psychiatry per se but parallel to psychiatry — into the fields of city planning and achitecture, of social planning and economics, of educational planning, and into government. I thus found myself in an entirely new area — a sort of arena for those whose minds and interests overlap, intermingle, and intertwine in a common search for "wholeness" and increasing "competency."

The participants in what Derek de Solla Price[2] described as the "invisible colleges" are the sociologists, scientists, architects, philosophers, lawyers, doctors, educators, and so on, whose avocation is "change" and how it may be effected. Though all are intimately involved in reality, many having key and critical roles within their own profession, agency, or institution, they are primarily interested in the *constant redefinition of problems*. This in turn, implies a corresponding *constant reformulation of both solutions and their management*.

During my years at the National Institute of Mental Health[3] I found that as I talked about the "para" issues of mental health — those of slum conditions, overcrowding, rapidly changing social structures, the breakup of the extended family unit, technological innovations, educational lacks and strides, freeways, rapid transit, etc. — and as I considered what services were going to be demanded by an ever changing society, I could really bring about

[2] "Collaboration in an Invisible College," *American Psychologist*, Vol. 21, No. 11 (November 1966). Actually, "invisible college," as a name for a group is of historical derivation — a loosely organized group who met in the pubs and coffee houses of London around the mid-seventeenth century and later became formalized as the Royal Society of London.

[3] Twelve years as a psychiatrist, Professional Services Branch; two years as chief, Office of Planning.

a redefinition of the problems. While discussing these matters with a range of people within and outside the government structure, I discovered that my information input of what was happening, together with their contributions, brought about an awareness that mental health could no longer be the sole province of the psychiatrist. The remarkable outcome of all this is that a tremendous amount of outside pressure was brought to bear upon the NIMH so that hoped-for changes did begin to occur. (These changes in direction continue, as demonstrated by the recent creation of the NIMH Center for Metropolitan Studies, which includes a Center for Social Policy Planning.)

This is perhaps proof positive of one of my most basic beliefs: that the power of ideas and the power of redefining a problem through information input can have profound impact upon the long-range direction of an organization — even if one is not among the decision-making hierarchy. (If one would take the time, innumerable "changes" in fields from education to garbage collection could be shown to have resulted from information input, even from just correlating or regrouping available data, so that the very problem is thus redefined.) In fact, few of the members of the "invisible colleges" head programs, though, as I have already noted, each is vital to the efforts with which he associates himself.

Communication lines for the members of the "invisible colleges" are the telephone, the Xerox machine, and the jet. Their value lies in both their access to information and their ready dissemination and utilization of that connected and correlated data. They link up, connect, and interchange ideas and theories and concepts as well as information. Operating on many different levels at the same time, they create links between business and government, between the private and public sectors, between the different layers of government — federal, state, city — between government systems and the neighborhoods, between the money givers and the potential receivers, between the theorists and the activists. Being tied to neither time, location, nor job position, they actually join their counterparts in a multitude of "para" areas in a sort of confirmation of their basic "ecological"[4] orientation.

[4] "Ecology" may be defined as that inter-intra confrontation of biological, psychological, physiological, social, and historical factors that embrace one's

The "floating crap game" — differing combinations of these change agents — may assemble in the West to plan a community school, in the East to plan for a new town (as was the case with Columbia); they may get together informally to help one of their members solve a particular problem, possibly with regard to a new community health facility or a transportation system, or even the impact of systems technology upon social policy planning. The range and scope of their interest and application of knowledge would seem to be boundless. Their *expertise* is in combining and reformulating data and information, in redefining the problem, and, perhaps most importantly, in causing others to believe that they must do likewise — simply because of the way in which additional information is presented relative to the issues at hand.

These planners have a penchant for *performance criteria*, while they rebel against the traditions of *specific standards* that are not possibly multiapplicable. They have the ability to "feel" data; they have an appreciation for the ecological implications of decisions. For example, they realize that a single administrative decision to extend the hours of a particular service agency (perhaps even the Welfare Department) will affect not only staffing patterns but also clientele and, potentially, transportation systems, purchasing trends, education and health systems, unemployment rolls, and so on.

The really crucial factor inherent in these "floating crap games" is their self-renewing and self-perpetuation capacities. They are a continuous and ever expanding flow of diverse personalities and orientations. They group and regroup; they bring in new members and rid themselves of those who do not or cannot measure up.

Sir Geoffrey Vickers has cited the one characteristic that, more than anything else, sets these people apart from those who are

---

family, school, neighborhood, the many overlapping communities that teach values, defenses, and offenses, the meaning of oneself and one's existence. Ecology contends that as man creates and alters his environment, he in turn is affected by that environment. For example, many of the pressing social and economic problems of the aging today exist because of advances made in the field of medicine. "Ecology" connotes *wholeness* — that all has effect on all else, that education is tied to housing to transportation to employment to discrimination and on and on.

merely of today and yesterday. Sir Geoffrey credits these members of the "invisible colleges" with the *art of judgment* — the ability to make judgments in the present which dramatically change the future. They radically differ from such groups as the Commission on the Year 2000 in that they do not become preoccupied with "predicting the future." For the planners and forecasters who constitute these "invisible colleges" the concern is how the present can be altered so that the future will become one in which we shall want to live.

All of this brings us to an important point: Where is the major formal symposium(s) for change in our society today? The halls of Congress and of the state legislatures and the political and business areas are where the allocation of funds and resources take place, where the real process of change is being either aided and abetted or hindered and starved. For business and industry, long-range planning, projections, and keeping as far ahead of the trends as possible — hopefully, setting some trends — are crucial to continued existence. Thus they are, for the most part, by virtue of their profit-motive incentive, creatures of change. In somewhat stark contrast, state legislatures, city councils, and even the federal Congress have demonstrated little ability or inclination to plan and to act in terms of the future — particularly with regard to urban policy. In general, all are responsive to immediate demands placed upon them, to crises occurring at the moment, rather than to any search for and determination of future policies.

In fact, most politicians frankly admit to the potential danger incumbent upon those who would publicly plan too far ahead. One example of the potential implications of an urban policy that would place great import upon *integration* is the "bussing" factor, sadly a grave political danger in today's world. The politician is perhaps a cautious agent of change — if a generalization may be made; there are, of course, the notable exceptions.

All layers of government do have one common denominator, the Bureau of the Budget, which forces them into a position of at least planning one fiscal year ahead — not necessarily policies but program expenditures. With the advent of PPBS[5] we shall cer-

[5] Planning, Programming and Budgeting Systems promote horizontal thinking and action — not unlike the procedure by which the three branches of the armed services were "McNamarized."

69

tainly see more planning, that is, more integrated and coordinated planning. The tangential implications are here vital in that there are inherent and immediate demands not only to conduct the business of every day but also to change — somewhat radically — the very philosophy upon which that business is being run.

Coordination of efforts, of monies, and of personnel can become a problem. Whereas just a few years ago many of us worried at the lack of coordinating instruments, what is happening in American society today is that we are seeing an era of "umbrella agencies." It seems that agencies are being funded to coordinate other funded agencies, which were funded to coordinate personnel, and so on. This is producing a number of heretofore nonexistent linkages as well as the phenomenon of disappearing boundaries — jurisdictional, professional, programmatical, even political. In some ways, I see this as a promising trend in that we are each beginning to touch and affect each other; but the dangers of duplication through overcoordination must also be considered.

We are seeing coordination not only of facilities (physical aspects) but of personnel (social aspects) as well. My fundamental concern with planning is that these linkages and coordination occur as well as when, where, how, why, and to what end they occur. Information input at crucial moments certainly is a causative factor. Moreover, as I have previously implied, information is power, and that power is not necessarily negative, for if the planner is concerned with implementing plans, with causing change in current institutions and people, then he must have leverage and power. His greatest source may be found in his information and his informational sources.

The minute he becomes aware of and concerned with power, he enters the arena of politics; the minute he enters the political arena, he engages in the constant battle of confrontation between the various systems extant. At this moment in time he finds himself forced to declare his basic values; and then he is in a battle for his life.

It is particularly for this reason that I cannot too strongly advocate "consumer"[6] participation in those questions and deci-

6 "Consumer" is here used to denote those users of a particular service or facility — whether they are welfare recipients or Sunday picnickers at the

sions which affect the life and environment of the consumer. In fact, I believe this may be the highest value to be stressed by any social urban policy. When the systems are opened up, when people are encouraged and enabled to participate (and educated to do so), then we shall not have welfare inspectors "visiting" recipients at four in the morning; nor shall we have training programs for which only high school graduates can qualify, nor urban renewal that becomes Negro removal coupled with tripled social costs to local communities and agencies.

The real planner is he who opens up the system (using every trick of the trade) so that the democratic processes can be applied. True, this often results in a pitting of one value system against another. HUD has been facing this problem in its transition from the old primary concern with building of the Housing and Home Finance Agency to HUD's increased concern for people. I readily admit that this process usually muddies the waters of "perfect plans" or of "master planners" who prefer to bulldoze through what they feel should be done. They have found fault with the likes of me in the past because of my beliefs in involving people before decisions are made, as well as afterwards.

One of my favorite stories in this regard concerns an Israeli planner I know. He became extremely agitated when the first three hundred people moved into *his* beautiful city in the desert where everything had been perfectly planned. He told me: "You know those Jews, they like to run the country. The minute they moved in they started changing my plans" — and so they should. All of this relates to some very basic values, which we are fond of expostulating but often find difficult to apply — those having to do with human dignity and social equity in which the assumption is made that people should have the opportunity to be treated as people should be treated and should have some say about the way in which they live.

The planner, then, is a multifaceted personage in that he defines the image as he collects information and links people, as he brings about constant redefinition of the problems. He must be a politi-

---

neighborhood park, out-patients at a local clinic, or students of an adult education class.

cian in that his understanding of complex ecological systems (the very relationships of agencies and people and governments) brings him an awareness of leverage points — both inside and outside that system with which he may be primarily concerned. He develops links with the "invisible colleges" thus expanding his own abilities. The planner must also be a technician so that programs may be implemented and policies may be carried out. The crucial point is that the planner must never be guilty of "closing the system" so that his ideas alone can develop. Problems, ideas, or plans must all be constantly evaluated and re-evaluated, defined and redefined, over and over again.

What I am really talking about is the concept of the planner as a change agent whose job is very much like that of the psychiatrist. While remaining virtually (or publicly) anonymous, he helps to redefine the problems put to him by the patient (or community). He helps his patient see what new data are needed. He helps him collect and correlate the additional information. Thus, while helping to reformulate the problem, he helps the patient (or the community) make its own decisions. Then he proceeds to help evaluate the effect of the decisions through "feedback."

What is vital here is "feedback" — responses to what is happening. Some may be idiosyncratic, irrational responses, others may be very well thought out and developed, others may even be organized (as in hearings or marches). The planner must be able to evaluate this "feedback" — the impact of change upon any of the systems. He must be able to see and understand the tangential changes in the total ecological system.

This is a difficult and very delicate task for any planner who would be a change agent. My profession of psychiatry has prepared me for some of the situations into which I find myself drawn or catapulted in this whole process. Because once you're in, you are dealing with man's irrationality, with his fantastic anger, his hostilities, and his misunderstandings or misconceptions. You find that the very people you are helping may suddenly turn on you in anger. The gap between aspiration levels, thanks to mass media and TV, and ability levels is often a cause of uncontrolled or uncontrollable hostility. You find that the tools of language are inadequate when talking of change to a Federal Housing Administration appraiser.

You find that working through thoughts and ideas — "playing them out" — can help in understanding. Everybody plans in some way or another. What I am advocating is that the planner promote as much of this planning as possible and that he facilitate people planning together about that which may ultimately affect them. This is the contrast between a *society that plans* and *a planned society*. We can succeed in our planning, as I have already stated, only if we as planners continue to change and if our plans continue to change.

At this point it must be rather obvious that when I accepted your kind invitation to participate in this conference, I also accepted the invitation to speak on those issues which I feel are crucial today. They are no less crucial to architects than to psychiatrists or to planners. For these reasons (and all I have heretofore stated) I want to encourage the establishment of a number of interdisciplinary institutes whose concern would be with these issues. Called by any name that you might feel proper, they would be linked one with the other — rather informally so that the system would be fluid and promote change.

We must begin to train architects and planners and all whose interests are in making the systems more effectively open and operative. Those whose interests lean more toward the technical aspects must be so trained, but with an appreciation for those whose concerns are more for evolving policy. We must begin to develop new kinds of curriculums for those whose interests lie in helping to develop long-range policy, and we must set up the systems that would achieve this end.

Because there are really no experts in this field, our training ground — our very classrooms — must be the community. We must be willing to wade in, to get our feet and our hands dirty through involvement with every aspect of our ecological setting from the slums right on up to the mayors' offices and from there to the state house and then to Washington. Our involvement on all levels is as vital as promoting the involvement of people on all levels in making the decisions and setting the policies that ultimately affect them.

DISCUSSION

DAVIDOFF: There seems to be some conflict between your high valuation of participatory democracy and your description of the "invisible college." As long as it is invisible, the college may be quite destructive of democracy. Would you comment on what you think the relationship should be and whether that "invisible college" should become visible or not?

DUHL: The group I was talking about range through government, academia, cities, and foundations. Though they share no one specific ideology, they do share many of the same values; that is, when you are dealing with a sort of gigantic operation in government, trying to develop new kinds of concepts, you must work rather hard to make democracy work.

Now, ideally, this so-called "invisible college" should begin to connect every interested group. As you are probably aware, some of these people who are concerned with the problems of poverty are in foundations like Ford Foundation, and some of them are in CCAP (Citizens Crusade Against Poverty). Really, what I am saying is that I am not concerned as much with the word "invisible" as with the linkages between almost all the different segments in society. I am concerned that we provide a *forum* in which the real arguments and battles and confrontations can take place.

There still remains a large segment of our society who are unable to participate in the confrontation, partly because they don't have the data, partly because they don't have the skill, and partly because they can't get into the system.

DAVIDOFF: The nature of the group you discuss still seems unclear. First you say that it is a group of people with your values, and then that it is sort of a political party, and then that it is the social critics which most societies have had, and the social critics work in a number of different institutions.

DUHL: Let me redefine it, Paul. Derek Price has written about the "invisible college" in the field of biochemistry, where there are about twenty or thirty key people who are really tuned in to the advances. They are in continual communication with each other — so much so that when basic decisions are made, somehow this group is always in the forefront, influencing students and policies in that area.

THE PARAMETERS OF URBAN PLANNING

You will find a small group like this in every field — be it in architecture, social action, city planning, or poverty warring. What I was saying was that the man concerned with comprehensive long-range policy must connect all these others from differing orientations.

Now, the values of each group are characteristically very different. I am sure among the biochemists there are those who are really not concerned with the issues we are exploring here, just as there are those of us whose chief concern is not biochemistry.

Though I believe the concept of the "invisible college" to be sound, one of the problems it faces today is that it does not include large segments of our society. As long as they are not included, we must have advocates for them — advocates who are really fighting to see that the values they represent are given visibility and included in planning or programming.

The more diverse the members of the "invisible college" are — as long as they share some basic values as to the need of societal systems to change in response to their human elements — the more effective will be its import. I am really issuing a clarion call to get into the forum, get into the act, and let's start stirring up the systems and see what the impact will be.

S. ANDERSON: The advocates will themselves be one invisible college.

DUHL: Some of the advocates are members of these invisible colleges and show up in many places, like this place.

Professor HAROLD BARNETT: I want to clarify what you didn't quite clarify in your last comment. Is the invisibility of the "invisible college" something of positive value, or is the invisibility the result of not being in one institutional area?

DUHL: It is the latter.

Dean SAM HURST: It seems to me that you left an apparent contradiction in your concept of the planner as a change agent, in which his prime role is that of agent, which implies a certain neutrality, and the concept of him as a value delineator, which implies a rather different responsibility.

DUHL: If I may here be permitted a personal reference, when I first began my training in psychiatry, I was told by some that I must not allow my value system to infringe upon my treatment of patients. However, I very quickly discovered that I still had to be very aware of what my values were.

If I really believe that each individual has the ability, once freed, to make decisions that affect his life, this will affect my role as a change agent. If, on the other hand, I essentially believe that the individual patient really has no competence whatsoever, that my role is to impose competence on him (which is a different value), I shall treat his case in an entirely different way.

It is really very basic to the change agent's efforts that he be aware of his own value system. If he is to fit into the kind of value system that promotes change and nourishes competence, his values must be predicated upon the notion (1) that he is not the God of the system and (2) that people have the ability to make decisions that can affect them. Even as I become more involved in the urban area in the Department of Housing and Urban Development, I can't tell you how to run HUD. That is not my objective; yet there are certain values that I stand for in the social arena which I would like to insert into the HUD decision-making process. And I intend to keep pushing these values on them. So you are right in the respect that there is a certain value element ever present.

BARNETT: You spoke of the need of the consumer to express himself in a democratic way. What role do you have for the traditional notions of economic freedom, consumer choice, free-enterprise market, the conventional market economy concept? What role is there for consumers simply to express their choices in the market place or workers or college professors to express their choices individually as workers or buyers in the market place and not democratically?

DUHL: First of all, let me say I am not an economist; I don't know much about it, but I do feel that very often there are really no choices in the market place. When you give a choice to a Negro in the slums to buy a big Buick or a Chevrolet, you are not giving him a choice. If you consider the situation today in which less than 20,000 low-cost housing units are built in the United States each year, the poor are not receiving very much choice in terms of housing. This means that the market-place system is really not working in the low-cost housing area.

If today the poor were made part of the decision-making

forum — if the poor really had a voice in determining housing policy — we undoubtedly would be forced into a situation where we would have to start producing what we really need. Roughly estimated, this would mean the construction of a million units each year for the next fifteen years — just to keep up with the low-cost market. I don't think the market place is going to handle that one.

I believe the only way we are going to begin to escalate our construction is when people start screaming and demanding satisfaction for their needs. The fact that the poor are beginning to protest against housing conditions, the fact that the poor are beginning to complain about conditions in Harlem, may very well lead us to a change in policy so that we will start building low-cost houses in Harlem. The point here is that the market place has not met this need. Thank God the poor had some advocates around who would help them begin to voice their demands and aspirations.

Certainly, the pressure is going to build up so that, within a very short time, we will probably see a low-cost housing market, but it is going to be a different arrangement, for I don't think the market is going to handle it itself. Once the demands are there and once we see that we can produce a million units a year, I predict that all the big industries in the United States will flock in immediately.

Professor CHARLES KINDLEBERGER: I think what you are really saying today is that there is a clash between planning and action, and you want the planners to take over the action.

DUHL: Not take over.

KINDLEBERGER: In my view, you feel, deep in your subconscious, unhappy at being cut out of the action. It is not so much that you wish to bring the people in but that you want to join the "power elite" yourself, if I may use the term. If I may interpret what you have been saying in psychoanalytical terms, the planner claims to want to bring the people into planning, and the planner into decision making, because he himself has a taste for power. The planner is basically unhappy that he is not running things in the minister's place. There is a basic clash between planning and day-to-day decisions and action which cannot be resolved by having the planner take over the day-to-day decision making.

77

I can give an example from the Department of State, which has a policy-planning staff. Time and time again, the effectiveness of this body is reduced by bringing it into day-to-day policy making or continuing negotiations. But there are frustrations. When I saw something of the Office of the Economic Adviser in the department in the early 1940's, the office was advising as to the desirability of stockpiling. But there was no one to take the advice and carry it out. Ultimately, the Office of the Economic Adviser ended up as the stockpiling agency of the department, but this meant he had to give up planning.

The general difficulty, I think, is that the planner often psychologically wants power and wants to take an action — this is what I think you were saying. But if he does, he has to stop planning.

DUHL: No, if I know myself, I know one thing: It is that I really don't want to take over the action, but I do want to influence the action. If I am giving an argument for the planner, I say that too often the planner is dealing with abstractions that have nothing to do with day-by-day decisions. The planner must become so deeply connected with action (not that he does the action) that he contributes at the critical points when action decisions are to be made. This is the critical issue here.

I have no desire to run an organization; nor do I want to plan for it in such a way that I can tell you where the organization is *definitely* going to go. However, I do feel that at the critical points, where the decisions are made up and down the system, there should be planners' inputs — inputs from planners not like myself and not only myself — in fact, a whole range of planners other than those presently so involved.

What happens in places like the State Department today is that the planners are completely disconnected from the reality of planning policy in the department. They are operating in an abstraction; they are way off in a corner, and they are completely locked out.

To reiterate, I should like to be a planner where the action is, though not actually taking part in the action. Maybe it is a very hard point to explain, but I think it is a little different from what you were saying.

About "Mankind 2000"

ROBERT JUNGK

In my family home we had an engraving showing a theater audience as seen from the stage through the eyes of the players. In that picture, as I remember, the theatergoers looked like perfect monsters; from here at the rostrum you in the audience look a bit like them to me. But I shall try to overcome my stage fright because I feel that it is important to start a dialogue between the New and the Old Worlds about the shaping of the future. We should not only do that in an abstract academic style; we should also risk progressing from factual, "objective" extrapolations to the realm of values — from exploratory prognostication to normative planning. Dr. Duhl has already indicated this direction. That is why I was so impressed by what he had to say earlier. "Mankind 2000," the organization I was asked to talk about, is very much involved with values. It is an international, interdisciplinary, and interideological venture dedicated to the invention of desirable future conditions of life and to the design of institutions likely to ensure the survival of the human race.

Mankind 2000 was first discussed and promoted by the ICDP (International Confederation for Disarmament and Peace), whose central office is in London. The ICDP tries to coordinate several dozen non-Communist peace groups which represent a great number of countries and continents. It was, as I see it, set up partly in order to counterbalance the very active and well-funded World Peace Council, which is strongly influenced and probably run by the Communists.

When the ICDP began to look for purposes transcending its immediate defensive aims, the fight against the armament race and war, it contacted many intellectuals, including myself, and asked them: Could you help us find and define some positive goals?

As a newspaperman, and especially as a writer who had devoted much time to studying the impact of science and technology, I felt like some of the scientists who had tried in vain to stop the use of the first atom bombs and, later on, the nuclear arms race. We were always on the defensive, trying to make responsible people change their dangerous policies when it was too late. Would it not be possible, I wondered, to anticipate and eliminate dangerous events by the early study of trends and the formulation of alternatives?

At about that time I found an article in the English monthly *Encounter*, written by the eminent physicist Dennis Gabor, which struck a similar chord. Mentioning *The Treason of the Clerks*, which had been quite influential after the First World War, Gabor said that "*les clercs*," the intellectuals, had again committed treason after World War II, because they had not even tried to provide the public with a vision of things to come.

Strengthened by Professor Gabor's polemic, I proposed that the ICDP take up that challenge and ask their members in over twenty different countries: What probable and desirable images of future conditions could you draw? How would a peaceful world actually look? In a world without armies and war, toward what efforts and goals might people work? What should and could be done with the mental, material, and financial resources set free from their bondage in the warfare states? Finally: Would it not be stimulating to present such images of a peaceful future in a world exhibition?

Of the important personalities to whom we had sent the first outline of our ideas, it was surprising how many responded and how positive the answers of most member organizations were. The answer of Johan Galtung, the Director of the Institute for Peace Research in Oslo, was typical. He based his reply on what he had learned when studying the reaction of people to the idea of peace: "Most of them see 'peace' only a something negative, namely the *absence* of war. People feel that peace is something desirable, but also that it is something dull, stale, and static."

This gave us a clue to a riddle, which had startled pacifists for a considerable time. The riddle is why young people, in general, are so little interested in political action aiming at a peaceful future. Is not that lack of interest in a large part caused by the purely defensive and therefore unappealing nature of the peace movement? We live not only in an age of immense dangers and terrible brutality but also in an epoch of intense creativity. Mankind 2000 is an appeal to that creativity.

We try to tell our friends: "Think about social inventions for a different kind of world. Think about powerful incentives that might motivate society as much as the armament race — for example, the building of new cities fit for people to live in and a new working environment that would be a far cry from the barracks- and beehivelike factories and office buildings of today."

In order to inspire and direct that "peace race" (if I may borrow that excellent slogan from Seymour Melman), we feel that some kind of "think factory" not unlike the RAND Corporation would be necessary. It would be an intellectual powerhouse devoted to the study and the design of a future based on the common need for peace rather than on the assumption of a never-ending chain reaction of international crises and military conflicts.

From the very start we knew that ICDP, as compared with the high degree of competence of the military "think factories," was much too weak to do the necessary studies; but we felt some kind of beginning had to be made. We compiled some of our ideas outlining the scope of work to be done by an organization specializing in "peace games" and circulated that memorandum to several hundred persons all over the globe.

Perhaps most impressive — and most unexpected — was the enthusiastic response we received from the countries of the Third World and from the other side of the badly torn Iron Curtain. Leading personalities in the Soviet Union, Poland, Czechoslovakia, Rumania, and Hungary were extremely interested in discussing the future with partners from the "other side" and in finding out what the future might hold for all of us. That in itself is an interesting development. The old certainties about a future rigidly determined by some laws stated through the "scriptures" of Communist doctrinaires seem to have been shattered. The "new men" in the socialist camp are less tradition-oriented than their fathers. They feel that their counterparts in the Western world might hold at least some interesting and worth-while ideas about the world to be.

As a delegate of Mankind 2000 I was in Moscow only two weeks ago at a conference called "The World between 1970 and 2000." At that rather disappointing meeting, which was sponsored by the Disarmament Section of the Academy of Sciences and the Soviet Peace Council, we discussed the possibility of calling an international East-West conference devoted to the future in the autumn of 1967. Mankind 2000, The Institute of Peace Research, and my own small Institut für Zukunftsfragen in Vienna will sponsor that meeting, which we hope to hold in Oslo.[1]

Originally, as I have told you, Mankind 2000 set out to promote an international exhibition. In trying to contact persons and institutions that might counsel us, we found out that there existed many more agencies concerned with the future than we had surmised. We were not the only ones to come to that conclusion. In a broad survey on "technological forecasting" that Dr. E. Jantsch did for the Organization for Economic Cooperation and Development (OECD) in Paris, he wrote:

When the work on this Report began, it was believed that technological forecasting was practiced in only a few places and that a survey of techniques and organizational forms could be carried out on the basis of the limited amount of information that was to be gathered. This turned out to be a poor forecast indeed. Not only did the information expand in volume virtually to the exploding point, but also the scope of the enquiry broadened to take on new dimensions. . . .[2]

The number of institutions devoted to the study of the future has increased so rapidly in the last five years that it has become more and more difficult to know them all. Moreover, there exists so far quite insufficient communication among these different "lookout institutions." So Mankind 2000 found itself thrust into

---

[1] The meeting took place in Oslo from September 10 to 15, 1967. It was attended by 65 scientists from 12 countries.

[2] E. Jantsch, *Technological Forecasting in Perspective*, unofficial edition (Paris: OECD Publication, October 1966).

a position it had not striven for; we began to act as a switchboard for "futurists," who wanted to know about each other.

Therefore, as a branch of Mankind 2000 in Vienna, I started a contact and documentation center devoted to this new inter-disciplinary branch of research, which has been called by a friend of ours, Professor O. K. Flechtheim of the Hochschule für Politik in West Berlin, "futurology."

This institute in Vienna is being sponsored by the Austrian Ministry of Education and has an office in one of the government buildings; so far it has worked "with no strings attached." It is doubtful if this state of complete freedom (which has its dark side in the scarcity of financial support) will last when it dawns on the politicians that nowadays the old saying "Knowledge is power" should really be changed into "Foreknowledge is power." Anyway, so far, nobody is bothering us — "us" meaning about forty young graduates who have recently completed or are near-ing completion of their doctoral degrees. Our main activity thus far has been the collection and indexing of the growing literature concerned with a serious study of the future. We already have several thousand recent books, magazine articles, scientific papers, and reports devoted to the "world of tomorrow." We have also started an abstracting service and hope to publish soon an inter-national interdisciplinary bibliography on "futurology." We are also preparing a weekly news service (in German) presenting future-oriented news and articles.

Trying to do all this with almost no money — to supplement the meager government support we have had to subsidize our-selves from our own pockets — I feel sometimes like a village potter in the middle of the Industrial Revolution. Is it at all worth while to dabble in this field while a "knowledge industry" using all the modern devices of information gathering and retrieval is growing not too far from us? Perhaps it is, because many impor-tant institutions have had to start in a small way and only later on were developed by better organizers with more money into something more efficient and more lasting. We hope our little intellectual "pilot plant" will be discovered by some people who might exclaim, "That ought to be done better." All right, they are welcome to us. The main reason for my coming over here is to find such "better-doers."

Finally, I should like to mention a series of books that I began to edit two years ago and that are devoted to the ideas of Mankind 2000. The title of the series, which should eventually have at least twenty volumes, is *Modelle für eine neue Welt* (*Models for a New World*). So far five volumes have been published in Munich. The editors (Dr. H. J. Mundt and myself) have asked a large number of people who are knowledgeable in their own fields to think up proposals, visions, and designs for the future in such critical areas as education, public health, urban problems, leisure, international cooperation, and so on.

Though the books have been rather successful so far, we have also run into a number of difficulties in preparing the books; my coeditor and I wonder if we shall be able to publish the twenty volumes. First of all, we learned that the ability, even of outstanding persons, to outline concrete and consistent alternatives to the present state of affairs was much scarcer than we had thought. The habit of social invention and the practice of formulating imaginative and bold plans must be acquired, it seems, through learning and exercise. The field of utopian creation has been in disrepute for such a long time that it has become barren. Today's experts are so afraid to lose their standing as serious members of their professional community that they no longer dare to go out on a limb.

Even worse, we discovered, is the deeply ingrained mental passivity of the general public. If one asks the dissatisfied and grumbling "man on the street" — as we did in Vienna, for example — what kind of new solutions or institutions he would like to propose, he will answer with very fuzzy generalities or clichés. But in running "workshops of the future" we were able to improve on that. Such "brainstorming" groups discussing desirable futures are what Mankind 2000 will try to promote among its member organizations, because inventing the future environment must be more than the effort of a few chosen experts in a few days. We shall have to overcome the effects of decades of mental passivity before we can hope to involve more people who would be sufficiently confident to trust their own intelligence and imagination in a democratized effort of social model building.

I shall end on a somewhat lighter note: Once when discussing the subject of the growing lack of concern about public issues in Vienna, somebody said, "The root of that decay must be attributed to the disappearance of our coffeehouses." The Viennese coffeehouse, you must know, used to be a place where you could sit for hours in the most pleasant environment without consuming more than one cup of not very expensive coffee and many glasses of fresh water. You could find there not only many newspapers from all over the world but also friends and discussion partners. But since real estate in the city has become expensive, coffeehouses have either disappeared or have become too expensive. Furthermore, the proprietors of the few old places that survived have become impatient with customers who consume too little in too long a time. They have to look for sufficient turnover in order to break even.

Now, it may sound outrageous to some of you, but why should not the public subsidize coffeehouses the same way it supports schools, museums, theaters, and other institutions of cultural importance? A coffeehouse, it is true, does not exhibit paintings, but it helps the painters to discuss their problems. It does not stage plays, but it provides a breeding ground of ideas for new plays. It is not such a representative environment as a parliament, but it fosters democratic debate.

The inventors of the future environment should be concerned about such places because there we might tap the one resource we are nowadays neglecting too much: human creativity deeply buried under layers of distrust and passivity induced by the *hubris* of the expert.

If you architects build new communities, think about these millions of dried-up imaginations in millions of individuals and create conditions that will make them come back to life.

DISCUSSION

NEWMAN: I am rather interested in the problems you list: the loss of the coffeehouse, the rejection of the suburbs, the need for an infusion of spirit, and a few other things. To what extent are these your own projected values?

JUNGK: I believe we have not made measurements in as exact

a way as the social scientists. I feel that the collecting of an enormous amount of social-psychological data is an American superstition. Perhaps four or five good journalists could quickly bring in more information than big task forces that collect data somewhat mechanically, only to find the data antiquated at the conclusion of the study.

I feel something must be done to develop a new kind of investigator — one who has a little more of what we in the newspaper trade call a "nose," a feeling for the data not yet quite out in the open. When I read modern sociological studies, I often feel that the investigators have overlooked phenomena which cannot, or cannot yet, be quantified. You have to have a special gift for finding out facts, especially those pointing toward the future.

HURST: I am very interested in what you say about the avoidance of involvement by people. It seems to me that this is one of the symptoms of urban society today that we don't pay enough attention to and haven't evaluated adequately. It extends itself into *the avoidance of community* or the lack of desire for community, and I think if that is a trend at all, then it challenges the whole basis for the concept of planning the city around community. I think we see it extended into the avoidance of responsibility, and perhaps we see it in Los Angeles as much as in any city. I wonder if you would extend your remarks about that?

JUNGK: There I have some data about the citizens of Vienna. Every year the city of Vienna organizes an international symposium. In 1963 the theme concerned urban problems. Prior to that occasion we asked the people of Vienna, through posters and all other means of mass communication: "How do you want your city to be? Please send us criticisms and suggestions." We found that the participation was much less active than we had anticipated. This was so, despite the fact that, for example, the most popular television commentator had on several occasions talked about this experiment in direct democracy. We asked a number of people who were known to be critical and imaginative, "Why didn't you write to us?" Most of them answered, "That would have been wasted time. Nobody in city government would take our advice anyway." This terrible feeling of resignation is at the bottom of civic disinterest. Unless we can show the citizen that his word may count, we will lose our democratic way of life — in fact, we may have lost it already. We also contacted the people who *had* written in, and we discussed with them the feasibility of their ideas. Later, some of these ideas were implemented by the city fathers. The ideas that were not accepted were also discussed with their proponents, and we tried to make them see why these ideas could not be pursued. They always understood, and they were willing to accept the arguments against their proposals. From that experience, I had hoped there might develop a new department of the city of Vienna which would encourage closer contact between the citizens and their executive in matters of social planning. Vienna was a pioneering city in social innovation, but now the governing socialists have become afraid of anything really new; they are afraid that such increased democratic participation might shatter their position. Thus the experiment, despite its successful beginning, finally came to nothing.

Professor JOHN MYER: I would like to extend the previous question. It seems to me that the desire for community has to be examined carefully. We are living in an age in which affluence has permitted many of us to reduce the number of people with whom we have close daily contact. We no longer live with our aunts, uncles, grandparents, etc. We no longer live among or near other economic or ethnic groups. We have tended to select a very thin kind of homogeneity in which to live.

We have elected a way of life which minimizes an intimate connectedness to people in the first place and any connectedness with people of different origin from ourselves in the second. It may be that we are really electing something else, isolation being the by-product of that other election. Or it may be that we seek this removal of ourselves from others. Would you care to comment on this point?

JUNGK: I would first say that you really have to undo what thirty or forty years of making people passive has wrought. You certainly can't do that in one year. It will be extremely difficult to give confidence to people to come back and talk to you.

As you say, some social processes have gone in the direction of isolating people more and more, and some housing developments have unfortunately supported that trend. In European housing developments you increasingly find immense buildings where people don't know each other. I feel that one necessary purpose of social inventions will have to be the fostering of an atmosphere of closer contact.

One common argument I will not accept is that we have too many possibilities of distracting ourselves and therefore are no longer interested in public affairs.

Public affairs, if you are able to present them in a vivid, even dramatic, way, can catch the attention of people. This may not even represent a primary interest in the public good, but rather an interest in fights; many men and women like discussions, and they like to take part in them. In our age, you may have to develop showmanship in order to make public affairs attractive, although this may go very much against the grain of purist social reformers.

One of the reasons the Italian Communists are popular in Italy has nothing to do with communism; it has to do with the fact that the Communists are able to put on all kinds of meetings and festivities; they are excellent at giving the people a feeling of community.

DUHL: I believe the question of community to be a critical one. Because of its importance, its analysis is bound to reoccur as a discussion point. I think one of the problems we get into is this: What we mean by a "sense of community" is something that really doesn't exist any more. It is an image of the past in which all sorts of things take place within one small geographic area — all participating functions having to do with life, business, and so forth.

Actually, the situation today is one in which we find active participation in many separate communities within a community. Apathy really comes when one is actively operating in a particular community and has no impact on another community in which one is perforce involved. What I mean by this is that you will find some very significant and important people deeply involved in the national community (having to do with health, planning, urban policy, and so forth). They have a deep commitment and a deep sense of responsibility to this involvement, yet they are completely disconnected from responsibility or commitment to their immediate urban environment — to the geographical area of their urban environment.

CAZES: Is that bad?

DUHL: I am not saying it is bad. I am saying what happens now. This, in itself, is one of the reasons some of us are concerned with connecting these various communities. For once the linkage points between the varieties of communities are established, critical issues can be better confronted.

Now, the second point I want to talk about is the one that you raised about apathy and participation. When the situation exists where life is as complicated as it is, it is extremely difficult to know how to "plug in" the system and have any impact on that system.

The problem of involving the general citizen in a decision having to do with schools or urban policy or land planning or roads or other problems is that the general citizen doesn't fully realize that he might be able to have an impact on the situation. In many cases, he probably doesn't even have any possibilities of having any impact. He has really never had the experience of first learning that through participation he can have an impact, even on a small issue. One of the exciting aspects of the civil rights movement, the advocate planners, and all the rest is that we are beginning to see people have an effect. With a little energy and organization and a little learning of what the middle-class population knows how to do very well, people who have up to now been relatively apathetic are learning that they can have an impact on small segments of issues that impinge on their lives. Starting with that, they begin to increase their effectiveness so that as they gain more and more skills, they increasingly participate in the infinite complexity of life around them.

This is really an education problem. This is why I think Dr. Jungk was talking about the education of the total environment. He is quite right that the politicians are uncomfortable with this situation. Anybody who runs a bureaucracy is uncomfortable, because these efforts begin to shake the very foundations of our society.

KINDLEBERGER: Dr. Jungk and Dr. Duhl have talked about the broad mass of people as if they all spoke with one voice and had one point of view. I suggest that politics means conflicts of particular interests. Various groups are involved through the political process in varying degrees because their interests are engaged in varying degrees.

Dr. HASAN OZBEKHAN: What you are saying is there is a conflict between vested interests. I do not feel that this specifically means the same kind of involvement that has been talked about.

Professor BERNARD FRIEDEN: There is a three-way discussion between the people, the technician, and those involved in the political process. Many of the kinds of issues we talk about, such as highway planning, aren't carved solely out of a political relationship; they are influenced by technical studies and by the advice of technical experts. I think that much of the self-criticism in the technical professions today comes from a realization that at the time the technical decisions are made, the relationships between the people who are affected and the technicians are very weak, practically nonexistent. At the point at which highway plans are made, there is practically no contact with the people who are affected. But there is evidence that people can become positively involved in decisions that affect their lives.

I think the paper that Norton Long gave recently called "Violence as a Form of Communication," is relevant here. We can see many examples of his point, for instance, the civil rights movement and other kinds of protest. However, it seems to me what we have to search for is some better relationship between the technical people who are doing the planning and the political process. At the same time the technicians seem to be dissatisfied with their own plans and with the political process as in the case of the highway route in Cambridge. We are searching for some better way to represent these interests.

DAVIDOFF: In Dr. Jungk's talk, the question arose, "How do we involve the people in the process?" That may be part of the enormous problem of political apathy. How is this applied in what we think is proper political behavior? People may be political in many different ways. Thugs throwing stones at Negroes are breaking through political apathy. In one sense they are keeping issues alive and making them more explicit. That may be a healthy thing — at least the issues are no longer buried. The proper questions are: "How are you developing a theory of the future? How do you work to understand what the people want?" The problem is not how you make the people come to understand what you want.

For example, Dr. Jungk, when you publish something, is it published for the laity or for us? Is it for the technicians or for the working man to understand the nature of the planning process? Will your work appeal to the layman?

JUNGK: Yes.

DAVIDOFF: That is good, and very unusual. In general, we are publishing for and talking to ourselves at the level of expert or technician. We are not trying to involve the laity in the literature or in the writing of pamphlets. Who is writing the pamphlets?

Professor BRUCE MAZLISH: Dr. Duhl, would you like to see your "invisible colleges" become more like Cazes' institutionalized planning group for the year 1985? In HUD specifically, or in America generally, do you think planning by the invisible college approach is the right approach?

DUHL: If the process became formalized, I would very quickly go out and try to create a new "invisible college."

MAZLISH: M. Cazes, in comparison to your Group 1985, I would like to set up three groups: the first two composed of members with the same backgrounds, and the third one of people with different backgrounds. For example, would it be useful to have a group of planners in this country doing the 1985 planning who were mainly from the conservative spectrum of American politics — I mean the William Buckleys and the Senator Towers? Really, we have not yet touched on the question of identifying basic attitudes toward the future, such as whether one welcomes it. We tend to think that what we "liberals" see coming ahead in the future is, in fact, what concerns most people. Their concerns, however, may be quite different.

CAZES: Assuming a 1985 Group of a quite different membership, I do not know how the report would have differed significantly. If one were to have several groups each with its own orientation, it would be very important that they work along parallel lines and that each such group draw its own image of the future. Concerning the 1985 Group, Professor Mazlish is quite right: there were no fundamental disagreements among the various members, no dissenting opinion in their report.

JUNGK: Just a complement of information: In France there was considerable discussion of your plan, and in some instances a very critical stand was taken. There was even a brochure published: *Le Contre-plan.* There was an article in *Esprit* about *Reflexions pour 1985* — also in *France-Observateur.* They said that all this was too conservative, that it took too much of the existing societal structure for granted. This criticism showed that the future-oriented proposals and the discussion of the future cannot be one-sided. Such considerations must come from many societal groups with very different basic points of view. In Germany the trade unions are only now beginning to realize that they will have to conceive and publish their own hypotheses of what they want in the future. Only then will they be able to contradict or complement what the government is planning. In a democracy, discussion of the future is one of the most important issues.

MAZLISH: Don't you draw a distinction between the plan of the possible future and its projection by different groups? I wonder whether, for example, a conservative planning group, as well as the Americans for Democratic Action, in this country and the Social Democrats in Germany unknowingly share a great deal in common. The long-range trends, if Mr. Cazes is right, ought to be the same for all of us, and I would like to examine the way we ourselves look at them. You might get, independently, a good deal of unanimity of thought; whereas, once the plan is produced by one group, then all the old clichés come from the other groups.

DUHL: Actually, gaming procedures take separate groups from different orientations, and given the same data, the few experiments I have heard of end up with markedly similar plans, as you said. I feel this is, in large part, due to the fact that the rules of the company game given to each of the several groups were the same. Even though the groups may have had different complexions, they were following the same rules. One of our challenges may very well be to set up separate groups in which each may create its own rules of the game — which has never been done.

As the rules of the game are critical to planning, if we can really redefine the rules, then the products will be different. I suggest here that if the rules of the game say that any highway cannot be planned without the direct involvement of the people, we will get entirely different planning with the same technicians.

KINDLEBERGER: You would get no highway.

DUHL: Yes, you would, but through different means.

CAZES: You would have more roads. In France, if you invoke the people, they will advocate more highways.

KINDLEBERGER: The highway would not go through; no town would have it. The communities would veto you, and the communities could veto any highway.

FRIEDEN: This is the same thing that is involved in the planning process; it is the right to reject any plan drawn up. However, it seems to me that a good planning process might have very different outcomes, such as community bargaining, trade-offs, and concessions to various points of view. It doesn't necessarily have to follow an obstructionist line.

BARNETT: I want to do a little classification that might improve this discussion. Let me define the two arenas for social decisions. One is that in which political decisions are made. The decisions include public economic decisions, such as subsidized low-cost housing by the government. Second, there is another arena where private economic decisions are made. Each of these arenas has structural relationships, attitudes toward goods, money, and work, and relationships among groups.

Now, to the extent that planning has positive scientific aspects (and I think this is what we think of in the academic sense, as opposed to normative behavior), it must be viewed relative to these two arenas. Examine these two systems of structural relationships with regard to some possibilities like growth in population or change in technology or new products or possible new consumer preferences; and, with or without a computer, simply play out what results are presented. By this method you obtain a set of alternative plans, possible futures, based on the structural relationships in either of these two areas. This planning is done without the injection of value judgments, except in two minor respects. One of them is that the planner has a concern for society, or he wouldn't be in the game; but that is latent. He tries to do his work in such a way that it would be subject to replication by somebody who didn't share his personal views. And the second point is that he is limited in his ability, for example, to read people's preferences as he sets up the structural relationships according to what he can recognize himself. For this he consults himself to some extent. But basically he is engaged in describing in the most objective sense the relationships of these structures, and that is, I think, positive science; I understand that as planning. If you agree with it, that is one piece of communication.

Another part of planning activity is simulation. The planner tries to assume changes in certain structures. He says: Let us assume that people become radical in the popular sense of the word, so there is much less done in the *private* market and much more done in the *public economy* market. Let's say that people are greatly concerned about the Negroes and try to break up existing political relationships. They pass laws against segregation and so on. Then the planners outline these changes, and this is a playout with change in the structural parameters; this, I think, is also planning. And again, latently, there are some values, because which changes he chooses to play out are ones he can recognize. But he is a neutral scientist, if you like, in the social sense. Furthermore, it is obvious that any scientist (the positive scientist I am speaking of, the planner) would like to be understood. He is motivated by concern for society, so he will take the trouble to write popular articles, presenting his computer runs and the implications of various decisions. This again is still a neutral, scientific planning activity.

Finally, still another point that keeps coming up is the question of what the new society should be. This is deeply embedded in the talks of both Dr. Duhl and Dr. Jungk, in which they reach quite clearly into their own social motivations and values for change. At this point I want to suggest that they are being politicians, but not in a bad sense of the word. They are being political activists; they are being citizens, and not being planners as such. I believe that this is what reconciles much of what I heard, and what seems to have been the point of some of the arguments that have been made.

This final category — a good deal of what Dr. Duhl said — is neither planning nor science but political action. It is not improper, but it is different from planning as a rather positive science.

DAVIDOFF: I am going to give a talk later about planners and advocates. Perhaps I am not communicating with you, or perhaps we are going to communicate in two different arenas. You can make a case for acting as the planner, acting as the objective observer; you can also define a role for the planner as a political animal who is planning in accord with his own values or those of the group he is representing. He doesn't try to represent everybody's values.

My objection to what you say is based on the experience of previous planners; that is, those who claim to act according to your suggestions are, in fact, selecting the values that they consider important. Many values are never represented in the schemes of planners for the localities, states, nations, or the world. Planners tend to be narrow in their vision of what the objective truth is. So it may be possible to create a whole host of roles for the planner. I believe he does not need to be a pure scientist, as you suggested.

BARNETT: Is there, then, ever a case in which it is useful to distinguish the planner as an objective scientific analyst? If there is, it pays to identify such a case.

DAVIDOFF: We get confused because the long-range planner has to make value judgments right at the inception. The most political act in the process is setting the objectives.

FRIEDEN: It seems to me that, as you point out, there are problems of time — of the range for which decisions are being made. But there are also differences depending on the numbers of people involved in the geographical scale in which decisions are to be applicable. In this sense the problem for architects is different, possibly easier, than for planners. That is, in making decisions about a single building, one is dealing with a relatively small number of people who might be consulted directly; in making a decision about a highway network for a metropolitan area or about national housing policy, the problems are altogether different. I feel that thinking of relationships with the consumer on national or metropolitan or state levels calls for innovations in these relationships in order to create arrangements that we don't have now or that we have only in rudimentary form. It is possible that existing techniques for direct consultation or for the use of social science methods to study the impact of decisions might be quite readily applicable to architectural decisions.

KINDLEBERGER: May I just summarize what I was trying to say? I am afraid that some of the discussion has been in terms of general welfare, but I believe there is no general welfare. There is a political process. There are many particular welfares in conflict with each other, and appeals to the general welfare have little relevance. The hard problems come when you try to reconcile the particular welfare in a big way for a small group with the lesser welfare of the larger group. These are very difficult questions, which social science is very far from solving; but they can't be ignored. This is all I am trying to suggest.

Dean ROBERT GEDDES: Many of us here don't understand the operating definitions of the other fields. Bernie Frieden has made one. For example, he assumes that a highway planner is concerned with the highway and that the architects or builders are concerned only with the intersection, when, in fact, architecture has the same concern with the network. I think we have to be wary of inadequate definitions for the fields.

DUHL: I don't want to summarize, but I am thankful to Mr. Barnett for having reminded me that in the whole process of planning one of the most interesting things that happens is that the planner himself changes. If you are a change agent and you are trying to change somebody else, if the process really works, you have also changed yourself.

What I am really struck by in our discussions is that all of us are products of our own particular culture. Our profession or our particular group in some ways locks us into a specific way of thinking. We use the same words, but we use them quite differently. There are preoccupations as to what is planning and what is not; and there is substantial reaction, as was demonstrated earlier, when some people, including myself, touched on other people's strongly held viewpoints they thought unshakable. What ultimately comes out of an experience like this, even if we were all a group of planners, each with a different set of values interacting with each other, is that all of us change.

96

JUNGK: Perhaps we have somewhat neglected to point out our concern about peaceful solutions for the future and about the fact that so much civilian planning today is blocked in an open or a hidden way by the war machine and the war economy. I wonder if we couldn't tackle this question, at least privately.

Two Broad Substantive Issues
in Planning for the Future

Whether seeking a test for a bold hypothesis or presenting data about the emerging situation, all discussions about planning or the future return to at least two fundamental problem areas: demography and resources.

Since studies in these areas appear quite "hard" by comparison with most long-range studies, it is chastening to see how complex even these problems prove to be — for example, the frequency with which extrapolations from past performances elicit doubt.

Nevertheless, in the following papers, Herbert Moller on demography and Harold Barnett on resources suggest that any limits on our future are not physical ones.

The Population of the United States in the Last Third of the Twentieth Century

HERBERT MOLLER

The present population of the United States of 200 million is likely to increase to about 300 million by the year 2000. More exactly, the latest census projections for the turn of the century give a range between 280 and 356 million. These projections take into account the decline of national fertility during the past ten years.

The average number of children per couple rose after the Second World War, and so did the mean ideal family size. Most American women hoped to have families of three or four children, whereas their mothers had a family image of three or two. In the past few years both the actual mean family size and the family ideal have come down slightly, even among Catholics and Negroes, who have the highest growth rates.[1] However, the average number of children per couple is only one factor determining the national fertility level. More important causes of the "baby boom" were an increase in the proportion marrying and a trend toward marrying at younger ages. Nothing has changed in these respects. From now on we shall have an increasing number of thirty-six-year-old grandmothers. The *average* age for first marriages is now around twenty for women and twenty-two to twenty-three for men. This represents an amazing cultural change, with psychological implications that have not yet been investigated.

[1] Judith Blake, "Ideal Family Size Among White Americans: A Quarter of a Century's Evidence," *Demography*, Vol. III (1966), Part I, pp. 154–173. Ronald Freedman and Larry Bumpass, "Fertility Expectations in the United States: 1962–1964," *Population Index*, Vol. XXXII, No. 2 (April 1966), pp. 181–197.

Earlier marriage, of course, means earlier childbearing; in addition, postwar couples spaced their children more closely. In other words, more Americans are marrying, marrying earlier, having more children than their parents, and going through the reproductive cycle faster. Thus roughly four, instead of the traditional three, generations have to be counted per century.

The most important factor making for rapid increase in the immediate future is the fact that the larger year cohorts born after World War II are now entering the marriageable age and are becoming parents. In 1970 there will be 7 million more women of childbearing age (fifteen to forty-four) than there were in 1960. In 1980 there will be 18 million more potential mothers than there were in 1960. These additional millions of women of childbearing age are not statistical estimates; they are the women and girls of today.[2] As a consequence of the rise in the number of marriages, there will be a vast increase in the number of households; 800,000 to one million new households will be established every year for the coming ten years, and a larger number thereafter. The dwelling units needed by these newly married couples have to be added to needed renewals of obsolescent housing.

The tremendous growth of our population from 200 to 300 million in forty years or less is bound to change the quality of our lives, since it necessitates increasing rational direction and social planning. In the present decade high school enrollment is swelling from 10.1 to 15.1 million students; the college population is doubling from 4 to 8 million and is expected to rise to 12 million in the 1970's. In 1964 the federal government began to provide funds for education at all levels on an entirely unprecedented scale. In addition to education, national health, old age care, the reduction of poverty, highways, etc., will require such vast capital outlays as to make it unavoidable for the federal government to become involved in community affairs, thereby guiding and restricting options for local action and bypassing state governments. Likewise, it is questionable whether a million or so new heads of

[2] Charles F. Westoff, "The Fertility of the American Population," *Population: The Vital Revolution*, Ronald Freedman, ed. (Chicago: Aldine Publishing Co., 1964; also paperback, New York: Anchor Books, 1964), Chap. 8.

households every year will be able fully to pay for their housing needs. In these and other areas demographic growth necessitates rapid utilization of technological inventions, which requires large investments of capital. If private savings are not sufficient to accommodate these capital demands, the government is expected to become more active in the formation of capital.[3]

How sheer bigness changes the traditional quality of life may be illustrated by the discrepancy that there is only one President of the United States, whereas the number of mentally disturbed persons who focus their aggressive impulses on him is presumably growing at the same rate as the general population. As a consequence, the danger to the President has greatly increased and is constantly increasing. In 1965, over 12,000 telephone calls were referred by White House operators to the Secret Service; the White House was picketed on 166 occasions; 7 persons were apprehended climbing the fence; 341 unwelcome visitors were interviewed at the main gate, and 112 of these were arrested or committed for mental observation.[4]

To preserve our freedom and economic well-being we have to accept more and more direction. The social functioning of individuals has become so important that government agencies and public schools are setting up special services to develop in children a sense of security and self-worth and to foster intellectual curiosity and spontaneity. In this way, the upbringing of children is not left entirely to the family, and parents find themselves being helped and sometimes being pressured into accepting therapeutic interference. It does not follow that restrictions of personal liberty necessarily increase in modern mass society. Many of the governmental responses to bigness and complexity are designed to liberate the citizen from poverty, fear, and ignorance. In fact, it is tempting to argue that, basically and in the long run, legislation in complex societies has to aim at smooth functioning, reducing avoidable frictions, or plainly getting things done. Rationality is functional in a complex society, and it is becoming irritating, even for people who are not themselves involved, to find restrictions

[3] Simon Kuznets, *Capital in the American Economy* (Princeton, N. J.: Princeton University Press, 1961), Chap. 10.
[4] *The New York Times*, January 23, 1966.

and penalties imposed without any demonstrable benefit to the community, for example, to have persons imprisoned for drunkenness and nonsupport of their families or to find the police spending their time ferreting out individuals practicing homosexuality with consenting adults.

Rapid demographic growth entails certain disadvantages that have been referred to as its aesthetic consequences, because they amount to a deterioration in the quality of human life. State parks and recreation areas are teeming with fellow humans, and it becomes harder and harder to enjoy unspoiled nature. Entire animal species have become threatened with extinction. Legislation to preserve the nation's wilderness areas is helpful, but its effectiveness is impaired by the doubling of our population in the past fifty years, and again in the coming fifty to seventy years. The "development" of wilderness areas attracts crowds of tourists and easily makes them resemble city parks. Cultural facilities, theaters, exhibitions, and libraries become disappointing because of crowding, long waiting lines, unavailability of tickets, parking difficulties, and noise. Growing traffic makes our streets less and less safe for children, who cannot go anywhere without adult protection. High school students seem to adjust emotionally to the unlimited size of their schools, but school life among thousands of peers involves a loss of certain growth experiences in that it offers fewer positions of importance and responsibility. Training for participatory democracy is encumbered by the very bigness of schools as well as colleges. The annual meetings of professional associations have lost much of their original usefulness as meeting grounds of independent scholars because of size. In numerous situations social overcrowding makes for superficial contacts which preclude genuine human communication outside the nuclear family. "It is not very relevant," writes Joseph J. Spengler, "to ask how many people a given country can support. It is relevant to ask why population continues to increase in a country after population growth has ceased to confer a net advantage upon the country's inhabitants."[5]

[5] Joseph J. Spengler, "Population and World Economic Development," *Science*, Vol. 131, No. 3412, pp. 1497–1502. On the same problem, Peter Blake, *God's Own Junkyard: The Planned Deterioration of American's Land-*

Of the momentous historical movement from country to city we are witnessing, in the United States, the last great rush. During World War II, over 5 million people of labor force age left the farms, and after the war the movement away from rural-farm areas continued. The Depression policy of encouraging subsistence farming ceased, and agriculture became modernized. For the future we visualize huge, highly capitalized farming enterprises run by college-educated managers who use a computer programmed to make 5,000 decisions per year.[6]

In 1965, the farm population was only 6.4 per cent of the total population. In this country, therefore, most of the movement from rural-farm areas to cities has now taken place. On a reduced scale, it will probably continue for another two decades, and the majority of today's farm boys will never become farmers. At least 60 per cent of those who leave the farming areas are under twenty-five years of age; this has led to a distorted age structure in many rural-farm areas. There are now two large sections of the United States where the remaining population is not even replacing itself, because the average age is so high that there are more deaths than births: (1) the southern fringe of the corn belt (southern Iowa, northern and western Missouri, and eastern Kansas; and (2) parts of Oklahoma and Texas.[7]

Although many small towns survive and even thrive, two thirds of the population of the United States, that is, about 130 million people, now live in metropolitan areas. This number is likely to double within the next 35 years. With the addition of another 130 million, metropolitan areas of greater spatial extension and increased density will be more vulnerable to breakdowns, accidents,

---

scape (New York: Holt, 1964). Lincoln H. and Alice T. Day, *Too Many Americans* (Boston: Houghton Mifflin, 1964). Alfred Fabre-Luce, *Men or Insects?*, translated from the French by R. Balkick (London: Hutchinson, 1964). S. N. Afriat, "People and Population," *World Politics*, Vol. XVII (1964–1965), pp. 431–439.

[6] *The Christian Science Monitor*, August 22, 1966.

[7] Calvin L. Beale, "Rural Depopulation in the United States: Some Demographic Consequences of Agricultural Adjustment," *Demography*, Vol. I (1964), pp. 264–272. Donald Janson, "Boys Lack Chance to Stay on Farms," *The New York Times*, September 25, 1963, p. 51. Many of the prospective migrants belong to the 3.5 million Spanish-speaking Mexican-Americans living in southern California, Arizona, Colorado, New Mexico, and Texas.

or sabotage, in peacetime as well as under war conditions. Even a major failure in the supply of electricity or a heavy snowstorm can paralyze one or several of these vast agglomerations of people. There is, of course, no need for all the present disadvantages of city life to multiply. Air pollution by motorcars and industry may be eliminated; highway deaths, which at present are still mounting, may conceivably be reduced in the future. The traditional antiurban ideology which pictured cities as the peculiar breeding grounds of crime, corruption, disease, and mental illness had never more than partial validity. Poverty and slums, of which there also exist rural varieties, can be abolished by a dynamic, technologically advanced society.

What seems hard to overcome is the moral atomization of city people, the loneliness of a large proportion of individuals, and the isolation of families even from neighbors, which increases with socioeconomic status. People flee into privacy as a protection against the "attention overload": being exposed to too much information, too many problems and good causes, and meeting too many people to become genuinely interested in them.[8]

Another disadvantage of vast urban agglomerations is the problem of commuting, which, in fact, is taking on a new aspect with the trend toward decentralization. As long as only private homes were built in the suburbs, it could be expected that an improved public transportation system would absorb much of the home-to-work traffic. However, since the end of World War II, an increasing number of industrial enterprises have also moved away from the cores of cities, either to suburbs or along highways such as Route 128, the industrial semicircle around Boston. As a result of this general dispersal, dependence on the private automobile is by necessity increasing, because more and more people are not commuting simply between a residential suburb and the downtown industrial and business district, but are moving in all directions; even bus lines cannot satisfactorily link the widening dispersal of places of work and residence.[9]

[8] Karl W. Deutsch, "On Social Communication and the Metropolis," *Daedalus* (Winter 1961), pp. 99–110.
[9] See the final part of Leo F. Schnore's *The Urban Scene: Human Ecology and Demography* (New York: Free Press, 1965).

Apart from urbanization and suburbanization, another pattern of migration in the United States is the movement from the interior to the peripheries. The areas along the Atlantic and Gulf coasts have gained in population, and so have the areas bordering on the Great Lakes and the Pacific Coast. People have moved from roughly one half of the nation, where either forests and minerals have been exhausted or where farming has become mechanized and consolidated, to the more prosperous half.[10]

Two movements are operant to make the American people more homogeneous: (1) the migration of Negroes out of the Deep South, which began in earnest only after 1910 and soon became so rapid that within fifty years Negroes were more urban than the white population; (2) the movement of much industry to the Deep South, which is now catching up economically with the rest of the country. Although it is still the least prosperous part of the nation, per capita incomes are increasing faster in all but one of the twelve southeastern states than in the country as a whole.

Until 1930 the Negro population grew at a slower rate than the white population; since then it has been increasing more rapidly, and most of the increase accrued to the northern cities. Negroes have moved to cities in both the North and the South: in 1960, 73.2 per cent of Negroes lived in cities, against only 69.5 per cent of whites. The mechanization of southern farms and the diminished importance of cotton culture in the South are the major reasons for this rapid urbanization. The Negroes who moved out of the Deep South were very young: in the 1940's these migrants had an average age of twenty to twenty-four. Naturally, they had, and still have, a very high birth rate, which intensified their economic, educational, and civic problems. The cities outside the Deep South have thus developed their own home-grown Negro population, living largely in ghettos and without any cultural contact with the South. By 1960 this indigenous contingent formed already the majority of the Negro population in non-

---

[10] On internal migration see Donald J. Bogue, "Population Growth in the United States," in *The Population Dilemma*, Philip M. Hauser, ed. (Englewood Cliffs, N. J.: Prentice-Hall, 1963); reprinted in *Population Bulletin*, Vol. XX, No. 1 (February 1964), pp. 17–25.

southern cities. They constituted a very young population; their median age was about twelve years.[11]

Since 1940 Negroes have slowly advanced in the social structure; the proportions of Negro white-collar employees and craftsmen have risen in the nation as a whole, but they have risen faster among nonsouthern than among southern Negroes. However, the great majority of Negro migrants moved into low-wage occupations and encountered heavy risks of unemployment. Apart from racial sentiments among whites, the greatest obstacle to integration is the Negro birth rate, which is among the highest growth rates in the world.[12] This alone tends to perpetuate the Negro-white socioeconomic differential. In the last few years birth rates have dropped slightly for the Negro as well as for the white population, but not yet as much as would be desirable.

Since Negroes are now moving into white suburbs, they are apparently going in the same direction as other ethnic minorities. It is a fact, however, that voluntary ghettos of Armenians, Irish, Jews, and others remain in existence, because their denizens prefer it that way. Large minority blocs such as the German Catholics of the Middle West or the Pennsylvania Dutch have persisted for long periods. It can be taken for granted that, in the foreseeable future, sizable Negro neighborhoods will survive, with or without the feeling of being uniquely excluded and rejected by white citizens.[13] The extent to which Negroes will be dispersed among the vocational and status groups of American society is largely dependent on educational and — perhaps even more — on employment opportunities.

If our national economy has a sustained high annual growth rate (of 5 or more per cent), disadvantaged people generally find themselves accepted. High school "dropouts" are discriminated

[11] C. Horace Hamilton, "The Negro Leaves the South," *Demography*, Vol. I (1964), pp. 273–295.

[12] Negroes are increasing at a true rate of 2.7 per cent per year, compared with a white true rate of natural increase of about 1.9 per cent. Charles F. West, "The Fertility of the American Population," *Population: The Vital Revolution, op. cit.*, p. 119.

[13] For a similar prediction of reduced but continued segregation see Charles C. Moskos, Jr., "Racial Integration in the Armed Forces." *American Journal of Sociology*, Vol. LXXII (1966–1967), pp. 132–148.

against when employment lags. There is no evidence whatsoever for the widely held idea that persons without high school diplomas are fitting less and less into a modern economy. On the contrary, between 1950 and 1965, the number of jobs suitable for dropouts increased; and as of 1960 at least half of the American labor force were dropouts.[14] During the labor shortage of World War II, men and women were adequately trained for many industrial jobs within a few weeks; and at the present time, technologically modern factories are set up in underdeveloped countries and, apart from a few managers, are staffed by a labor force trained on short notice from among people who have had very little formal education. Employers easily reject people with adequate capabilities if they can hire workers with longer schooling but in no way better trained for the specific job. Likewise, vocational associations and labor unions are tempted to set up restrictive entrance rules, which are presented as indispensable training requirements but are actually hurdles erected in order to monopolize a sector of the economy.

While automation does not create a redundant labor force on a national scale, the specialized work of highly trained individuals, such as engineering personnel, becomes obsolete if such work can be performed by high-speed computers for a fraction of the cost in wages. The answer to this problem obviously lies in continued education for older specialists. Adaptability to advancing knowledge has become a requirement not only for professionals but for skilled workers as well. Inability to learn new things will lower a person's economic value and employability, and this is true for adults as well as for children. Provided, however, that the economy expands with the population, the Marxist bogey of a "reserve army" of unemployables is no more an intrinsic feature of a non-Communist economy today than it was in the nineteenth century.

Big blocs of people who are really hard to absorb are of two kinds: (1) unusually large year cohorts of young people entering the labor market with a sudden impact, as at present the large number of young Negroes, and (2) mentally deficient people

[14] A. J. Jaffe, "Education and Automation," *Demography*, Vol. III (1966), pp. 35–46.

(I.Q. under 50 and to some extent even under 80) and psychotics, whose economic usefulness was always low but who are even less adaptable to a modern economy.

The U.S. population is becoming increasingly homogeneous in styles of life and behavior patterns. Income differentials, however, remain high in America, which is not surprising since even in Great Britain, with higher taxation of individual incomes, apparently little redistribution of wealth has been effected.[15] In America as in England, the welfare state does not hurt the high-income groups, who find ways to exempt substantial portions of their incomes from heavy taxation.

The need for trained professionals is increasing; and, among these, *salaried* professionals are increasing faster than the self-employed, especially physicians and lawyers. Another large-scale change in the occupational structure of America is the increase of government employees in federal, state, and local administration by almost one third between 1950 and 1960. Furthermore, women have joined the work force in rising numbers, on all levels from professional work to unskilled labor. This trend is bound to continue because of the early mean age at marriage and the rearing of children so early in the lives of women that — in addition to the primary interest in a second family income — life would become boring for many married women without any vocational activity.

The age distribution of the American population is not likely to change greatly in the future. The absolute number of children is still going to increase in the next few decades, but not out of proportion to the total population. Unless the birth rate returns to the high level of the 1950's, the proportion of children under fifteen is likely to decline by the end of this century from the present 31 per cent to as little as 25 per cent. This would make the age structure of the American population similar to that of Western Europe. Since the Second World War, the middle-aged population between fifteen and sixty-five has been relatively shrinking. This movement is now likely to be terminated and even to be reversed. The number of people sixty-five years and

15 Richard M. Titmuss, *Income Distribution and Social Change* (Toronto: University of Toronto Press, 1962).

over is not likely to increase out of proportion to the entire population. Unless decisive medical discoveries occur, the increase or decrease of the present 9.3 per cent of older people will depend mostly on the future birth rate. In any case, it is projected to stay somewhere between 10 and 8 per cent.

Two other developments, however, have to be taken into account. First, there is a trend toward earlier retirement. This trend prevails even though in the past decade the incomes of older people have increased at a slower rate than the incomes of younger age groups. Second, older people have been enjoying better health in recent decades. Both economically and in respect to health, older persons have become less dependent on relatives and institutional care and increasingly maintain their own homes.

The proportion of teen-agers and young adults in the total population affects the cultural climate. This proportion is smaller in the Western world than it is in the now-developing countries. Still the continued decline of infant death rates and the recovery of birth rates after 1940 have created a relatively large teen-age and young adult population also in the United States. Among young people in this country there has been considerable involvement in social causes and also a vocal and occasionally active rejection of the "establishment." Yet, despite the ferment and professed alienation, the great majority are eager to prepare themselves for personal advancement, economic independence, and early family life. Their readiness to adjust to the existing social system agrees with the great opportunities and rewards offered by an expanding economy. The difficulties faced by American youth are largely problems of personal adjustment to a rapidly changing and more demanding society.[16] The overwhelming majority of young Americans, in and out of college, marry and have children early in their lives. In this way, young people of all social classes are continuously casting their votes for a life not only without revolt but even without prolonged intellectual and vocational experimentation.

Furthermore, they opt for privacy. Just like the older generation, who avoid living with their adult children or their in-laws,

[16] Talcott Parsons, "Youth in the Context of American Society," *Daedalus* (Winter 1962), pp. 97–123.

young people want a dwelling place of their own. This is true today even of unmarried sons and daughters. In this respect, a generational change occurred between the censuses of 1940 and 1960, when the proportion of young men who were heads of households markedly increased, and it was very surprising that this change came at the same time that young people were staying in school longer and starting their working careers later.[17] Historically, as far as we can look back, people in Western civilization have always valued the privacy of a home of their own. That so many couples and single people now can realize this desire is a by-effect of the high productivity of modern economy. It follows that, short of a national economic disaster, this preference for a private home will be permanent.

Lastly, there is evidence to indicate that mankind is growing not only in quantity but also in quality. It is well known that the average height of man has increased slowly over the centuries and then more rapidly in recent decades. Americans have grown taller and bulkier quite conspicuously. The size of standard beds is still unchanged, but there seems to be a growing demand for king-size mattresses. This development toward larger human size may not be entirely advantageous; however, it is clearly connected with better nutrition and improved health as reflected also in a longer mean life span. In the world of sports, records are broken every year.[18]

Another physiological change which is an indicator of what is happening in the present century is the earlier onset of the menstrual cycle and the postponement of menopause. At present, in America, menarche begins mostly at eleven or twelve years of age, often at ten. In the eighteenth and nineteenth centuries, menarche began between fourteen and sixteen years of age, in the seventeenth century between fifteen and eighteen, occasionally

[17] John C. Beresford and Alice M. Rivlin, "Privacy, Poverty, and Old Age," *Demography*, Vol. III (1966), pp. 247–258.

[18] *Life*, September 2, 1966, carried an article that was entitled "The Kids Keep Going Faster," in which it was pointed out that in the constant speeding up of the world's 1,500-meter swimming record the women's record of 1940 had overtaken the men's record of 1920, and again in the 1960's women's time was shorter than men's time had been in the 1940's.

even at twenty.[19] Corresponding physiological changes seem to have occurred in males. Objective evidence for the lengthening time span in male sexual activity may be seen in the greater incidence of sexual offenses by older men between fifty and seventy years of age. This fact has been noted in several European countries.[20] The improvement in the health of older people is certainly accompanied by emotional changes.

In the pessimistic period between the two world wars, certain physical anthropologists assumed that the intellectual level of modern populations was declining from generation to generation owing to the higher fertility of the lower and less intelligent classes. This notion has been disproved.[21] It is even likely that "the frequency with which children are born with brain damage attributable to malnutrition or infection has been declining and will continue to decline."[22] A general reduction of mental retardation may be attributable to growing medical knowledge, better nutrition, and not least to psychological factors connected with more devoted maternal care, increasing family stability, and better familial and cultural stimulation.

There is today another kind of stimulation which the vast majority of mankind has never before received. Modern society needs much more intelligence than any traditional society did. Throughout world history only a tiny fraction of the available human intelligence could be utilized, the masses remained uneducated, independent thought was discouraged, and a surplus of intellectuals existed from the later Middle Ages to about 1940. Since then high intelligence is in short supply, positions are available for well-trained people, and creative and experimental thought is encouraged in many places. This situation, together with the availability of a great variety of educational institutions, can have only a most stimulating effect on the development of

[19] Hans Heinrich Muchow, *Jugend und Zeitgeist* (Reinbeck bei Hamburg: Rowohlt, 1962), pp. 83–85.

[20] M. Grunhut *et al.*, *Sexual Crime Today* (The Hague: Nijhoff, 1960).

[21] J. Maxwell, in *Advancement of Science*, Vol. VI (1950), pp. 357–362. P. E. Vernon, in *British Journal of Educational Psychology*, Vol. XX (1950), pp. 35–42. Ernest M. Gruenberg, "Epidemiology of Mental Retardation," *International Journal of Psychiatry*, Vol. II (1966), No. 1, pp. 105–108.

[22] E. M. Gruenberg, *op. cit.*, pp. 78–126.

human intellectual potentials and on dominant styles of thought and of taste.

Another change that, I think, is becoming visible might be called "mental urbanization." During the nineteenth and early twentieth centuries, cities grew rapidly through in-migration from the countryside and small provincial towns. In this way they became, to a large extent, inhabited by "urban villagers," whose artistic tastes, style of life, and religion were still shaped by a rural or small-town environment. In the future, in-migration to metropolitan areas will become a trickle in proportion to the vast populations living and born there. Traditionalism and anti-intellectualism can be expected to lose much of their appeal.

Altogether, it appears that a new type of man is emerging. The old idea of "overman," or *Uebermensch*, a human type who transcends past limitations of his species, is becoming more than fantasy.[23]

DISCUSSION

CAZES: I was struck by your contention that between 1950 and 1965 the number of jobs available for "dropouts" increased despite automation and technological advance. In what sectors of the economy did this take place — in the private or in the public sector or in both?

MOLLER: In both the public and private sectors. There are many positions in federal, state, and local services that do not require a high school diploma — from the Armed Forces and the Post Office to local fire departments, sanitation departments, and custodial jobs. Not every improvement in services diminishes employment. If a second daily mail delivery to private homes were again provided in the United States, 60,000 additional mail carriers would be needed immediately.

CAZES: Yes, but all this is in public sectors.

MOLLER: Also in the private economy there are ample oppor-

23 Ernst Benz, "Der Uebermensch: Grundprobleme des heutigen Menschenbildes," *Zeitschrift für Religions- und Geistesgeschichte*, Vol. XIV (1962), pp. 19–35. John R. Platt, *The Step to Man* (New York: Wiley, 1966).

tunities for people without high school diplomas, for instance, in the expanding construction industry. In New York City alone there are about 35,000 licensed taxi drivers and close to 5,000 garage and parking lot attendants; there are over 17,000 restaurants or other places serving food or drinks. However, there is not much of a point in listing individual industries employing large numbers of persons of low academic achievement — almost all industries, in fact, are doing so — and I wish to refer you to the statistical evidence presented in the enlightening article on "Education and Automation" by Professor Jaffe. [See note 14 of Moller's essay.]

S. ANDERSON: Would you please comment on the relationship between recent advances in birth control and your population projections?

MOLLER: I did not specifically consider the problem of birth control. In my study I proceeded from the demographic situation of the United States as it is at present and as it is likely to develop to the year 2000, and I tried to show the social and cultural implications of this development.

S. ANDERSON: With the significant changes in birth control during the last decade, isn't it necessary in looking at future populations and demographic patterns to take into consideration the possible discontinuities brought about by birth control?

MOLLER: Family limitation is, indeed, an important factor of this demographic trend; it is the major reason for the difference between the highest and the lowest census projections which I quoted.

Other problems that I have not touched upon are the motivations for birth control and the desirability of modifying the mores of procreation. Even though this country will not have any serious shortage of raw materials in the foreseeable future, the satisfaction that parents derive from a larger number of children than are needed for the replacement of the population will finally have to be balanced against the liabilities of an increasingly congested country. The primary question is how many children people really want. The questioning of various population groups in the United States has shown that most people actually get the number of children that corresponds to their ideal family image. The exceptions, of course, are illegitimate children. They are usually not planned.

HURST: That is a big exception.

MOLLER: If you wish to consider population policies, there are several basic approaches. At the outset, I think, certain unsocial suggestions have to be rejected, such as the idea of depriving parents of tax exemptions for their supernumerary children or burdening them with special taxes or denying aid for dependent children to unwed mothers. Such measures would deprive exactly those children of material support who are in greatest need of it. The regulation of births for eugenic reasons will almost certainly command increasing attention in the not-too-distant future. At present, a simple and humane population policy would above all eliminate the births of unwanted children. These children are neglected and reared without affection in their formative years and thus become the greatest reservoir of emotionally maladjusted juveniles and adults in our society. In addition to unwed mothers there are many very young persons who face the responsibilities of parenthood with dismay; but middle-aged couples can also find a pregnancy most unwelcome when it occurs several years after they had considered their family completed. The legalization of abortion on demand of the mother would be one of the most wanted and medically simplest steps to the improvement of our society.

Natural Resources in the Changing U.S. Economy

HAROLD J. BARNETT*

This essay is aimed at architects and urban designers. They design and plan for construction operations using a set of "inputs," such as cement, steel beams, paint, space, trees, gullies, and labor. The purpose is to produce some "outputs," specifically effects upon other variables, such as quantity of shelter space, visual beauty of form, and access to living facilities. These inputs and outputs are the variables with which architects work. In this "production function" architects try to maximize output through time, subject to availability of inputs and various constraints — subject, that is, to a set of social and economic factors in the external environment. The purpose of my paper is to discuss trends in the *economic* variables — that is, the availability of inputs and the character of the economic constraints architects may face. Some subsets of resource availabilities and other economic constraints are more likely on economic grounds than others, and it is possible that economic analysis can guide us.

I shall discuss the following questions:

1. What is the prospective shape of the national economy in, say, the year 2000?
2. How will demand in the sector of primary interest to architects — construction — grow relative to the total economy?

* I am indebted to my Washington University colleagues, Professors David Felix and Murray Weidenbaum, and to Dr. Hans Landsberg of Resources for the Future for helpful criticisms and suggestions on an earlier draft. In addition, as noted later, the bulk of the data — both tables and charts — is based on Resources for the Future research.

3. What will be the demand and supply situations for the key construction inputs?
4. What is the land availability for future needs?
5. How do my projections reconcile with the historical record of material and natural resource availability?

1. PROSPECTIVE NATIONAL ECONOMIC GROWTH

If we peer a substantial distance into the future — say, to the year 2000 — shall we visualize radical structural change in the society? Shall we contemplate very great changes in the trends of such variables as income; relative preference for material goods, services, and leisure; labor force size and productivity; relative prices, etc.?

To the general question, the general answer is no. Alfred Marshall, father of neoclassical economics, wrote in his famous *Principles of Economics* text, *natura non facit saltum*, which means "nature does not proceed in jumps." We've improved economic knowledge since 1890 when Marshall wrote. But I'm not aware that any economist has ever quarreled with his cap-stone generalization, which he put on the title page of the first edition and maintained through the eighth in 1920. One should entertain only with caution those grand economic generalizations in which sweeping and very rapid changes are foretold. Of course, Marshall's and my emphasis is on the relation of magnitude and speed, and I am speaking of the three decades from now until the turn of the century.

To illustrate, let us consider the past thirty to forty years of our lives. The advances in scientific knowledge and scientific tech-niques have been blinding; in military destruction and potential, devastating; in certain technologies like cybernetics, nuclear fis-sion, and rocket propulsion, almost unbelievable. But since 1929 income per capita in real terms has not even trebled; population concentration in so-called urban places has not even doubled; the work week is not much different in length; and man is no less an individualistic, self-seeking "economic man" in his activities.

Three or four decades back (about as far in the past as is our concern here today for the future), the technocracy movement

118

examined science and technology and predicted revolutionary economic changes. So did the great Norbert Wiener in his cybernetics book and Buckminster Fuller in his work. Their scientific genius correctly predicted new technologies, at least in part, but they did not correctly appraise economic structure, processes, and institutions.

This economy has 200 million people, and 2 trillion dollars of capital goods in place, and 200 locations with great, dense networks of sewers, water pipes, wires, buildings, and roads. The rates of change in these omnibus economic magnitudes will not enormously accelerate or vastly decline.[1]

Table 1 presents a set of "medium" projections for the over-all dimensions of the U.S. economy in the year 2000. In all the charts and tables that follow I use the Resources for the Future data compiled by my former colleagues or myself.[2]

TABLE 1. THE U.S. ECONOMY

	1950	1960	1980*	2000*
Population (millions)	152	180	245	331
Households (millions)	44	53	73	99
Labor force (millions)	65	73	102	142
GNP (billions of 1960 $)	363	504	1,060	2,200
GNP per capita (1960 $)	2,390	2,800	4,330	6,650
GNP per worker (1960 $)	5,620	6,920	10,400	15,500

* Medium projections. These are the intermediate of three sets of Resources for the Future projections, the other two being labeled "low and "high."

In these projections the population growth rate is about the same as the 1950 to 1960 rate, and the projected labor force and gross national product growth rates are somewhat more rapid than the 1950 to 1960 rate. The chief measure of economic welfare, real income per capita, more than doubles from 1960 to the year

[1] I should also add that my presentation here is one in positive science, not normative. I am not advising on how activist anyone should be in trying to change economic or other social parameters.

[2] These appear in *Resources in America's Future*, by H. Landsberg, L. Fischman, and J. Fisher; *Trends in Natural Resource Commodities*, by N. Potter and F. Christy, Jr.; *Scarcity and Growth*, by H. Barnett and C. Morse. All these volumes were first published by Johns Hopkins University Press for Resources for the Future in 1963.

2000. The chief measure of the nation's economic activity, gross national product in constant prices, more than quadruples. These projections may be read as the economic context for the architects' professional activity.

2. PROJECTIONS OF CONSTRUCTION

Our interest here, however, is not in the total economic activity of the nation (GNP) as such. It is rather in the fact that over-all economic activity generates demand for construction volume. Table 2 projects construction demands by major classes.

TABLE 2. U.S. CONSTRUCTION (BILLIONS OF 1960 $)

	1950	1960	1980*	2000*
Total	59	76	166	348
New	42	56	130	281
Maintenance and repair	17	20	36	67
Residential new (including additions and alterations)	19	23	55	126
Nonresidential	23	34	75	155
Private new	33	41	90	197
Public new	9	16	40	84
Components of public, new nonresidential:				
Schools and hospitals	2.3	3.2	5.0	7.4
Highways	2.6	5.5	16.1	34.6
Military and industrial	.6	1.8	5.1	12.3
All other (water, sewer, etc.)	3.6	4.8	11.0	23.5
New residences (thousand units)	1,880	1,540	2,650	4,210
Average value per unit ($ 1960)	8,880	11,500	16,900	24,600

* Medium projections.

The projected increases in construction are relatively larger than the projected increases in total economic activity by a small degree. The greater increase occurs primarily in new residential and in public construction. The latter, however, is concentrated more in engineering projects, such as highways and sewers, than in architectural projects, such as schools, hospitals, and military and industrial facilities. But the major observation, as the table shows, is that construction demand, which is the consumer of architectural services, is expected to grow slightly more rapidly than economic activity in general, to 4½ to 5½ times the 1960 level.

3. DEMAND FOR AND SUPPLY OF CONSTRUCTION INPUTS

Construction activity generates demand for construction inputs. Will these be ample, at approximately present relative prices, to satisfy the demands? Or will persistent shortages arise which would increase prices and induce substitutions, or even require significant reductions in planned construction? The availability of construction inputs will affect volume and types of construction, and volume and types of architects' "output."

To begin our answer, we can rather quickly dispose of the prospects for certain construction inputs:

a. *Construction labor.* Over the long term, real wage rates in the economy can be expected to rise at about the same rate as labor's productivity, projected at about 2½ per cent per year. Labor will flow into construction as demanded, at wage rates competitive for the skill involved with nonconstruction sectors. It is conceivable, of course, that labor monopolies could dictate greater increases in wage rates in construction than in other sectors. If so, the cost of construction might rise in such degree that the quantity of construction demanded would be less than what was presented in Table 2. But I do not anticipate this. In summary, I believe that an ample supply of construction labor will be available at competitive wage rates, wage rates will rise in construction as elsewhere, and there will be incentive to economize on the use of the labor input.

b. *Capital equipment* used in construction (such as tractors and cranes), and *capital goods* installed in construction (such as fixtures and air conditioners). Profit-seeking entrepreneurs will try to economize on use of labor, by substituting relatively cheaper inputs and by improving laborsaving technology. Over the long term and in the national economy, can capital goods be expected to fall in cost and/or increase in productivity or quality so that they will be substituted for labor, whose wage rates have been and will be rising? The trend picture is very clear and persistent. Capital costs — interest and depreciation per unit of capital of a given efficiency — have been declining relative to labor cost. In general, I expect the trend of decline in cost of capital equipment relative to wage rates to continue. Continued substitution of capital for labor may therefore be expected. In summary, we expect construction techniques to become more heavily capitalized and finished construction itself to become more heavily capital laden, with laborsaving and other quality improvements.

c. *Miscellaneous services,* such as construction financing, insurance, and license fees. These inputs are not specialized to the construction industry, and we expect them to be available at competitive market prices; their costs will not frustrate construction demand.

This leaves us with certain projected demands for major materials, to support the volumes of construction previously shown (see Table 3). Can we expect availability of materials to meet these projected demands without major increases in cost? If so,

TABLE 3. U.S. DEMANDS FOR CONSTRUCTION MATERIALS

	1950	1960	1980*	2000*
Lumber (billion bd ft)	33	28	46	76
Plywood (billion sq ft)	3	8	27	63
Building paper and board (million tons)	3	3	6	11
Steel, including railroad (million tons)	24	23	39	59
Copper (thousand tons)	518	522	1,094	2,396
Aluminum (thousand tons)	295	678	1,760	4,566
Portland cement (million bbl)	223	308	742	1,644
Aggregates (million tons)	550	1,130	3,830	9,000
Asphalt, tar, and oil (million bbl)	66	111	224	448

* Medium projections.

then the architect may design on the basis of approximately present relative prices for the different types of inputs. (We are abstracting from general price level changes which affect all commodities, since these do not affect choices among the various inputs.) If we foresee shortages in particular items — lesser quality or rising prices or nonavailability — then the architect and builder must turn to substitutes. If the substitutes permit construction of equal economic value at relatively constant prices per unit, then the shortage was without economic significance.

The answers are easy for most of the materials. Cement and aggregates will be plentiful; these supplies will be suitably forthcoming. Asphalt, tar, and oil are a small part of the output of the oil and coal products industry, and they will be available as long as hydrocarbons are generally. They may rise somewhat in price, but there are ready, fully satisfactory substitutes, and thus they are not of great economic importance in architectural construction.

Iron ore and aluminum ore reserves are in very great supply abroad and, in lesser grades, in this country. Copper ore reserves abroad and at home, on the other hand, are not publicized or even marked out for thirty- to forty-year production periods. The practice of the half-dozen companies that dominate the industry is to estimate and develop reserves only as needed and sharply to limit availability of statistical information. It is believed that copper supplies to meet domestic consumption needs will be forthcoming without significant increase in price. For all three metals it is estimated that supplies would accommodate the construction demands previously given, as well as all other projected U.S. demands. Total demands are shown in Table 4.

I must point out, however, that the copper projections are based not on reserves estimates but on general hypotheses of

TABLE 4. TOTAL DEMAND FOR METALS IN THE UNITED STATES

	1950	1960	1980°	2000°
Steel and ferrous castings (million tons)	74	72	121	194
Aluminum (thousand tons)	910	1,560	5,650	14,720
Copper (thousand tons)	2,060	1,810	3,550	6,830

° Medium projections.

mineral occurrences, past trends in the opening of new reserves as needed, and technological trends in mining lower-grade ores without increase in cost. If there were shortages sufficient to force significant price increase, then the least valuable or most substitutable uses of copper would of course be rationed out. Particularly in view of availability of aluminum, steel, and plastic substitutes, relatively rising copper prices, if these did develop over the long term, would be unlikely to have very significant impact on construction activity.

This brings us to the question of supplies of timber products, primarily lumber and plywood. When the estimated demands by the construction industry are added to other demands, the projections of net domestic consumption of forest products in the year 2000 shown in Table 5 result.

TABLE 5. U.S. DEMAND FOR FOREST PRODUCTS

	1950 Total	1960 Total	2000 Medium Projections Construction	Total	Low Projections Construction	Total
Lumber (billion bd ft)	42	37	76	98	26	31
Plywood (billion sq ft)	14	22	63	133	29	56
Pulp (million tons)	17	27	11	110	5	76
Total timber (billion cu ft)	12	12	—	32	—	15

Total U.S. "medium" consumption is projected, as shown, at about 2½ times present use. Present U.S. public and private commercial forest area is, however, very inefficiently used, so forest land area would not have to rise proportionately. It is estimated that the so-called "medium" needs of the year 2000 could be met by adding about 300 million acres to the 500 million acres presently in commercial forests. But, with regard to other land uses, this volume of additional land for forests is not easily available — the present commercial forest acreage is already one fourth of the U.S. land area.

Thus we have identified the only materials shortage that, possi-

124

bly, could significantly constrain the volume or the input structure of U.S. construction, by forcing wood price increases or substitutions for wood. We very briefly note the various possibilities of response, adjustment, or error:

a. Imports from Canada and elsewhere could increase substantially.

b. Multiple use of land acreage — forest products from reservoir and grazing lands, nonproducing agricultural acreage, recreation areas, etc. — could provide very large cuts of timber, under sustained yield practices. (See Table 6, showing land use in the United States.)

c. Much saw timber could be released for economically significant end uses by diverting it from less valuable uses. For example, more than half of pulpwood and a third of fence posts and mine timbers were made from saw timber in 1952.

d. Improved technology and new products could economize on timber use by utilizing residues and present wastes in wood products to a greater degree. Also re-use of lumber could grow.

e. Of course, metals, aggregates, plastics, and chemical products could, suitably and economically, still further substitute for construction timber products.

f. Finally, I think the RFF (Resources for the Future) medium projection is rather high. For example, the U.S. forest output hit its peak more than fifty years ago and has been level or declining since. I am not convinced that the past trend will so greatly change as henceforth to cause demand for timber products to rise at a rate half as fast as that of U.S. economic activity and twice as fast as households. If one were to use RFF's so-called "low projection," the demands for forest products would require no more than the present forestry acreage, used only a bit more efficiently. (Researchers at RFF also now feel rather uncertain about the forestry projections and think there may be an upward bias from the use of an inflated time series on residential construction.)

In summary, architects and construction engineers may find timber products relatively more costly than other construction

125

materials in the future as compared with today. This development, if it occurs, will be gradual and foreseen.

4. LAND USE IN THE FUTURE

We shall now turn to land availability and its uses. In a sense, land is the major input in architects' "production functions," particularly in their efforts to shape the physical form of cities and the nation. The present and projected land uses appear in Table 6, prepared by RFF. After allowing for growth in cities, recreation facilities, transportation, etc., the supply of land is plentiful, although, of course, availability of unused or little used land is not uniformly distributed over the nation.

The figures are fascinating. I have become increasingly conscious of U.S. congestion problems, yet 37 per cent of the land

TABLE 6. LAND USE IN THE UNITED STATES*

(MILLIONS OF ACRES)

	1950	1960	1980	2000
Cropland (including pasture)	478	447	443	476†
Grazing land	700	700	700	700†
Farmland, nonproducing	45	45	45	45
Commercial forest land	484	484	484	484‡
Recreation (excluding reservoir and city)	42	44	76	134
Urban (including city parks)— 2,500 population and over	17	21	32	45
Transportation	25	26	28	30
Wildlife refuge	14	15	18	20
Reservoirs and water management	10	12	15	20
Total specified	1,815	1,794	1,841	1,954
Total U.S. land area	1,904	1,904	1,904	1,904
Residual	89	110	63	—50

* Excluding Hawaii and Alaska.

† Increased land required for growth in food requirements in the future has been accounted for in the cropland figures, the grazing and nonproducing farm land figures being left unchanged from their 1950 and 1960 levels.

‡ See text discussion. A medium timber consumption projection would imply 300 million more acres. A low projection would imply smaller acreage than the 484 million acres shown.

area is reserved for grazing. Forest land is the second largest U.S. land empire — 25 per cent of the United States. I had no idea Pinchot and his followers had been so successful. For cattle and trees, the total is 62 per cent of the U.S. land area. The acreage now in cropland and pasture, 25 per cent of the nation, is unchanged from half a century ago. It is a coincidence that the projection of 45 million acres for urban area exactly equals the present and projected acreage in nonproducing farmlands. For the year 2000, RFF has projected that one acre out of each 14 in the nation will be devoted to recreation, in addition to city parks, national forests, etc. Our cities and transportation facilities, which, we have heard, are making the nation into a concrete wasteland, presently occupy 2½ per cent of the U.S. land area and are projected at about 4 per cent. Cutting across this pattern of economic use of land is the fascinating pattern of ownership. The United States government owns more than one fourth of the total land area. The largest land magnates are the Bureau of Land Management, the U.S. Forest Service, and other less-known land agencies, such as the Defense Department.

5. COMPARISON WITH PREVIOUS ECONOMIC THEORIES AND U.S. ECONOMIC HISTORY

How well do these projections of ample natural resources and extractive products reconcile with past U.S. trends and tendencies? The classical economists originated the idea of increasing natural resource scarcity, and conservation theories and neoclassical literature have carried it to the present. The doctrine states that the pressure of population and economic growth upon a fixed natural resource base leads to natural resource scarcity, and this tends to retard economic growth. As conceived by Malthus, when all resources are in economic use, each additional application of labor has fewer resources with which to work, thus resulting in diminishing returns per unit of labor. In the formulation of David Ricardo, also a century and a half ago, the best resources are utilized first. To meet growth in population and economic activity, additional resources are brought into use, but they are of inferior grades. This also results in diminishing returns in relation to increments of labor. In both cases the effect of natural resource scarcity is an increase in the amount of labor to procure a unit of extractive product. That is, the cost per unit of output as measured in man-days increases because of natural resource scarcity.

Figures 1 to 3 show that in the United States since the Civil War neither of these doctrines has been true for minerals. The charts have a vertical ratio scale. Each curve shows the amount of labor, measured in man-days, required to produce a unit of the respective commodity. On the left-hand scale we read the decline in labor costs per unit of minerals output from 1870 or 1880 to 1957. In Figure 1, the rate of decline is greater from World War I to 1957 than it was before, when unused resources were presumably more plentiful. The three curves immediately below the "All minerals" curve are, respectively, "Mineral fuels,"

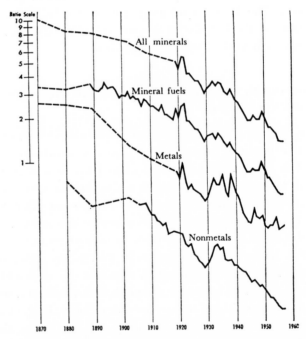

Figure 1   U.S. minerals: labor cost per unit of output, 1870–1957.

Note: Solid lines connect points in annual series; dashed lines connect
       points over a year apart.

"Metals," and "Nonmetals." The labor costs required to produce a physical unit of each of these has been declining at a substantial rate.

In Figures 2 and 3 are breakdowns of the record for the individual metals and nonmetallic minerals — iron ore, copper, sand and gravel, and stone. If one compares these data to the projections for construction materials presented earlier, it is apparent that the projection of ample supplies of metals and nonmetallic mineral materials for the future without increase in cost is consistent with the historical record.

The case of forestry is different. Figure 4 shows this record. The labor cost per unit of forestry output increased until the early 1900's, while forestry output increased. Because of the cost increase, substitutions of other commodities for lumber were invented or induced to meet the demands of economic growth.

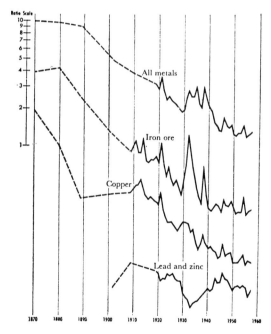

Figure 2 U.S. metals: labor cost per unit of output, 1870–1957.

NOTE: Solid lines connect points in annual series; dashed lines connect points over a year apart.

From before World War I to 1957, forestry output has been roughly constant, and so has labor cost per unit of output.

When the various extractive products are appropriately combined in accordance with the usual techniques for index number construction, the resulting record appears as shown in Figure 5. The top two curves on the left side show the output of extractive goods. The next two curves show that the inputs of labor plus capital and of labor alone required to produce the respective volumes of extractive goods increased until about the First World War *but at a slower rate than output.* On the right-hand panel of

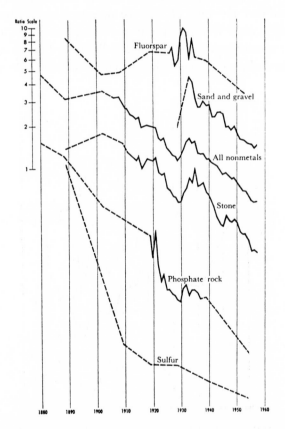

Figure 3   U.S. nonmetals: labor cost per unit output, 1880–1957.

NOTE: Solid lines connect points in annual series; dashed lines connect points over a year apart.

the chart, the output figures have been divided into the input figures, to show the cost in such real terms as man-days and machine-hours to produce a unit of physical output. For extractive industries as a whole, the cost to produce a unit of output has declined persistently since the Civil War, and more rapidly since World War I than previously. This is true whether one

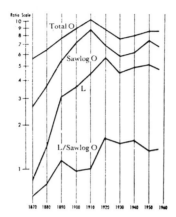

Figure 4   U.S. forestry: total output, sawlog output, labor input for sawlogs, and cost per unit of sawlog output, 1870–1957.

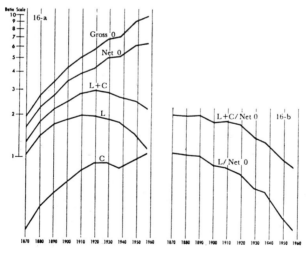

Figure 5   U.S. extractive industries: output, labor and capital inputs, and cost per unit of output, 1870–1957.

131

measures input cost as labor and capital, as I have done on the upper curve of the right-hand panel, or as labor input alone, as I have done on the lower curve.

Figure 6 shows the relatively declining importance of the natural resource sector in the economy as a whole. At the beginning of our historical period, in 1870 and 1880, the extractive industries required about 50 per cent of all the U.S. workers, primarily in agriculture. Since that time, there has been a steady decline in the number of workers required to produce for our extractive

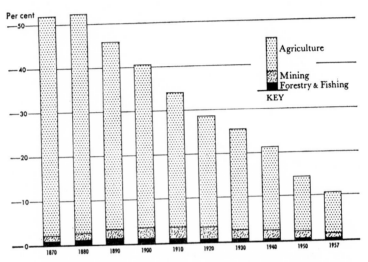

Figure 6   U.S. extractive workers as a percentage of all workers, 1870–1957.

needs to the present, when only 10 per cent of the U.S. workers are engaged in such industries. The reasons have been partly the rapid gains in productivity in agriculture and minerals; partly the gradual shift from being a net exporter of extractive goods to being a net importer of some minerals commodities; and partly the slow rate of growth in demand for agricultural goods which has increased at about the same rate as the population, rather than at the much higher rate of increase in the gross national product.

Finally, Figure 7 relates to our earlier projections of over-all economic growth. The curve shows labor plus capital costs per unit of gross national products in real terms (that is, after removing price inflation). There is a persistent decline in inputs required to get a unit of output, consistent with the projections of increase in national economic activity presented at the beginning

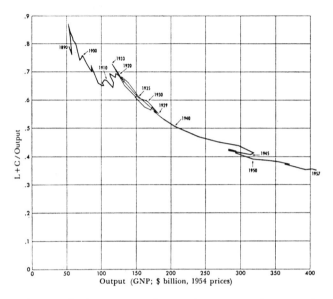

Figure 7   Trend of average real cost of output in the United States, 1890–1957.

of this paper. Since the vertical axis of this chart is an arithmetic rather than a logarithmic one, the rate of decline in input cost per unit of output seems visually to be slowing down, but actually the rate has increased since World War II.

I have tried to make plain that we live in an increasingly productive economy, today and for the future, as far ahead as we can see. It is possible to question our national devotion to growth and product, to doubt whether these make for a better society. The conservationists have questioned such a value for years, and John Kenneth Galbraith's *Affluent Society* has lent powerful new support to their view. More than a hundred years ago, John Stuart

Mill also had doubts, and with characteristic grace he wrote in his *Political Economy:*

A population may be too crowded, though all be amply supplied with food and raiment. It is not good for man to be kept perforce at all times in the presence of his species. A world from which solitude is extirpated is a very poor ideal. Solitude, in the sense of being often alone, is essential to any depth of meditation or of character; and solitude in the presence of natural beauty and grandeur, is the cradle of thoughts and aspirations which are not only good for the individual, but which society could ill do without. Nor is there much satisfaction in contemplating the world with nothing left to the spontaneous activity of nature; with every rood of land brought into cultivation, which is capable of growing food for human beings; every flowery waste or natural pasture ploughed up, all quadrupeds or birds which are not domesticated for man's use exterminated as his rivals for food, every hedgerow or superfluous tree rooted out, and scarcely a place left where a wild shrub or flower could grow without being eradicated as a weed in the name of improved agriculture.

At times I find this plea very persuasive. At other times I look at "Land Use in the United States." (Table 6), and am persuaded the other way.

6. SUMMARY

The national economy will continue to grow at nearly 4 per cent per year and income per capita at about $2\frac{1}{2}$ per cent to the year 2000. Barring very large-scale war, there will be a continuation of present economic trends.

New construction activity and demand for its inputs will grow slightly faster than the economy as a whole. Among the inputs, relative price rises are certainly expected in labor and might possibly develop in timber and copper products. None of these will frustrate growth in construction activity.

Land for future needs in the year 2000 is available in ample volume. For example, grazing land and commercial forests today account for more than 60 per cent of the nation's usable land area. Urban areas (cities with 2,500 or more people) occupy only $2\frac{1}{2}$ per cent and transportation facilities only 4 per cent. Present cropland is adequate for projected demand for agricultural products.

DISCUSSION

FRIEDEN: I should like to raise a question about the urban land use projections in your table. Projections for some individual metropolitan areas such as New York show a faster rate of increase in the amount of urbanized land than this table does. They usually assume continuation of present land development controls in the suburbs. Your projections probably assume some change from the current trend toward larger and larger lots.

BARNETT: The assumption and data include the following points: (a) The definition is land *withdrawn* from alternative uses for urban use, whether or not the urban land is actually used. Such a definition includes, in addition to actual urban use, whatever land has been made idle by its urban context, on the ground that while some may forever remain idle, none is likely ever again to revert to such alternatives as cropping, grazing, or forestry. (b) By the year 2000, 279 million of the U.S. population will be urban; this is 80 per cent of total population, as opposed to 70 per cent in 1950. (c) The urban density will be 0.160 acres per capita in 2000. This compares with 0.184 in 1900, 0.174 in 1950, and 0.171 in 1960. (d) The result is 45 million acres in the year 2000 (279 million people multiplied by 0.16 people per acre); the acreage is a bit more than double the 1960 level. By comparison, total U.S. population does not quite double between 1960 and 2000.[3]

If we were to assume the same density in the year 2000 as in 1960, the result would be 48 million acres. If one took the density at 0.184 (the 1900 level), the result would be 51 million acres. For any reasonable assumptions for the year 2000, the U.S. urban land area is a very small percentage of the total land available.

Land for the Future[4] is the primary source of the urban land use data. The Landsberg book[5] presents a summary of the Clawson model.

GEDDES: In the relationship between the total amount of construction in the year 2000 and the number of people and the

[3] See p. 119.

[4] Marion Clawson *et al.*, *Land for the Future* (Baltimore: Johns Hopkins Press, 1960).

[5] Landsberg, Fischman, and Fisher, *op. cit.*, pp. 370–372.

135

productivity per person of service industries (such as planning and architecture), is there any direct relationship between a five-fold increase in construction and a fivefold increase in the number of architects and planners necessary to do the job? Or is it likely that we are going to have an increase in output in the service industries?

BARNETT: The question is: "What is the ratio between architectural and planning input and construction output?" I guess that the ratio is declining, in terms of real cost as well as man-hours, but I simply have not looked at the figures.

FRIEDEN: Your general conclusion seems to be that our resources are quite adequate for meeting foreseeable needs through the year 2000. However, I wonder to what extent foreign needs have been taken into account together with possible changes in the relationship of the United States to the rest of the world. Specifically, if the United States were to decide to make much more use of its agricultural productivity to feed the developing countries, what would this do to the adequacy of farmlands and the other resources involved?

BARNETT: Foreign demands for United States agriculture are not significantly dealt with in my paper.

In general, I found that U.S. natural resources would not be the limiting factor in the nation's growth. This doesn't mean that we don't have problems, including concern for the food needs of the poor nations. I think that our problems are now in the institutional arena. That is, in one sense the classical economist says that nature will limit our welfare, and in my own studies I find that nature doesn't limit us. But our group and our men-to-men relationships do. As we solve our natural resource problems by making the society more congested, more interdependent, more specialized, and so on, we create institutional problems. The solution of our natural resource problem by technological advance has left us with problems of how to live with ten million people in an urban area. This is partly why we are so productive, but we also have a new set of problems.

FRIEDEN: My interpretation would be similar on the space question. I accept from your data that there is no absolute shortage of space in the United States, but it is a question of everybody wanting to be in the same place. There are enough girls to go around, but everybody wants the same girl. I think the question of rationing space has to be considered at least when we talk about urban space.

OZBEKHAN: Then we have to learn to want other girls.

S. ANDERSON: In both your writings and your paper today, you indicate that there are no great problems about supply — that we probably can do just about whatever we want in terms of resources. Doesn't this make the question of alternative futures, and normative decisions about which ones we prefer, all the more interesting and important?

BARNETT: Yes, it liberates you for the problems of choice. Society is not as constrained as it would be under a less advanced technology, so all of our institutional and choice problems become larger.

Bernie Frieden's comment triggered my realization that in this case I may have a unique comment to make from my own economic background. We may be on the threshold of a need for substantial change in what is a basic element in our laws and institutions, concerning land and political science. I wrote about this a few months ago in another paper. Let me read it:

"The increased pace of ecological change and the lesser willingness to bear it are two of the reasons for the growing public concern. Another reason is the uncertainty over whether the laissez faire or self-regulating market economy can satisfactorily handle the problems of environmental management. And it is this latter question that I want to discuss next.

"The competitive, self-regulating market economy is one of the fairest devices ever conceived by man. But it was conceived by man and not ordained by God or nature. While we may marvel at its performance over the past century and a half, we may also question the present validity and vitality of some of its elements. The complete subjugation of land to the impersonal force of the market place — its subordination, that is, to free market exchange and use — was a conception of both heroic and grotesque proportions.

"It was heroic because immediate economic welfare and progress was served magnificently in that land could be sold, mortgaged, foreclosed, built upon, planted, disfigured, irrigated, reclaimed, and disembowelled.

"It was grotesque because, as Polanyi has written, 'What we call land is an element of nature, inextricably interwoven with man's institutions. . . . Traditionally, land and labor are not separated, labor forms part of life, land remains part of nature, life and nature form an articulate whole. Land is thus tied up with the organization of kinship, neighborhood, craft, and creed — with tribe and temple, village, guild, and church. . . . The economic function is but one of the many vital functions of land. It invests man's life with stability; it is the site of his habitation; it is a condition of his physical safety; it is the landscape and the seasons.'[6]

"As I read the economic history of Western society, it may indeed have been necessary during the eighteenth and nineteenth centuries that land be torn from former uses, that tenants and small landowners be evicted, that fee simple title to permit unrestrained exhaustion of forest fertility and minerals, all in order to destroy existing society and to liberate nascent industrialism, urbanism, and economic growth into what we know as modern society.

"But it is not self-evident that unrestrained private ownership and use of land is still necessary in the now well-established industrial and urban society. Once we admit that land has a special role in society and that fee simple title in land is not now essential for the maintenance of a free enterprise system, then it is proper to contemplate very major revisions in the laws and rules which govern land ownership, exchange, lease, and use, subject, of course, to due process. Such revisions could extend to taxation of the full amount of economic rents and their use for land preservation. They could well permit governmental purchase and ownership of all land, with private leasehold use under restrictive conditions.

"Lest you think I should be credited here with very original thinking, I must point out the classical, neoclassical, and modern

[6] Karl Polanyi, *The Great Transformation: The Political and Economic Origins of Our Time* (Boston: Beacon Press, 1957), p. 178; originally published in 1944 by Rinehart, New York.

economists have always viewed rents as 'unearned increment,' which may be subjected to taxation without distortion or damage to the efficient working of the competitive self-regulating market economy. In uninterrupted line since at least the time of John Stuart Mill, who was head of the Land Reform Society, which had this objective, we have been teaching this notion to our children in their elementary economics course.

"The fame of Henry George — more than two million copies of his *Progress and Poverty* reportedly have been sold, and his single-tax doctrine is still taught in the Henry George Schools in most major cities — rests upon the notion of governmental intervention in land use and net revenues. The Conservation Movement of 1890–1920 strongly rejected laissez faire with respect to land, flatly disbelieved that private owners should have the privilege of disfiguring land, cutting timber beyond sustained yield, flooding, overcropping, undermaintaining, or permitting erosion. Finally, it is not accidental that many of the examples of external economies or diseconomies which occur to us relate to environmental effects. As Polanyi said, they relate to the site of our habitation, the landscape, and the seasons.

"In summary, I should like to emphasize that in the economic theory of a free-enterprise society, there is no necessary reason why due process appropriation of economic rent or land titles should interfere with classical economic efficiency nor why democratic decisions to place boundaries and rules on land use might not improve economic welfare."[7]

I will omit the rest of it, but I wanted to present the main idea to you.

[7] Harold J. Barnett, "Pressures of Growth upon Environment," in Henry Jarrett, ed., *Environmental Quality: In a Growing Economy* (Baltimore: Johns Hopkins Press for Resources for the Future, 1966), pp. 17, 18.

Two Themes on the Changing Style of Life

Demographic changes and resource availability, complex as they are, do permit quite strict examinations which can be formulated and tested by analytical and quantitative methods.

Other changes in society may be equally or even more important to the quality of our lives but are difficult to analyze. For studies of health, work habits, or leisure, one can find statistics that refer to such things as percentage of persons employed or average hours on the job. But complex interpretation is more significant than calculation in discovering the meaning of such figures.

As examples of such interpretive studies of changing life styles, we present the following essays on leisure and on obsolescence.

Leisure: Old Patterns and New Problems

PARDON E. TILLINGHAST

The world's population is growing too fast for the comfort of any of us, and the most serious problems of the next several decades will relate to our relations with our neighbors. This much is obvious; what is less obvious is how we are to invent an environment where overcrowded people can feel free to be themselves as fully as possible and deal with their inevitable frustrations in a creative way. To understand this, we must take a hard look at our present standards of behavior and dig out the real problems, as far as they can be found. A searcher in this field needs knowledge, imagination, and somewhat more common sense than is sometimes apparent in the policy statements, learned articles, and position papers that comprise much of the immense literature and non-literature on the subject.[1]

A small but growingly important part of this problem is what passes for leisure, or time away from work. At present, somewhere around 40 per cent of Americans, apart from students and housewives, have full-time jobs in the economy; by the year 2000 one prediction is that 10 per cent or less will.[2] In 1900 the work week averaged about 60 hours; today it varies from 40 to 36 hours, except for those with two jobs. By 2000 it may be 15 hours. How will society then keep people from each other's throats when most of their waking time is at their own disposal? How will a profoundly technological culture use this time in an intelli-

[1] For a complete bibliography to 1958, see E. Larrabee and R. Meyersohn, eds., *Mass Leisure* (Glencoe, Ill.: Free Press, 1958), pp. 389–419.

[2] *Time*, February 25, 1966, pp. 28 ff.

gent and creative way? Some people have always had a good deal of spare time; in the near future most of us will. How can we plan for a society where, for the first time, the population will be spending most of its days, not holding jobs, but in so-called leisure-time activities?

The problem has been dealt with at considerable length already. Commissions, such as the Ford Foundation, the Twentieth Century Fund, the University of Chicago, and several government task forces as well, have worked on it.[3] There has been a flood of earnest pamphlets, mostly driving at one question: "How do you fill leisure time? How do you occupy all those endless empty hours?"

As a historian, I was trained to look not so much at facts as through them — to try to find the unspoken assumptions behind the most obvious statements. The chief assumption here is that if we find enough things for people to do — more national parks, bowling alleys, motorboats, do-it-yourself projects — the problem will solve itself. Unfortunately, the solution is being given before the problem has been properly stated. The question is not how to fill vacant time; it is how to use the knowledge we already have to try to predict how people will behave when the pattern of society varies slightly; to discover what makes them work, play, relax, and, above all, what they think makes life worth living. This is not so easy for committees and commissions to decide. In summary, there are countless studies in the techniques of filling vacant time but very little material on the philosophy of leisure.

A few definitions may be useful at this point: work can be defined either as something one doesn't like doing (Mark Twain), as something that gets the goods and services produced (any economist), or as that which gives one status. I shall use all three. Recreation is time off from work that improves working performance, useful time: school recess, the coffee break, the two-week vacation. Leisure, on the contrary, is true free time. For some, it connotes a gorgeous scene: the country home, green lawns, Salem cigarette and cocktail in hand, the bronzed and amorous young couple running down the fortunately empty beach, the large egg

[3] Russell Lynes, in Larrabee and Meyersohn, *op. cit.*, p. 346.

with the golden chain in the affluent twilight years. This picture implies easygoing happiness, absence of pressure (and therefore also absence of reality), luxury and self-indulgence, but in a way no one can criticize. In actual fact, of course, what is called "leisure" means something more like cleaning up the sink, mowing the tiny front lawn, a traffic jam on the way to the beach, a struggle with tax forms. My own definition of leisure goes beyond that of time off from work, because most free time is not free at all. I shall define "leisure" as anything not done for the sake of something else, but for its own sake — a Kantian definition. It is something in which one is absorbed, tranquil without being bored: going fishing, watching baseball, doing some work one loves, just sitting on a hillside. It can also mean cleaning sinks or mowing lawns, if that is what one loves. The opposite of leisure is not activity or even work: it is boredom.

It is obvious that most of our time off is not leisurely, but there now arise some further questions. Usually, a change in the physical needs of a society has brought about a change in its moral standards. In our society, the center of our ethic is work. Ordinarily, the harder someone works, the more moral he is, and the more status and prestige he has. The reason for this is not ethical at all, but pragmatic; every society before our own has been concerned, once the peace is kept, mainly with getting work out of people. Just as we are having to change other ideas (such as the one that wedded morality includes having a quiverful of children), so we shall have to come to grips with the prejudice that the most upright man is the one who works the longest hours. "Moonlighting" is becoming a real moral problem; for instance, in Akron, Ohio, the fact that one man has two jobs may well mean that another will have no job at all.[4] It seems that each advance poses a new set of problems, and any attempt to do something about leisure means much more than drumming up projects to kill vacant time. Now we are beginning to realize that the very forces that have given us the spare time have made it impossible for us to treat it as leisure: a change in our social needs has *not* altered our moral standards.

[4] H. Swados in *ibid.*, pp. 354–363.

The historical development can be quickly traced. In primitive societies the pattern of work and leisure was seasonal and tradition-directed, and few choices were necessary; ritual and inherited status patterns kept the tribe together. Later came the great invention of slavery, which made leisure in the modern sense possible for the ruling class. In the Greek world the arts, sciences, and intellect in general developed astonishingly. To Greeks the highest human activity was *theoria*, or contemplation (and discussion) of the most abstract realities. Few people had leisure, but those who did used it gorgeously. In Rome, on the other hand, the same institution (slavery-based leisure) had a different outcome: growing restlessness and boredom, and as the Empire developed, bread and circuses for the unemployed.

By the thirteenth century, European slaves had usually become serfs, but the cultured class still believed in contemplation, which, like everything else, was worked out by the principles of scholastic philosophy. Among other scholastic products was an analysis of the problem of leisure, although it was not called that. The medieval ethic was not based on the righteousness of work, except for the lower classes; work was the curse of Adam. The highest good was not action to improve society, but contemplation of God in solitude. But in contemplative communities certain problems arose. A serious one was "accidie," the noonday demon, the terror of medieval abbots. Accidie or acedia was a kind of cosmic boredom, sometimes leading to despair and ultimately to suicide and Hell; its translation was sloth.[5] The point is that economic idleness itself was not regarded as evil, but only the things it led to when it was poorly used. Thus sloth had no connection with leisure; it was not the thing that made leisure possible but that which made it impossible.

But already by the thirteenth century a so-called "capitalistic" way of life, and therefore of thought, had begun. Capitalism looked at both time and money in a new way (new, at least, since ancient Rome): money was not to be enjoyed or used to support contemplation or to be given to the poor; it was to be used to

[5] A. Huxley in *ibid.*, pp. 15 ff.; J. Pieper, *ibid.*, pp. 340 ff. Cf. E. Waugh, "Sloth," in Angus Wilson, ed., *The Seven Deadly Sins* (London: Sunday Times, 1962), pp. 57 ff.

make more of itself. This slowly involved a mental revolution, and at the end of the Middle Ages even the desirability of leisure began to be questioned. The whole organization of a man's life, and the lives of his servants, was to be based not on contemplation or creation but on maximum efficiency. Leisure meant loss of money and was thus an abomination. Many medievals doubtless also held this view; the difference is that they did not ordinarily defend it. While I have no intention of taking part in the controversy over Max Weber's definition of capitalism,[6] it is worth noting that wherever Protestantism won, one of the first steps taken was to cut out the excess holidays that had disfigured the Catholic work week.

Eventually, northern Europe entered the Commercial and then the Industrial Revolution. This inevitably involved a further rationalization of time by those participating: leisure was time wasted. Virtue and hard work became very nearly the same thing. Finally, the idea of God as the Great Taskmaster was dropped, and work for its own sake, as a healthful, uplifting, and moral exercise, was adopted. This was the era of Carlyle, Samuel Smiles, and Elbert Hubbard. Work became a redemptive activity in itself, and leisure became not the end of all work, as with Aristotle, nor a gift from God to man, as with St. Thomas, but something that had to be earned in the sweat of one's brow and used very cautiously at that. It was this gospel on which the American economy was built. But such a gospel does not fit our present situation, and will fit the future even less. Machines work better and better now by themselves, and we are being relieved of labor faster and faster. Yet, as Walter Kerr has pointed out, we are not being relieved of the idea that work is our highest moral activity.[7] This paradox has to be dealt with in any sensible discussion of contemporary leisure. Perhaps free time, since it makes moral demands on us — demands for contentment and creativity that we are not in a position to enjoy — is something even to be feared.

[6] For those who are interested, R. W. Green, *Protestantism and Capitalism: the Weber Thesis and Its Critics* (Boston: Heath, 1959), summarizes the relevant literature.

[7] Walter Kerr, *The Decline of Pleasure*, quoted in M. Gunther, *The Weekenders* (Philadelphia: Lippincott, 1964), p. 44.

The result is our cult of busyness, the vital importance of proving not only to others but to ourselves that we are working terribly hard, endlessly occupied about important matters, in a word, indispensable.

This problem did not arise, except for a very few, until the unions — to the horror of the employers — began enforcing shorter hours, and gradually almost everyone began to have more spare time, except young mothers and Top People. There was more and more of what was called leisure; but somehow there was not more happiness about. The five-day work week meant that breadwinners were around the house much more, and possibly the result was something less than an increase in domestic happiness. In working-class circles, days at home are sometimes called "honey-do" days. A recent *New Yorker* cartoon shows a businessman firmly leaving home with his briefcase, while children can be seen screaming and carrying on inside the house. His wife is standing indignantly in the doorway, calling, "Come right back in here. You *know* it's Sunday!"

Much of our contemporary psychological folk wisdom stresses the evil character of inhibitions, although there is some disagreement on how they are to be done away with.[8] It seems to be one's duty to enjoy certain things: for example, family fun. It must, of course, be moral fun, for ours is a very moral society. Family togetherness is something very important not just to have, but to enjoy having. This point of view has been stressed in an excellent paper on "The Emergence of Fun-Morality."[9] Its author, Martha Wolfenstein, argues that since it appears to be one's duty to enjoy himself, not having a good time raises feelings of guilt. The advertising panjandrums, who in their practical knowledge of psychology yield to no one, assure us that "you owe it to yourself" to buy the product, usually a luxury product, being touted. This line of reasoning implies that the customers would not feel free to enjoy it unless a moral excuse were offered. How, then, does one enjoy himself properly? In every society leisure activity is related in some ways to work activity: our games parallel our work. Our society today is a manipulative one. Manipulators tend to de-

---

[8] *Ibid.*, p. 64.
[9] Reprinted in Larrabee and Meyersohn, *op. cit.*, pp. 86–95.

velop a "marketing personality" and find it necessary to like people efficiently, to be, and be known as, "people-liking." If they like their work, not only should their time off be spent with people, preferably manipulating them in more or less subtle ways, but they should also enjoy spending it that way.[10] It is as though there were an army directive: "All personnel will enjoy themselves in the following ways." The horrible thing is that we have been so thoroughly conditioned by this talk that we hardly notice it. Group adjustment begins in grade school with us, and by the time we are adults we have been completely accustomed to it. And so we spend our time with our family, our business contacts, and a group of carefully chosen friends, in that order. We have very little time to waste in what used to be the ordinary give-and-take of small-community life — and this in an age when interpersonal relations are more important than they ever were before.

At the turn of the century, Thorstein Veblen gave a new title to an ancient idea: "conspicuous consumption." A century ago the fact that someone had any time off at all to speak of meant either that he was congenitally shiftless or that he had made the grade: he was either at the bottom or the top. Now almost everyone has some, and the great middle group has much more than those at the top. Therefore, spending this time becomes very democratic indeed, whether one likes it or not. Much of our spare time today is spent waiting in lines or in traffic jams, than which nothing more democratic exists. But most people dislike being democratic; they prefer to find symbols that indicate various refined degrees of superior status: a less obvious form than Veblen's of conspicuous consumption. Leisure has developed a whole ladder of status symbols, and people scheme to get into cliques with the reputation of being where the fun is. A whole complex of industries supplies fun badges. At any given moment there are In and Out activities: at present golf, skiing, travel, family camping, and motorboating are especially In. But not only are we strongly encouraged to like doing certain things rather than others, in what is supposed to be our own leisure; we also have to do them at cer-

---

[10] Gunther, *op. cit.*, pp. 83 ff.

149

tain times, usually when everyone else is jamming the available facilities to bursting; the rhythm is not personal, but collective. The machine that has achieved the greatest personal effect on our lives is not the computer at all, but the alarm clock.[11] Our fun is not only clock-timed fun; it is also family fun (dependability), people-liking fun (management timber); above all, it must be fun that can be turned on and off quickly. The result is that what is called leisure often fills not so much creative needs as compulsive ones. As competition for status accelerates, we have to accelerate too or lose out. After a week on vacation we are often more tired than when we went away.

Thus, what has happened is that the new time off from work that our machines have provided for us, at least for those with ambition ("upward social mobility"), has become one more kind of work time — except that it is supposed to count as playtime. The controls over its disposition are much subtler than those that operate during the hours when we are officially employed, but they are even more effective. One chief reason is that so many people prefer status to leisure; they would like both, but in a struggle, leisure loses out. Status comes partly from the classification of one's job and, of course, one's disposable income, but also from two other things: how little leisure he has and how alert his antennae are on ways to spend it. So where a mark of good business sense used to be careful consumption of the firm's money, it is now conspicuous consumption of one's own leisure. And in so collective a society a desire for solitude often leaves one with a sense very much like guilt.[12]

One of the less beautiful aspects of our postindustrial society is that accidie is growing once again, not just in the United States, but over the whole industrialized world. The stigmata, among the young, are the old Roman ones of boredom, restlessness, and lack of purpose, shown in aimless driving about, hanging around drug-

---

[11] L. Mumford, *Technics and Civilization*, quoted in J. C. Charlesworth, *Leisure in America: Blessing or Curse?* (Philadelphia: American Academy of Political and Social Science, 1964), p. 14.

[12] As David Riesman, *Individualism Reconsidered* (Glencoe, Ill.: Free Press, 1954), p. 136, suggests, businessmen and professionals have very little reverie to balance their sociability.

stores with blaring transistors, motorcycle jaunts to nowhere and back, taking drugs for kicks, a noticeable fascination with criminals. All of these could be considered leisure activities, but the mood in which they are pursued hardly indicates either joy or tranquillity. Members of motorcycle groups pursue status too. The older generation shows many of the same signs but in subtler ways. We are less sure of what we are drawn toward than of what we are eager to avoid. It is said that medical students are not willing to put in the same years and labor as formerly; the same is true of young lawyers in the great law firms as well as apprentice garage mechanics and hotel waiters. The graduate schools, one hears, are less full of embryo scholars than of draft dodgers. In drama and literature, the accent is on fed-upness, rebellion without a cause, with no particular moral standards or the slightest interest in acquiring any. There is irrational anger and, behind it, a sense of waiting — for no one knows what. There are, of course, idealism and willingness to help others too: the peace marchers and Peace Corps, Vista and the American Friends' Service Committee, the war against war and poverty. But this idealism seems short-term; it means commitment for a month, or a year or two, not for a lifetime.

These things have happened in past societies too. Their cause, if any single cause can be found, is clearly not in a decline of morals; it is more deep-seated than that. A hedonistic ethic always appears in advanced societies where an old set of moral values is dying and nothing new has yet taken its place. The analogy of entropy might be suggestive: the energy is there, but something in the social situation has made it unavailable, diffused. All late civilizations — for example, the Hellenistic world and the fifteenth century in northern Europe — have had a cult of melancholy.[13] But whereas before it was always aristocratic, today it reaches all sections of society. It is perhaps worth noting that studies on aggression among groups of rats and monkeys have concluded that overcrowding causes a good many of the less at-

---

[13] J. Huizinga, who developed the play theme in his *Homo Ludens* (Boston: Beacon, 1955), has offered a classic study of late medieval melancholy in *The Waning of the Middle Ages* (Garden City, N.Y.: Doubleday, Anchor Books, 1954).

tractive social phenomena there that we observe among our-selves.[14]

One conclusion is that there are too many people living in too confined a space. We are also too civilized; we can find no direct way to take out our all-too-human frustrations. There are too many decisions to be made, a fact that was not true in earlier so-cieties. Today social pressure is very strong, but diffused. It tells us what we ought to do and not to do, but the reasons it gives, as our educational level rises, are less and less satisfying. There is a constant need to choose goals; but the paths to the goals and even the goals themselves change all the time. We have freedom to do more things than anyone has ever had before; but we somehow find we cannot do them when we want to, and often when we can do them, we must wait in line for the chance. Finally, we wonder how worth while the goals are, since whatever happens, it is not likely that any action of ours will change anything very much. As Erich Fromm has remarked, people do not die quietly from psy-chic starvation any more than from physical starvation.[15] Our very abundance has made us wonder just what we really want to do; and supposing we do it, so what?

It looks as though society, all over the industrialized world, is going through the first stages of a crisis, not so much of subsis-tence as of values. The old work ethic is dying, and nothing par-ticular has yet taken its place; the decisions that have to be made are becoming rapidly too complex to live with easily, or even for a nontechnician to grasp. The leisure problem is merely one as-pect of a broader problem, but its solution will affect every other aspect of social life.

So far, people have always, at least in our society, been judged mainly by what they do. Would it not make sense to judge them also by what they are — irrespective of what they do? In the Hellenic world a technician was held to be less than a full man. Technology is already our way of life; but, curiously, these very machines have made it possible for us to begin building a society where all men can be human. For the first time in history we are

14 See especially Konrad Lorenz, *On Aggression*, trans. Marjorie Kerr Wilson (New York: Harcourt, Brace & World, 1966).
15 Erich Fromm, *Escape from Freedom* (New York: Holt, 1941), p. 256.

now able to abandon most of the work to mechanized slaves and spend more and more of our time doing, not what society needs, but what we really want to. The implication of this, for many observers, is subsidized laziness, TV syndrome, uncultured loafing. But this takes too low a view of human nature. People are bored and restless, not because they are unusually sinful so much as because they feel defeated. This defeat exists on many levels and in very complex ways; but it is constantly with us.[16]

If the argument so far holds, leisure is possible only when a man is a whole personality — not defeated but creating. There is no other way for him to achieve tranquillity without boredom. As the machines take over more and more of the work, our function will matter less than our whole being. Our jobs ought to be so classified that they give us enough self-respect so that in our growing time off we can behave intelligently, not stupidly. Most unemployed men, with unlimited time off, have no leisure at all. The new society we are developing will be one whose members acquire wholeness, integrity, not by mass decision or arbitrary status but by personal choice. That has never happened before; it is possible now. The cycles of business activity are already leveling off: less boom and bust, less frantic work and unemployment. As social planning develops, there will come an awareness of a different dimension, where the growth and development of individuals is recognized as the chief end of social planning.

In summary, then, what matters to most of us is self-respect; leisure is meaningful only if it is based on sufficient status. Status used to come from family position, education, the kind of work one did. It still comes from job classification but, even more, from sheer spending power, as we come more and more to live among semistrangers who can be impressed only by the pure glitter of the legal currency. Thus the drive for monetary reward increases constantly, since most other rewards seem illusory and almost irrelevant. But after a while money rewards seem rather irrelevant too. People become restless and bored when they see no relation between their real goals and those they are supposed to have or when they cannot see any real goals at all.

[16] N. P. Miller and D. M. Robinson, *The Leisure Age* (Belmont, Calif.: Wadsworth, 1963), pp. 152 ff.

One reward that is not irrelevant is self-training, learning skills, education: the delight of growing and helping others to grow. It is creative and self-fulfilling, but in our society it counts, illogically, as work. More and more new factories and business concerns are being built near universities not only because high-level technicians and computers are handy but because of other, less tangible benefits. University communities with factories nearby seem to offer a kind of solution to many social problems that no other community does. It is superfluous to point out that the greatest concatenations of brains in the world today are reputed to be on the university- and factory-ridden coasts of Massachusetts and California.

Americans in the next few decades are not likely to develop a new taste for solitude; we have never been a solitary people. We prefer to do our learning together. The next generation may well learn how to combine their decreasing hours of work with rising hours of study and training for new skills, new creativity, a fuller life. This will take some of the status away from spending power and turn it to a more satisfying use of time. If I were an architect, I should try to find a way to put a work-study complex together.

Obsolescence and "Obsolescibles" in Planning for the Future

BRUCE MAZLISH

I

My topic is basically an uncongenial one,[1] not so much for me any longer, as I have learned to live with it since it was assigned to me, but for the general public. The notion of obsolescence goes against the time sense of both conservatives and liberals — I use these labels loosely — and it offends against our hopes of immortality. Let me explain.

The notion that obsolescence should be planned for, or will occur even if unplanned, violates the conservative's conviction that things should remain as they are or should change very slowly and very little. Ideas and institutions are expected to endure.

Now, at first glance, the liberal's desire to change society, and to change it rapidly, seems to run utterly counter to the conservative's view and to fit conveniently with the acceptance of obsolescence.

A second look at the matter, however, suggests otherwise. The liberal wishes only the *old* order to be treated as obsolete. (Indeed, as Webster's dictionary tells us, the synonym for "obsolete" is "old.") He does not wish his own "brave new world," his "new" order, to become obsolete. A glance at any of the utopias projected during the last 400 or 500 years will show us how unchang-

---

[1] Incidentally, the card catalogue of Harvard's Widener Library shows only two entries under this heading: one called *Obsolescence of Treaties* and the other, *Obsolete American Securities and Corporations.*

ing these societies are intended to be.[2] This state of affairs is natural. It is only when the idea of progress is in the air that the notion of obsolescence can arise.[3] Thus, the French revolutionaries knew they were fighting against an *ancien régime,* and the English liberals of the nineteenth century were aware that the "old order," that is, the "feudal age" (which is what they called it), was passing under the wheels of industrial progress. Yet the basic human desire for immortality, for that which endures beyond personal death, led both of these groups to postulate a form of millennium in which major change would be no longer necessary. Liberals, for example, assumed that liberal society and liberal values would persist.

Perhaps we can see this situation most dramatically if we look at Karl Marx and his followers. In Marx's case, obsolescence is built into the very foundation of his scheme. In the hundreds and hundreds of pages devoted to an analysis of capitalism, Marx tries to show how, inevitably, capitalism brings with it its own dissolution. Here, then, we have a form, almost a prototype, of built-in obsolescence, which goes far beyond the nineteenth-century liberal's conviction that the old regime was on the way out. Yet, with Marx too, the system that replaces the obsolete society is fundamentally unchanging and thus proof against obsolescence. Obsolescence, so to speak, as a way of life is no part of his scheme.

[2] For an excellent treatment of utopias, see *Daedalus,* Spring 1965, where the entire issue is devoted to the subject.

[3] The noun "obsolescence" is cited in the Oxford English Dictionary as first being used, with a social connotation, in 1828, then in 1869, and so forth. It is also used in biology, in 1852, meaning the gradual disappearance of an organ as a consequence of disuse.

The adjective "obsolescent," however, was first used in a social sense in 1755, and then in 1846 in a specifically biological sense. There is another adjectival form, "obsolete," meaning grown old or worn-out; this was used back in 1769 according to the OED. In the seventeenth and eighteenth centuries, we have the verb "to obsolete," as, in 1640, our "modern laws already obsoleted." There is also an adverb, "obsoletely," and another noun form, "obsoleteness."

For our purposes, however, it is the noun, "obsolescence," which is of importance. In its modern usage this term emerges, as we have seen, in an interesting relationship between the social and biological fields, early in the nineteenth century and directly in connection with the dominant ideas of progress, evolution, and industrialization.

II

There are two other groups in the modern period advocating obsolescence of some sort who ought to be noticed even in this brief summary. The first are the romantics of the early nineteenth century, with their heightened sense of the devouring nature of time and their quivering awareness of the omnipresence of ruins. One thinks immediately of Shelley's "Ozymandias," with these lines:

> Look on my works, ye Mighty, and despair.
> Nothing beside remains. Round the decay
> Of that colossal wreck, boundless and bare,
> The lone and level sands stretch far away.

As I analyze this, however, the romantics are deploring the *hubris* of technological man in thinking that his creations — his cities and civilizations — can endure for more than a flickering moment against the power of eternal nature. Thus, the romantics secure *their* sense of immortality in God or nature, while sweeping the whole of man's achievements into obsolescence. It is an interesting psychological approach to the problem but one that is too negative and too unreal for most of us.

More limited in their advocacy of obsolescence is our second group, certain manufacturers. While taking our technological civilization for granted, they do believe that obsolescence must be built into their products in order to ensure continued sales and production. Thus, automobiles as well as automobile batteries, Park Avenue office buildings as well as the equipment that goes into them are planned for fairly rapid obsolescence.

Alas, for the sake of my topic, this form of planned obsolescence also carries a pejorative air, and most of us regard such manufacturers as teetering on the edge of shysterism, dishonesty, and lack of respect for their own workmanship. Only in the area of taxation is obsolescence fully recognized and accepted. As is well known, a depreciation allowance is made on machinery and buildings, and good citizens and businessmen are allowed to write off the growing obsolescence of their equipment according to a planned schedule. (Even scholars can depreciate their library in this fashion.)

All in all, then, as I have suggested, with one or two exceptions

157

my topic is basically uncongenial and unrecognized. Yet it is growing in importance, as planning for the future itself looms larger in our lives. Therefore, speculative as they may be, some thoughts on the role of obsolescence in the future are very much in order.

III

A typology of obsolescence must start with a division into planned and unplanned obsolescence. For the first type, I suggest the term "obsolescibles," borrowed from Bertrand de Jouvenel's jovial notion of "futuribles," and emphasizing thereby the notion of *choice* among possible planned obsolescences.[4] For example, one can plan both for and against certain types of obsolescence: demolishing Fifth Avenue mansions or turning them into historic sites, eliminating given social classes, such as white-collar workers or preserving them. Moreover, once we become aware of the unplanned obsolescences taking place around us, they may thereby come under our control as "obsolescibles."

For the moment, there are few of the latter. Thus, I shall talk first about some instances of planned obsolescence, even though the notion of choice has not been importantly or realistically explored in them, and then of unplanned obsolescences. I need hardly add that "obsolescibles" are merely a part of "futuribles" but looked at from a special angle.

IV

A few examples of planned obsolescence that may illuminate our subject are: (1) military disarmament; (2) the abolition of poverty; (3) and depopulation, or, at a minimum, the control of population.

First, military disarmament is a deliberate effort to make war and its tools obsolete. It takes place in an area where obsolescence of the military "hardware" is already planned for in one sense; for example, planes are built with a lead time of four or five years and with the full knowledge that they will be outdated in another four or five. But this is obsolescence in terms of replacement.

---

[4] See Bertrand de Jouvenel, *L'Art de la Conjecture* (Monaco: Éditions du Rocher, 1964).

Total military disarmament per se aims at making *all* the "hardware" obsolescent. The effect on society of a successful disarmament program would be staggering, and here I must look in the direction of Dr. Jungk and his work. In reality, however, and to be paradoxical, the subject is "unthinkable" (shades of Herman Kahn), and, as a result, there is very little in the way of actual, hard-boiled studies to which one can point. Of course, everyone is aware of such things as the widespread social dislocation in various countries that followed the end of the Napoleonic wars, or World War I, but the end of *all* war has never been available for our observation.

To take the United States of America alone, one would want to know just the sheer amount of land that is held by the military for bases and armories — think of the outcry at Secretary Mc-Namara's closing of some of the "obsolete" armories — and what would happen to these properties and their surrounding communities if they became obsolete? Indeed, the subject of military holdings of land could bear comparison to the position of the Church in the *ancien régime*. And then what of the men involved — the hierarchy of officers and the two and one-half million men under arms? And the materials devoted to arming these men? The sixty billion dollars in the budget each year devoted to military purposes is vastly more than the total GNP of most countries in the world. To what purposes could and would these men, materials, and money be dedicated if war and military preparations for it became obsolete?

Unfortunately, in William James's terms, these are not "live" issues. At the moment, there seems little point in thinking about war as an "obsolescible," where we might choose between the total disestablishment of the army and the transformation of it into a "labor army," used to train young men in a certain way and to mobilize them for various social tasks. Only a form of world government, monopolizing the military instruments, could bring about an approximation to the obsolescence of war; that, or World War III, might do the trick. In summation, while military disarmament is a planned form of obsolescence, it is so only in the minds of a few powerless individuals.

Second, if we consider our next example, the effort to make

poverty obsolete, there is a nice irony to the present phrase "war on poverty." Clearly, with war obsolete and the resources now devoted to it turned to other social uses, we could be well on the way to abolishing poverty. But we have already indicated the chimerical nature of this notion.

Now in discussing poverty per se, there is a problem of definition. What standard of living would everyone in the United States of America, for example, require in order for poverty to be non-existent? I shall take only one aspect of this problem. Surely, a minimal consequence of the abolition of poverty would have to be the elimination of slums (defined in the layman's sense as what he sees when he takes the railroad train out of New York and goes past Harlem). On one level, slums today may be con-sidered the result of buildings becoming obsolete — if we use the term in the sense of becoming old though, alas, not disused. On another level, of course, the problem is to make the slums them-selves obsolete, by making poverty obsolete, and our definition of the latter includes the removal of the former.

With slums gone, what do our cities look like? At present, our cities mirror with extraordinary accuracy our social structure and its divisions. There are slums, middle-class areas, and upper-class enclaves — as well as the office buildings, shopping areas, and small businesses. The slums in many large cities — this is just an estimate — contain at least one third of the population and would often take up at least one third of the land area. With their ob-solescence, do our cities become like our suburbs today, a sort of classless or one-class area? (One must remember, however, the clever saying, "We are all equal, only some are more equal than others.")

Do we want to plan a city where the "more equal" of our day would live side by side with the merely "equal" and thus return, though in a very different sense, to the concept of the city in, say, seventeenth-century Naples, where, as E. J. Hobsbawm tells us, "The rulers and the parasitic poor thus lived in a sort of symbiosis. There was not even much need to keep the two classes apart, as in modern cities. The traditional medieval or absolutist metropo-lis has no *beaux quartiers*. . . . The city was a cultural unit."[5]

[5] E. J. Hobsbawm, *Primitive Rebels* (New York: Praeger, 1963), pp. 115–116.

160

The obsolescence of slums is only one small part of what might be involved in the obsolescence of poverty. The impact on social structure, education, and our general culture would be at least equally profound. While the end of poverty is being "planned," even in this putative free-enterprise country — and comparison with other countries where poverty is more or less abolished is very much in order — the social consequences of its abolition or obsolescence seem to me less directly confronted or planned for.

Third, and to be treated with equal brevity, is my last example of planned obsolescence: the notion that some people, or a portion of the population, may become obsolete. As yet, this idea has taken the form of mere efforts at birth control. With the prediction for the year 2000 set at six billion persons, however, it might be well to think of heading these efforts toward planned "depopulation."

For example, reverse tax incentives might be used in the advanced countries, so that one had to *pay* an extra tax for each child after the first one, instead of *deducting* from one's tax bill for every addition. (Earlier in our sessions, Professor Herbert Moller said that this was fantastic; but I disagree.) In the underdeveloped countries, of course, other methods would be required. The point is that, like demilitarization, depopulation may become a necessity once a certain saturation point is reached.

In the meantime, population will be growing alarmingly. How, for example, will the architect deal with it? Will his buildings seek to make more evident, or less evident, the dense population? Does he still seek to provide individuality in an increasingly mass society, especially in the physical sense, or to accommodate himself to the enormity of the population? Until people become somewhat obsolete, in the particular sense intended here, the architect will have to plan for their omnipresence in the future.

V

It is with a certain stoicism, but not pessimism, that I am forced to conclude that, at least for the rest of this century, military disarmament, depopulation, and, for most of the world, the abolition of poverty are abortive examples of planned obsolescence. The quality and style of life throughout most of the world will still be

161

marked by a high degree of militarism, population growth and density, and economic and social deprivation.

What about unplanned obsolescence? Will this change matters by means of one of those "still and secret" revolutions about which Hegel talks? Let us consider three possible instances, all somewhat linked: the unplanned obsolescence (1) of the profit motive; (2) of work; and (3) of ideology.

First, the profit motive has been one of the dominant springs behind the expansion of industry and the creation of an industrial society in the modern world. Indeed, it forms part of Max Weber's definition of capitalism, where he speaks about the rational pursuit of individual profit. Thus, in efforts to modernize underdeveloped countries, the West frequently finds itself trying to instill the "achieving spirit," in the form of the profit motive, into the native peoples.

Yet, in its own home base, the United States of America, capitalism finds its own profit motives being eroded. An initial reason for this is simply the growing complexity and interrelationship of industrial society. To take a crude and trite example, in earlier days a profit seeker could cut down a forest of trees, in pursuit of individual gain, without worrying about land erosion; there was always more land. Today the whole economic ecology needs to be planned more carefully. This trend toward "creeping socialism" is fairly obvious.

Less obvious, I believe, is the impact of enterprises like the space program on the profit motive. Here, a forty-billion-dollar program is training engineers, scientists, and industrial managers to think in dimensions from which production or sale for profit is totally absent.[6]

Another straw in the wind is the changing nature of student ambition at our universities. Mervin B. Freedman summarizes it by saying: "The Puritan or Calvinist ethic of hard work and success in competitive struggle is on the wane, and to some extent the ethic of social service, which nourishes the hunger to be part

---

[6] See, for example, *The Railroad and the Space Program: An Exploration in Historical Analogy* (Cambridge, Mass.: M.I.T. Press, 1965), p. 49 and *passim*.

of a community, is replacing it."[7] One can also look on the Peace Corps, the fact that young men are willing to give two years to that effort, as part of the ethic of social service replacing the profit drive.

Clearly, I have not substantiated in any depth my notion that the profit motive is on the way to becoming obsolete in the West. (Nor have I dealt with its absence, in theory, in the Communist countries and its creeping back there in practice.) Yet I should like to suggest that, as a trend, it exists and that further research would bear out this conclusion.

Second, closely connected with the profit motive, or, in Freedman's terms, "success in competitive struggle" is "hard work." Deeply rooted for most of us until now in the human condition — "Man earns his bread by the sweat of his brow" — this fundamental characteristic is beginning to become obsolete not just for a small elite but for large numbers of men. The introduction of machines has meant the exit, partly planned and partly unplanned, of man from the scene of muscular activity. With automation the process is extended to a wide range of mental work. Galbraith's "affluent society" and the problems of leisure thus emerge jointly.

If this trend toward the obsolescence of work, manifested most clearly at the moment in the United States of America, is accepted without further argument — and by the way, at this point the trend should become thereby an "obsolescible" — a whole host of social consequences need to be studied. Let me touch on only two. The first is the effect on social status. I can do no better here than to quote my friend, Dr. J. Bronowski, talking on the effect of automation:

Fifty years from now, the machine operator of any kind will be as much a fossil as the handweaver has been since 1830. Today we still distinguish between skilled and unskilled jobs of repetition, between office worker and factory worker, between white collar and no collar. In fifty years from now, all repetitive jobs will be unskilled.

The social implications of this change are profound, and I believe that they more than anything else that I have forecast will shape the

[7] Mervin B. Freedman, "Roots of Student Discontent," *The Nation*, June 14, 1965.

community of the future. For their effect will be to change the social status of the different jobs in the community. The ability to handle a column of figures will become no more desirable than the ability to drive a rivet; and even the ability to write business letters may become less sought after than the ability to repair the machine that writes them by rote. As a result, the clerk will sink in social status, and the electrical engineer will rise; and that in itself is a change as far-reaching as was once brought about by the dissolution of the monasteries.[8]

If we accept the seventeenth-century definition of a "gentleman" as one who could be idle — and this, by the way, is a definition from a book by Peter Laslett called the *World We Have Lost* — then it is clear that our social world will be turned topsy-turvy, and the present "working class" will become largely "gentlemen."

The second consequence of the growing obsolescence of work as we know it relates to the first. It is that the electrical engineer and his ilk may well become the elite of the new society. This would be to realize the Saint-Simonian and Comtean dream and prediction, only a century or two late. Something of this sort appears to be arising in the Soviet Union. However, we need to be very cautious on this subject. While scientists and engineers will undoubtedly take on more and more of the work load of society, with the present workers becoming "gentlemen," it is *not* clear that the new "meritocracy" will also rule. After all, Communist parties still seem to be headed by political, and sometimes military, figures. How this struggle for power will turn out may hinge on the end of ideology. For the nonce, we can say definitely that work and working relations, as we know them, are becoming obsolescent and, with some luck, might become "obsolescibles."

Our third candidate for unplanned obsolescence is the ebbing of ideology as a force in political decisions. It is held in some quarters, notably by Daniel Bell, that the "end of ideology" is at hand, with social decisions being made more and more on technical grounds.[9] Karl Popper calls it "piece-meal social engineering," and its possible connection with a scientific-technical elite is evident.

8 J. Bronowski, "The Shape of the Future," *Royal Society of Health Journal*, Vol. 82, No. 3 (May–June 1962).

9 See Daniel Bell, *The End of Ideology* (Glencoe, Ill.: Free Press, 1959).

This is hardly the place to argue in depth such a complicated problem. Obviously, there are straws in the wind, such as Rand Corporation's computer-type decisions, French technocrats, economists as premiers in the Soviet Union, which seem to lend support to the Bell thesis. Yet I feel that the "end of ideology" adherents both underestimate the psychological element in political-social life — the "metaphysical" need, if you like, of peoples and countries seeking to mobilize their energies — and ignore the ideological assumptions of their own end to ideology. In this, they are like the logical positivists, who dismiss metaphysics on metaphysical grounds, while claiming otherwise. It is probably no accident that logical positivists and analysts are anti-ideology.

It is true that industrialization, to be successful, imposes certain constraints of its own, whether in Indonesia or Communist China. Yet to equate this with the end of ideology is, I think, to ignore half of the factors involved, just as to emphasize *only* ideological considerations is to ignore the other half of industrialization. In sum, and all too briefly then, I do not believe that the growth of a technical elite necessarily implies the unplanned obsolescence of ideology.

VI

What sort of conclusion can I make? It seems to me that there are really two conclusions. The first is that the large issues of planned and unplanned obsolescences that I have scanned (and there are many others, such as the future of revolution as a means of social transformation or the effort to make our prison system obsolete, which I was tempted to consider) are too complicated and vague to allow us to say much with surety at this stage about the quality and style of life in the future.

Undoubtedly, however, the latter will change, and if I were forced to predict in this area, I should say that changes will occur in terms of the growing obsolescence of poverty, with its concomitant social effects; of the profit motive as a stimulus to economic-social activity; and of the present nature of work and the working classes. As I have already indicated, however, the

165

quality of our life in the near future will probably still be heavily colored by militarism, rising populations, and the activating of these conditions by ideology.

My second conclusion is that, vague and diffused as the subject is, the introduction of the concept of "obsolescibles" into our ideas of growth and progress would be useful. Thus, in planning our future, we might even be daring enough to allow for the temporary nature of our own desired ideas and institutions, to set up programs and ideologies that include their own phasing out.[10]

In summary, as I remarked earlier, the sort of thinking involved in obsolescence is difficult even to envisage successfully, for it runs up against the desire to avoid the awareness that our individual lives bear the stamp of obsolescence. Yet, uncongenial as the thought is, it is part of our coming to terms with the human condition. Part of maturing, individually and as a society, is to become aware of death. Put in its social form, the necessary concomitant of progress is obsolescence. Once fully aware of this fact, however, it may at least be possible to metamorphose obsolescence into "obsolescibles."

DISCUSSION

DUHL: I have a suspicion that the adolescent is the best prognosticator of the future that we have, since what they are concerned with, though quite amorphous and diffuse, might very

---

[10] There is an interesting comment by Donald Schon, made during the conference that the American Academy held under the direction of Daniel Bell on the year 2000, which suggests how difficult such an effort at "phasing out" is going to be. As Schon says, "If you look at the various agencies of the federal government, you can identify them with problems which are in general 30 years old. The Department of Agriculture is really even older than that. It goes back to the period of agricultural scarcity and the need for productivity. There are still 70,000 agricultural extension agents in the field. The Department of Labor goes back to the labor problems of the '30's. The small business administration goes back to a period, I guess, in the '40's, when we began to get nostalgic and worried about what was happening to the little entrepreneur. The Department of Commerce is a mish-mash, well, it's like a piece of geological strata where you can see all kinds of things together which were once relevant.

"I have spent in the last three years in government more time on how to stop things than on any other single problem."

well find forms in the future. I would suggest that adolescents are now less concerned with creating new material things and that they are beginning to talk about something else. This means that obsolescence does not become a critical consideration for them at all. What they are trying to do is to create a new set of values, which is what you were suggesting about the Peace Corps. I think this is a much broader question.

Professor MARX WARTOFSKY: If you intend to consider the concept of obsolescence, then it seems that you ought to be careful how you introduce it semantically. In one of the definitions, "obsolescent" means "old," and in the other you equate it with abolition, or with what is abolishable.

TILLINGHAST: It means old.

WARTOFSKY: In that case, the fact that it is obsolescent is no guarantee that something will disappear; and the fact that it is obsolescible doesn't mean it is going to be eliminated. It is not clear in your discussion. You talk about the military being obsolescible, or poverty being obsolescible; since these exist, then in one sense, "obsolescible" means "ought to have been abolished." But in another sense, you mean simply that we are capable of doing away with it, whereas in the past we weren't. But it seems to me we ought to be careful of talking about the obsolescence as if this meant actually abolishing or eliminating something. That something *can* be abolished is not the same as that something *ought* to be abolished. And this doesn't depend in either case on how "old" it is.

One of the problems with obsolescence is that we are burdened with a number of things that persist past their time. But much of what is old *is not* obsolescible, and much of what is new *is* obsolescible.

MAZLISH: I agree with you; the meaning of the word is fuzzy. I think you need to add to "old," "outworn" and "disused." All I meant by "obsolescibles" was that you had a choice. This is what de Jouvenel intends with his "futuribles." Thus, you might, in fact, decide you do or do not want to eliminate slums. I can see somebody arguing that one might want to have some sort of area that does deteriorate, because part of the population is going to have to live there, economically, and ought to live there, socially.

My intention is simply to introduce such matters as a choice. It seems to me what most planning (leaving aside slum clearance) does is to take only positive goals; that is, we will try to achieve this, and there are no plans to knock down the scaffolding that has now become disused from previous developments. For example, I would ask Mr. Cazes if there is any provision in the plan for 1985 for not only achieving new things in terms of the existing trends but for doing away with some other things.

CAZES: There is a whole chapter titled "Obsolescence" in our 1985 report. It is a curious chapter which reflects a rather frantic drive for modernity among some younger government officials who are impatient with things that they deem obsolescent but that are not considered obsolescent by others.

Professor JOHN W. DYCKMAN: I am confused about the definitional problems that are so formidable, especially because I was not certain whether you were talking about both the changes in forms and the changes in functions in obsolescence. Sometimes it seems — as in the profit motive discussion — that you were talking about changing the form, while implicitly the functions would remain unchanged. You would have motivation in some kind of efficient organizing or allocation devices, even though the form might change. But at other times, when you talk about the nation-state, the functions disappear entirely. The function of defense would then disappear; I don't know whether this eliminated the forms as well. I know it is possible to have planning for changes in the forms, but it seems much more difficult to plan for changes in the function. Also, would you have the form or the function on the planned side of the barrier and the other on the unplanned side?

MAZLISH: I am not completely sure myself, but I think I would allow for both form and function to become obsolescent by planning or unplanning. I suppose I am trying to say that we ought to give some attention to those things which are becoming obsolete in an unplanned fashion. Then we have choice. The instance I gave was the Fifth Avenue mansion. Now, in terms of various economic realities of New York, those buildings which have been torn down are considered obsolescent, and nobody worries or argues, or very little argument takes place. I can conceive of another way of looking at them in which we say that, although the initial function they served has disappeared, we shall redefine that function and change it into a historical function.

Professor GERALD DWORKIN: I wonder if you aren't eliminating Marx? As you mentioned in the very beginning, he saw quite clearly the contradictions within capitalism that, he claimed, would lead to its disappearance, and he said that the future would be always changing in this way. I wonder if Marx *is* opposed to the whole notion of the dialectical process, which he took over. Hegel is very congenial, constantly bringing forward the idea of things changing and nothing being constant.

MAZLISH: You open up the possibility of a prolonged discussion. I could take the easy way out by referring you to the chapter on Marx in my recent book *The Riddle of History*, but I won't. It seems to me that there is a logical contradiction in Marx. If Marx explains that the means by which the dialectic process works itself out is by the class struggle in history, as he does, then his next idea, the abolition of classes, which is to be achieved with communism, automatically eliminates this motive force, and logically that means you are no longer in history.

WARTOFSKY: I don't think that the notion that the dialectic ends when the class struggle ends is either in Marx or that it can be inferred from Marx's view. Certainly, if it were, it would be in direct contradiction to the notions of Heraclitus and of Hegel that nothing is permanent but change — views which Marx took to be central to his whole way of thinking.

MAZLISH: All I am trying to point out is that there is a contradiction in Marx; that in the end he becomes at least as utopian as those he criticizes. However, the only way one can settle this sort of question is by actual citation of the texts.

Plural and Normative Planning

In the face of our serious environmental problems, architects and planners must join other professionals in innovative programs like those which Jarvie has called "critical utopianism." But the active participation of the public is also needed. All possible futures will result from the interaction of these groups. Any desirable future will be the fruit of their mutually critical and mutually reinforcing interaction.

The essays of this section contend that our planning has, to our social detriment, evaded the implications of societal pluralism and competing values.

A practical proposal that mediates among the elitist tendencies of the professions and the plural interests of the citizenry is the "advocacy" method. As advocates, professionals offer their *expertise* to community groups and are themselves instructed and changed by this encounter. The professional then returns to advocate the interests of that group in a larger public arena. The considered confrontation of the advocates for various viewpoints would aid in the survival and flourishing, as well as in the evolutionary development, of a desirable diversity within our complex, urbanizing society.

Advocacy is thus a possible method for introducing multiple value systems into a rational planning procedure.

Normative Planning

PAUL DAVIDOFF

As we speak of inventing the future, it is revealing that we do not address ourselves to "preventing the future." The idea that the future is inventable suggests a bias toward both optimism and technological determinism. I question these biases.

As a planner, I am pleased that there is growing concern with thinking about the future. But I am afraid that much of this thinking may be devoid of knowledge and concern with the tremendous problems of poverty, discrimination, and war that beset our society at this time and will remain with us for some time in the future. I think that the futurists of today must be warned not to attempt to practice nonnormative planning.

Today's planning, both conventional agency work and the new concern with the year 2000 or beyond, tends to examine problems in essentially technical terms. But in masking the values underlying their proposals, the planners have weakened their plans. Contemporary comprehensive city plans are often quite unrealistic and appear so to the public precisely because their authors fail to come to grips with the basic issues that confront their society and split the members of the society into different political groups.

In city planning we have had a practice of a single planning body proposing a course of action. The community has then had a yes-or-no referendum: either they accept the plan, or they have no plan.

There has been strong reaction to this form of planning within our field in the past five or six years, and there seems to be a growing practice for planning agencies to make a point of considering alternative policies rather than a single "technically correct" plan. One who adheres to the recipe for good rational behavior would examine alternative policy choices rather than simply propose one rationally perfect plan.

A single agency, however, continues to be responsible for the discussion of alternative plans or alternative means for achieving a given end. The presentation of alternatives by a single agency still does not recognize the essential political element underlying a planning proposal, that the "general welfare" or the "public interest" is not a fact that can be discovered upon deep research. The identification of the public interest is always a contentious point. There are different views about how the public will best be served. Our practice in physical planning often has not accepted that debate; instead, there has been a concept that the technicians, the planners, might be able to develop a good plan or series of alternatives for the community. (The planning staff and planning commission may, of course, develop a good plan, but there is no objective measure of its goodness. Its evaluation in terms of serving the public is necessarily a political judgment. It is a choice of policy and a choice of what ought to be done for the community; as such it is subject to debate, or in a democracy it should be subject to debate, so as to permit different interests to react to the solution offered.)

The alternative to this monolithic agency proposal of plans is "plural planning," in which the determination of how the society ought to develop would not be the sole responsibility of a single public agency. Instead, many different groups within the society might participate in determining policy. "Determining" here means proposing, debating, deciding.

Plans for community development should be included in the platforms of political parties. For many reasons, however, the political parties want to remain as general as possible in their commitment so as not to lose popularity. They do not want to support specific ideologies. Since the political parties are incapable of developing plans themselves, other interest groups may be capable of proposing plans. The development of what has been called "advocate planning" recognizes this need for interest groups to express their demands in the form of plans.

Planners have begun to operate as professional advocates for neighborhood groups, developing alternative plans to the plans proposed by some public agency. This is a very healthy development, and one that we should take note of at this conference. As we find ourselves more and more concerned with the year 2000 and with specific commission plans for the year 2000 or some later time in the future, we should not expect that a plan for that year can come alone from the "best minds" in the country. One of these plans, that of the Commission on the Year 2000, prepared by a group of "experts," seems to represent a group of characters in search of a future. Here is a group of intellectuals, who, aside from the fact that they have some common background and training in being concerned with intellectual matters, have no real reason for coming together. They do not represent any interest at all, and it is not surprising that, at least so far, they do not seem capable of yielding a plan. There is no common interest that ties them together. They do not have a common political base.

The concept of pluralism in planning has both positive and negative features. In establishing a plural planning system, we have to guard against the abnegation of leadership. In proposing plural planning, we should not say that there is no role for the central planning agency. It will still have a vital role to play. The agency that produces the government plan will be better informed if it produces plans in the context of a societal process of considering what ought to be. The agency does have an important job in recommending what courses of action should be followed. It would be a mistake to minimize that central planning function or to recommend that it be transferred to the many different interests in the society. That would be an unwarranted dissipation of responsibility.

The central agency's role is to give direction; but it must recognize that its views are only one possible set of views. If the central planning agency is sophisticated, it will know how to take advantage of the alternatives proposed by outside groups. It will educate itself, both technically and politically, toward improving its own recommendations.

I should like to highlight my remarks regarding the need for pluralizing planning by suggesting in their definitions of major problems central planning agencies have tended to accept value orientations favoring the present distribution of opportunities in society.

First, let us look at the present concern with urban life. We know that there are problems in the city because *Life* and *Look* have told us so. If we feel insecure with those magazines, the *Saturday Review* has also told us so. Recently, *U.S. News & World Report* told us that there was a crisis in our cities and indicated that we have to spend perhaps a trillion dollars in ten years to combat this problem.

The concern with urbanism is misplaced. The real crisis of our times is not an urban crisis. Instead, the crucial problem is a national problem, an international problem, a social problem. It is the fact of great social injustice. It is the fact that there is vast discrimination, poverty, and hunger. It is the fact that there is great hate, that the world is ready to blow itself up and is very close to doing so, and that very few people are trying to prevent us from destroying ourselves.

Many of these social problems are presently located in urban areas. The poor live increasingly in urban areas, both in our nation and in others. The problems may thus seem more apparent in urban areas, so we call them urban problems. We discover, though, that in "dealing" with urban problems, we are not often dealing with the problems of injustice, discrimination, and poverty. In fact, we are dealing with *other* problems peculiar to urban areas: the problems of congestion, problems of "uglification," to use Lewis Carroll's term, problems of high density and of pollution. But the basic problem that must be confronted is the unjust distribution of opportunities in our society. We cannot hope to solve this problem at the urban level. By focusing on the urban aspect of social problems, we avoid dealing with national distributional questions.

In all our discussions of the future so far at this conference there has hardly been any mention of distribution, whether of the present distribution of opportunities, of education, of health, of leisure time, of wealth and income, or of knowledge.

We live in a society that has accepted the conventional

wisdom of modern economists, whose main concern is with growth. The quality of our economy must be determined in terms not only of growth but of how the economy distributes its resources.

In our discussion earlier no one said that the present distribution is wrong or that we should do something to see that the poor get a greater share of what our society and other societies have to offer. Our assumption is that of John Kenneth Galbraith, who wrote in *The Affluent Society:*

. . . Few things are more evident in modern social history than the decline of interest in inequality as an economic issue. . . . While it continues to have a large ritualistic role in the conventional wisdom of conservatives and liberals, inequality has ceased to preoccupy men's minds. . . . In the advanced country, . . . increased production is an alternative to redistribution. And, as indicated, it has been the great solvent of the tensions associated with inequality. . . . Yet in this case the facts are inescapable. It is the increase in output in recent decades, not the redistribution of income, which has brought the great material increase, the well-being of the average man. And, however suspiciously, the liberal has come to accept the fact.[1]

The inescapable fact to which Galbraith alludes does not lead to any inescapable conclusions concerning proper public policy. Galbraith comes to grips with the basic value problems by describing what has happened in economic thought, but his implied conclusion is that it is no longer necessary to consider the propriety of present distribution patterns. This is wrong. At a minimum a responsible evaluation of the quality of the national economy would always have to account for the distributional pattern as well as for the absolute quantity of wealth.

Our society is concerned with full employment and with economic growth. We argue whether we ought to have 4 per cent or 2 per cent unemployment, but the amount of employment or unemployment is itself not so significant as the question of who gets what from the society. In a society in which the unemployed were given a decent income, the problems of unemployment would have a different meaning than they do for us today.

[1] John Kenneth Galbraith, *The Affluent Society* (Boston: Houghton Mifflin, 1958), 15th ed., pp. 82, 96–97.

I ask for a greater sharing of the goods of the society: of knowledge, health, and wealth. I do not think it is necessary to argue, however, that everybody must have the same. We do not have to consider whether the society that we create will be too bland or whether we shall eliminate incentive.

What we should discuss is the question of whether it is or is not appropriate to maintain the present distribution of social goods. That issue, however, is never discussed. We assume that the present distribution is correct. It is probably a familiar fact that in our society the top 5 per cent of income earners earn three times as much as the bottom 20 per cent. The top 5 per cent earn 15 per cent, the bottom 20 per cent earn about 5 per cent, and the top 20 per cent earn almost ten times as much as the bottom 20 per cent. During the course of the period from the New Deal to the present, whatever redistribution has taken place took some money from the wealthiest group and gave it to the upper-middle-income group. Some resources went to the second quintile and some to the third quintile, but hardly anything has come down to the bottom 40 per cent. The figures since 1948 or 1950 show almost no change in the proportion the bottom 40 per cent received.

In the distribution of knowledge, of the opportunity to enjoy leisure time, we can find patterns quite similar. We know very well that the poor have very little opportunity to get out of the city to enjoy the great resort areas our country possesses. Dean Seifert has mentioned the great increase in airplane traffic. Only about a third of the American people have ever taken even one flight. We have a vast industry serving those of us who fly fairly often. We are only a small percentage of the population, yet a great deal of money from federal funds goes into support of the air travel industry. It is a fine industry, but the question is: Who has the opportunity to share its benefits?

Many may say that economic growth is enough. Some of us may disagree with that point of view; but the crucial point is that we should be debating the distribution issue. It shouldn't be hidden from view.

It is quite irresponsible on the part of any technician to come before the public to make a recommendation about how things ought to be, unless he states very explicitly that the distribution pattern he proposes is the best one. He should say explicitly that in the society he proposes it is right that the poor shall get only their pittance and that this is the best solution for everyone.

It is quite apparent that many people who make solutions today would rather not be so explicit. It is difficult, even if you do believe that ours is the best distribution pattern, to have to admit it.

In our discussions of the future of a particular society or of world society I hope that the underlying social issues, of resource distribution for rich and poor, for warlike and peaceful purposes, for benefit to persons and institutions, will provide the focal point of discussion. This exploration of underlying issues will help us to avoid the myth of the planner as technical specialist, privy to vast secret information banks, who can set out futures for whole societies in a political vacuum. We are all politicians and ideologues, and I hope our conferences and our planning documents will admit and face this fact.

DISCUSSION

OZBEKHAN: A few years ago, I was hired to do rather basic research on the methodology of planning for General Electric. In none of my writings for the corporation was I allowed to use the word "planning," because it sounded socialistic. A great deal of difficulty is encountered in this field, especially when so many are engaged in planning. But I agree with you that many groups must plan, that pluralistic planning is a very good idea.

However, two fundamental things will have to change: the first is our mores. In this instance, the supposed liberalism of the nineteenth century has to be broken down in our minds before we can approach what you were talking about.

The second thing derives directly from the first. It is that the relationship between work and income has to be changed. That is the only way we can achieve any kind of more equitable distribution today, other than through growth.

DAVIDOFF: There are two issues here. First, about pluralism: I don't want to be understood as saying that everybody *has* to plan. We are not going to make people plan. I hope that by suggesting that there can be more than a single central planning agency, it will be possible for the real estate boards, the Chambers of Commerce, the AMA, and the NAACP to get into the process of determining the future.

As to your last point, of course, there has to be a very great change in our mores. The very first group that has to change is the liberal intellectuals who for too long have accepted the liberal conventional wisdom of group growth and who haven't demanded that government concern itself at all times with the question of the propriety of any allocation of resources.

OZBEKHAN: No argument there. I believe Dr. Duhl touched on exactly the same point.

FRIEDEN: I am also in agreement with what you said about the importance of issues of distribution, but I would like to comment on the earlier part of your presentation. You spoke about the urban crisis and questioned whether it really exists and whether it is separable from these social issues.

It is one thing to say urban problems are very deeply embedded in social values and in issues of national policy. I agree with that. But if you mean to go further and to say that there really is nothing that needs to be done at the urban level, that we just have to worry about national policy and social values, I can't agree.

The way we build cities and the way we manage cities have a great deal to do with the distribution of opportunities and with issues such as racial and economic segregation. Our present urban arrangements have a great deal to do with denial of opportunities. If you want to take a broad national approach, there is an urban counterpart to it, and there should be urban policies consistent with national goals.

DAVIDOFF: We do have many functional agencies: HUD, HEW, and others. We spread out the responsibility for national social planning. We have no group responsible for developing a national social policy plan. The only thing that comes close to it is the Bureau of the Budget, which operates in secret. It doesn't open up issues for public debate. The Bureau of the Budget is not involved in a *public* planning process. What we desperately need is an agency at the national level to do comprehensive economic and social planning for the nation; and we need its counterpart at the city level as well.

What I am really saying, though, is that I have a hunch that the concern with urban crises is moving us further away from coming to grips with the essential social problems.

FRIEDEN: But concern with the urban problems might be a way of broadening this.

DAVIDOFF: If so, I must cite a prediction that William Wheaton of the University of California made: If you want to create any progress, do it in the 1960's. By 1970 the suburbs will be in control of metropolitan areas. The suburbs will want metropolitan government, so they can control it. We will not have very liberal urban policies when that happens. I hope you are right about the need to deal with the urban issues. In any case, we have to establish the political coalitions to work toward the ends we desire.

S. ANDERSON: In Chicago, for example, there have been certain changes in policies about financing and ownership in Negro communities. This represents a partial redistribution; but, perhaps more importantly, it demonstrates that the Negro community is becoming effective in the transformation of even socially entrenched problems.

DAVIDOFF: Unfortunately, I have to say that, in fact, what the Negro gets in the North is very little. There has been very little progress, very little change. What really has happened to the Negroes in Chicago? How much has been opened to them as a result of all this tremendous pressure? What have they received? If we assume we are in agreement here, that the Negro deserves a better share of things, then I am not so sure we are making progress.

We allow relatively few people to get out of the slums and ghettos, and we don't yet have a conscious national policy to permit the Negro to live anywhere within a region at housing prices he can afford. That will take strong federal action.

S. ANDERSON: Are you saying that this condition argues against advocacy planning as mere mitigation of serious situations? All that operates through local communities is inadequate, and you want central government planning to redistribute things dramatically?

DAVIDOFF: Yes. Many people will have to work very hard for a long time before we have a national policy that will accept that, but the end result should be greater equity.

S. ANDERSON: You are saying that advocacy planning has as its main role not the change, or mitigation, or improvement of the life of people in specific communities but rather the change of the political climate so that the central authorities will induce change.

DAVIDOFF: I think there is need for both activities to go on simultaneously. It may be a long time before there is a major shift in our national or international policies about the distribution of the goods in the world. In the interim we may be left to try to make things just slightly better in each community. But while we do that and while we continue the type of community work that advocate planning has represented in some communities, at the same time we must push for something much greater. Because he has not pushed hard on the essential issue, the liberal has no real policy, no strong conviction about what a better society would be.

BAUER: I guess I am in favor of humanity, justice, and the welfare of mankind, too; however, I want to be critical of uncritical criticism of conventional wisdom. I refer here to the joint issues of *distribution* and of *contribution*, and there is no more usual way to confuse the issues than to talk about the fact that only one third of the people have flown in an airplane and that a very small portion of the people fly their own airplanes; so, according to the rest of the argument, why should everybody else suffer because these people can afford to fly airplanes?

There are two assumptions. One is that flying in airplanes is a function of personal wealth, and the other is that the person is flying for his own pleasure. I don't know the precise figures, but I will guess that 90 per cent of the airplane-miles traveled are paid for by somebody else to get a man to go someplace and do some work. This is not consumption on the part of the flyer. This is supposedly related to his contribution to the general welfare. I do not pretend for a moment that the inequities in the distribution of income reflect contribution to society. But I do think that there are some key places in our society where the demand for certain types of contributions by people exceeds what these people can genuinely contribute and that we ought to see whether or not the maintenance of some pretty stiff system of incentives is not required there. I would encourage a group such as the one we are in to think about this particularly when we consider the problems of leisure.

NEWMAN: The problem that we are faced with is that for the poor, the ability to express themselves by buying something or not buying it doesn't usually come into play at all. They just do not have the market mechanism for dealing with the problem.

You [Davidoff] suggested another mechanism, when you proposed alternative planning. You listed a series of agencies, and you said that they could prepare plans and various communities could prepare plans. But then the whole idea of the very poor competing in the plan-making market seems to be a problem again.

DAVIDOFF: I am glad you picked me up on that. The major reason why I became interested in advocacy planning was to see that the poor got some adequate representation in the planning process. In the last few years, there has been a rapid growth of advocacy planning in Negro communities, in ghettos, and in poor white communities as well. We have good examples of it here, such as Bob Goodman's work in Boston.[2] In New York the Architects' Renewal Committee in Harlem has been working with neighborhood communities in developing their own renewal plans. Advocacy groups have come into existence in San Francisco, Syracuse, and probably in a number of other places. I think there is no question that it is the poor who are beginning to come into the planning process as a result of advocate planning. One of the problems is that they don't have the money to purchase any experts.

Foundation support is one obvious source of money for these efforts. The OEO [Office of Economic Opportunity] is also giving some thought to working in the field of planning this

---

[2] R. Goodman, "Advocacy: A New Role for Architects and Planners," *World Architecture*, Vol. IV (1967), pp. 22–23.

year. It may want to move into the field of planning as it moved into medicine or as it established neighborhood law offices and sponsored legal action to help the poor. One of the things a number of us in planning education are trying to do — Bernard Frieden at M.I.T. and our group at Hunter — is to help develop planners who will be capable of working as advocate planners with community groups.

MAZLISH: I wonder if there isn't a logical inconsistency between something you said here and your other statements. Perhaps I misunderstood. I thought you said that what is public interest or public good was not a settled question; and, indeed, this point has come up in many of the conversations earlier. Then you go on, however, to talk as if, in fact, it were clear what the public interest was, in reference to equality, to integration, and so forth.

Now, I think most of us agree with your version of the public interest, and I would go so far as to say that we do know there is a general good. You may not be able to achieve it in public life. For example, I am against the oil depletion allowance for the petroleum industry. I have no doubt in my mind that it would be to the public good to get rid of this. As a practical matter, however, I can't bring this to pass. In short, we are playing games if we say we don't know what the public good is, and then say we want equality. The problem, of course, is complicated. For example, we want advocacy planning for the Negroes. Fine, but what about advocacy planning for, say, the Italian population in Boston, who, I am quite sure, don't want the Negroes in their area, and who see their whole way of life threatened by Negro integration — and the Italians, of course, are larger in number? We have to face a possible logical inconsistency, then, in our own values.

DAVIDOFF: I don't find an inconsistency. I believe everybody has a right to a lawyer. Maybe someday everybody will have a right to the services of an advocate planner. Certainly the group that opposes the Negro coming into the neighborhood has as much right as those who are proposing that the Negroes have a greater access to it. I don't believe our objective must be to verify some concept of the public interest or the public good. I know what I believe, and I have expressed what I believe; but I can't state that it is true. I have no way of verifying the existence of that truth. Other people can certainly contest my version of the truth and argue on other grounds or about other things. I am asserting my own belief. All we can do is to be as persuasive as possible about our own beliefs. We can't impose our version of the truth on others.

BARNETT: I will try not to assert any of my own beliefs, merely facts. There are a number of studies that manifest concern for distribution. The authors include Robert Lampman and Burton Weisbrod of Wisconsin, Sar Levitan of Upjohn, Gunnar Myrdal, Herman Miller of Census, and many others.

Milton Friedman of the University of Chicago, for example, has come up with the notion of remedying the social injustice of poverty (which he did not define as you did; no one cares about the millionaire; what one cares about is the poor man). He came up with the notion of a negative income tax. He said: If you want to remedy poverty, focus on the *poor* people, not on farmers or the aged, many of whom are not poor. If it is poverty you want to remedy, then, just as you have a progressive income tax on high incomes, make payments on a progressive schedule to the people you identify as below the poverty line.

I want to ask you one question. How would you try to implement, in a rational way, any of the proposals that you described for a better distribution of the income?

DAVIDOFF: The easiest way would be a guarantee of a minimum income, a decent one, say $7,000.

BARNETT: Then, what you are proposing happens to have been originated before by the advisor to Mr. Goldwater, who proposed a negative income tax.

DAVIDOFF: Any program that achieves the end of redistribution is fine with me. Taxes should be established to control the wealth passed from generation to generation. That money can be given back in the form of special programs or subsidies for the poor. I don't think it is difficult to establish the kinds of subsidies and remedial programs that are needed. Let me give you an example. I should like to see people with present incomes of less than $3,000, $4,000, or $5,000 — you set the figure — have

185

decent housing in a decent environment. We need much more than 20,000 low-cost housing units a year. We need a million units or up to five million units a year to take care of the inadequate housing in our society. Everyone of any income should have access to a decent education. And one of my first goals in establishing distribution would be to work toward a situation where the distribution of deaths from sickness and accident would be the same for Negro and white.

BARNETT: You mentioned three things, and every one of them is now being decided in a political process. The question of education is being decided, and it may be that you want to change the process. If so, how or where? Education decisions are now being made. Maybe you know how to improve education — tell us how. The second thing is the taxation system. The federal tax system is decided in Congress in accepted political ways, and at the local level taxes are decided in various ways. Third, the decision concerning how much housing there should be of various kinds is determined in a legislature, which in our great wisdom is an imperfect political place. What do you want to change? You have identified three cases in which you would like to improve the mechanisms of our society. What shall we do?

DAVIDOFF: The issue is very simple. My speech is political. I said the issue is normative. I believe that we need greater equity in the society and that we haven't achieved it. We have lost in the political market place, and now we must develop our power and make coalitions so that we can alter the political results. You gave us what you said was an objective appraisal, an objective projection of what would happen. This was based upon the norms of our present society. Your projection was guided by what is currently accepted. It didn't have to be that way. You could have proposed alternative ranges that could occur in our society if we pursued different policies.

We have choices to make concerning how we act and what we choose to study. I come here today on a political errand. There is great social injustice. We planners are here to invent the future because we don't like it the way it is. It is necessary for people like ourselves to make explicit the issues that underlie social changes of the future. I wish that everybody were on my side on the issue. Since that is not the case, I think the people involved in discussing the future should see that the issue of distribution — of who gets what — should be made explicit and not constantly swept under the carpet.

Ideology and Architecture: Dilemmas of Pluralism in Planning

LEONARD J. FEIN

As the three blind men in the old Indian folk tale each saw something different in the elephant, so does the community confuse the role of architect. Happily for the elephant, he was not aware of what transpired, and so, despite the disagreement over what he was, we may assume that he plodded placidly along, remembering everything and being frightened of mice. The architect cannot afford to be so casual, for it is we blind men who make demands of him, demands so widely discrepant that he may be excused if he is no longer sure of what or who he is. We ask that he be artist, by which some of us mean more Michelangelo and others intend more our neighborhood cake decorator. We ask that he be planner — one day of Lincoln Center, the next of our second-floor bath. We expect him to translate our visions into realities, but we ourselves cannot articulate those visions. We ask that he be creative but require as well that he be responsible.

And now we ask him to be a social scientist as well. Artist, engineer, planner, prophet, interpreter, and now social scientist. The burden is staggering, and I confess that I am not optimistic that it can be borne. I have altogether too much respect for the guts of what an architect must master and, indeed, for the stuff of the social sciences to believe that the two can be as readily absorbed as either alone. I am aware of the ecumenical ideology that pervades these times, but I have even stronger doubts about its utility in professional training than in the theological realm. Indeed, if our concern here is dominated by the concept of

188

pluralism, one could well argue that the architect himself is a representation of the community writ small. Somehow he must come to terms with contending and often irreconcilable demands; he must in himself comprehend diversity, preserve it, and order it into a viable whole. It is perfectly plain that each of us ought to know a great deal more than we now do; it is equally plain that the limits on our capacities would quickly be exhausted if we took seriously the endless pleas for greater scope.

I suspect that the answer, if answer there be, lies not so much in the constant multiplication of demands on professional training but rather in the creation of new institutional frameworks in which we can talk to one another and which are based on just enough breadth in the training process so that we can understand the conversation.

I shall return to this matter presently, but I want first to consider the question of pluralism in planning. To come to terms with the concept of pluralism, either as norm or as description, requires a prior understanding of certain aspects of the social structure. Pluralism, of course, speaks to the issue of how to create diversity in an ordered society or, if you will, how to create order in a diverse society. But somewhat differently, in the words of Henry Churchill, it is concerned with "making the city tolerable and still keeping it a city." But the issue of order and diversity is no simple matter. On the contrary, a reading of American criticism reveals two rather discrepant views of the American experiment, each of which bears directly on the desirability and the possibility of pluralism.

The first of these views suggests that major emphasis must be placed on ordering the American chaos. Owing to this view, brotherhood has become our national slogan, ecumenicism our ideology, and the reduction of difference our central preoccupation. Our folk hero, curiously enough, is Shakespeare's Shylock, whose most famous speech we delight in paraphrasing to each other: We are all "fed with the same food, hurt with the same weapons, subject to the same diseases, healed by the same means, warmed and cooled by the same winter and summer. . . . If you prick us, do we not bleed? If you tickle us, do we not laugh? If you poison us, do we not die?" And so, we assure ourselves, the differences that set us apart from one another are indeed trivial; if not trivial, they are subversive. Differences are, in fact, only manageable when they are seen as either meaningless or quaint. We worship the same god, salute the same flag, and march to the same drummer. Where we do not, we become either unsure of ourselves or cast out by the others, for the system cannot comprehend meaningful diversity. This, if you will, is the normative theory of the melting pot.

It is not a particularly pleasant theory, as such things go, and it is easily caricatured, as I have just shown. It leads to a politics of the mainstream, a politics unable to cope with those who insist on meandering through different and isolated river beds. It leads as well to the city of sameness, the Colgate-Palmolive city as interpreted by Price Waterhouse, the city without guts. But the theory cannot be lightly dismissed, for not only is it widely accepted but its acceptance also ensures a minimal degree of harmony. It is, after all, the same theory that has led us to the civil rights revolution of the 1950's and 1960's, for has not the liberal argument through all these years been precisely that Negroness is irrelevant, color an accident of nature, to be utterly disregarded by all men of good will? In fact, one might argue that it is the theory of the melting pot, or the theory of anti-differentiation, call it what you will, which has been the basic argument employed by every minority group seeking admission into this society, and the same theory has been employed by the majority in determining the price of admission. However we try, none of us can truly comprehend America's awesome diversity, and perhaps indeed our best defense is to reduce it to irrelevance.

Yet, at the same time, there is available to us a rather different reading of the American experience. Here the argument is not at all that our distinctive quality is diversity but rather that ours is fundamentally an anonymous, privatized, lonely culture, in which the doctrine of universalism has cast men adrift on an endless and bottomless and fearful sea. Although in hailing distance of each other, our craft never join, and we remain alone, unknown and unknowing.

It is clearly this approach that has dominated much of the sociological criticism of the past century, and it is clearly this

190

perspective that dominates the humanistic critique of architecture today. It is out of this appraisal that the current faddish plea for community within the city arises. Indeed, if there is any one central theme to the vast sociological literature on the city, it is precisely that the intolerable quality of urban life is its terrifying loneliness and that what is required for redemption is community.

The scholar is wont to reconcile these two discrepant views. He may conclude that one man's utopia is another man's nowhere or simply that the pendulum has swung too far, that in our effort to bring order to the societal chaos we have been more successful than we intended. Such attempted reconciliations, however accurate, are not very useful. They may diagnose well, but their prescriptions are wanting. Their weakness is best revealed in the words of those who press community upon us, for, with rare exception, no one of the critics takes his own remedy seriously enough to spell out the positive attraction of community. Community as a response to anomie, as a defense against loneliness, indeed. But these are only the urgings toward community. What, once we have clung together, will bind us to one another, save our shared aloneness? Is the image one of strangers huddling in each others' arms, seeking thus to stave off the cruel coldness of mass society? I find little meaning in such an image, either as a definition of pluralism or as a real hope for the future. Yet, I submit, that is what we are left with, by and large, upon a reading of the literature in this area.

A viable plea for pluralism, which is, I think, the same as a viable plea for community, must add a specification for the cement that will tie the lonely crowds into meaningful entities. Without such a specification the plea for community reflects a condition of the central nervous system whose victims I have elsewhere described as "moral hemophiliacs, who bleed for mankind at the slightest provocation, but whose indiscriminate hemorrhaging leaves them weak and ineffectual." To rail against the city on the grounds that it is a city does not take us very far, nor do we progress by mystical stipulation that redemption lies in deurbanizing the city. It is not sufficient to call for cities with clearly demarcated neighborhoods, set apart by highways or parks, unless we are prepared to specify what manner of creature will inhabit our neighborhoods. The communalist dogma, which replaces faceless cities with faceless neighborhoods, inhabited by randomly selected people, is a flaccid dogma, solving nothing and having little to do with pluralism.

Pluralism does not speak idly of artificial difference, but rather it speaks of giving sustenance to that which sets men apart. Pluralism seeks neither chaos nor order but a delicate, and most unlikely, balance between the two. It does not urge that walls be torn down, for it knows that the walls are there to stave off the uprooting flood. Nor does it speak of walls so high that only the intrepid can scale them. With Robert Frost, it argues that good fences make good neighbors, and it recognizes as a good fence one that is both solidly built and easily scaled. As distinguished from the melting pot, the plural society calls for a beef stew, a loose and pungent gravy connecting identifiable chunks of this and that. In such a culinary preparation, little bits and pieces are constantly breaking off from the larger coagulations and getting lost somewhere in the general mess. It is hardly orderly, but in its lack of order lies its strength as well as its weakness.

Let me have done, for the moment, with analogy and imagery. A social system may be defined according to two properties of its group life. Groups may be more or less cohesive and more or less interactive with each other. Where groups are internally cohesive but do not interact with each other, we have a caste society, or, in terms of contemporary America, a city such as Boston.

It is to the problems of this sort of system that the bridge-building, brotherhood-oriented ideology is addressed. But instead of *building bridges* from group to group, the ideological ecumenicists managed to promote interaction by *tearing down the fences* which separated them. The result was a system of low intragroup cohesion and high interaction, which goes by the name of mass society.

It is mass society that has called forth the sociological critique of our urban structure and the cry for community or walls. Where that critique fails us is in its innocent assumption that he who says community says all that need be said. Pluralism is, indeed, concerned with maximizing both cohesion and inter-action, but the pluralist must recognize the costs of his per-suasion. The plural society seeks to ward off two threats simultaneously — the threat of absolute self-ghettoization and the threat of absolute rootlessness. But in order to stave off both, it must make some concessions to each.

Thus a mature pluralism recognizes that the bases upon which men will choose to associate with each other, at least for the time being, and for the most part, will be race, religion, and ethnicity. There is no escaping this. For most people, most of the time, the roots that matter are those that tie them to their ancestors and their ancestors' descendants, and not those de-rived from passing taste and fancy. A pluralism that involves the legitimation of such associational ties may not be quite what those who have urged community upon us intended, but there is little point in talking of community as if men anywhere were equally comfortable with men everywhere.

Even more, the pluralist must face the risk his doctrine brings upon us, the risk of fences built so sturdily that the groups living within them are turned wholly inward. These concessions to what many free-floating intellectuals see as atavisms will leave the intellectual dissatisfied. For those committed to a vision of the completely rational society, the notion that ethnic and religious ties are to be preserved — worse yet, encouraged — may be distasteful.

By the same token, for those committed to the preservation of group identity, increased interaction among groups may be seen as threatening. Pluralism is, in short, no casual panacea for all our ills. Before we are carried away by the current voguish acceptance of the doctrine, we ought to be aware of the costs and risks it implies. To answer Shylock with Shylock, the doc-trine of pluralism is in a less-known speech, Shylock's response to Antonio's invitation to dinner: "I will buy with you, sell with you, talk with you, walk with you, and so following; but I will not eat with you, drink with you, nor pray with you."

Such a system is extraordinarily difficult to construct and, once constructed, needs constant attention to maintain its balance. How can we build at the same time for apartness and togetherness, how can we educate at the same time toward universalism and particularism, how can we rhapsodize simultaneously both unity and diversity, how can we maintain the sought-for balance between liberty and fraternity? Yet that is pluralism's mandate, and that, I suspect, is what we are all after, despite the difficulty, despite the risk.

What has this excursion into the esoterica of sociology to do with architecture? There are, I believe, three lessons to be learned from it. These lessons follow if it is accepted that the architect is one among the several planners of tomorrow's social order. I take that as axiomatic, since some architects are engaged in large-scale projects, whether measured by the number of buildings involved or the number of occupants of any single building, and all architects, whatever the scope of their work, are subjects of the law that function, to a marked degree, follows form. (It may need saying parenthetically that the fact that function follows form does not mean that form ought not to follow function; the fact that both propositions may be accepted means only that we are engaged in a feedback relationship between function and form.) If it is agreed that architects are, *de facto*, engaged in social planning, then the discussion of pluralism has several things to offer.

First, the issue of pluralism is of substantive social importance. It underlies, or ought to underlie, much of our conceptualization of the social problem with which we are engaged. The architect himself may stand at the periphery of the issue, but he cannot fully escape its import. Clearly, there are visual and physical correlates of the theory. More important still, acceptance of the norm of pluralism forces upon the architect, as upon us all, a heightened sensitivity to the diverse tastes and life styles of others. He who views the task of urban planning as that of bringing enlightenment to the unwashed masses, be he architect or sociologist or philosopher, violates thereby the pluralistic assumption that differences in taste and temper are legitimate.

Second, the issue of pluralism is closely analogous to the architectural issue of unity and diversity. An impressive body of research now indicates that unrelieved perceptual sameness inhibits intellectual development and, indeed, encourages psychosis. There is, then, increasingly good reason to believe that the question of architectural diversity is a matter not merely of aesthetics but of sociopsychological significance as well.

If that is true, then any discussion of architectural function must include not only the relatively simple matter of space utilization but also the infinitely more complex problems of social and psychological uses — and misuses — of buildings and spaces. Bare-bones architecture may well respond to the simpler definition of function but may be widely off the mark of the broader definition.

Third, the issue of pluralism suggests something about the style of architectural decision making. If we take the problem of pluralism seriously, then we see immediately that it is not resolvable into a set of technical questions of the kind that can be dealt with easily by experts. Because pluralism requires both concessions and balances, it is a continuing problem, never finally resolved. Moreover, it is a problem that impinges on our most personal sensibilities. Those who would participate in the planning process, if the planning process must deal with such issues, are obliged to become aware of the ideologies that are at stake in the debate. They are so obliged because they themselves are caught up in ideological positions, as are their colleagues.

I am not here suggesting that the architect himself must master the social sciences, for such counsel would have little practical utility. I am suggesting that anyone engaged in the business of social planning must be sufficiently alert to the ways in which values impinge upon perspectives to be able to distinguish between positions and proposals that grow out of *expertise* and those that reflect private value commitments. Anyone who has both the audacity and the power to impose his views on others must regard himself with suspicion, must be trained to self-analysis, lest he confuse his role as expert with his natural propensity toward advocacy of personal causes.

This leads me to a rather important point, but I prefer to approach it from a slightly different direction. In speculating about the role of architect, I have sought to find some other, more familiar professional role that shares its essential characteristics with the architect's. I thought first of the architect as a physician, possessor of an occult wisdom designed to make us well. But, though it may be true that many architects deal in concrete placebos — innocuous buildings that offer the illusion of well-being — the physician does not fit very well. His role, after all, is too circumscribed; there is at least a crude consensus as to what constitutes good health and what illness is. Then, too, the patient's role is typically, if incorrectly, viewed as entirely passive: to be well, he must do what the doctor orders, however those orders violate his desires.

I thought next of the lawyer. There is here some analogy since the lawyer takes the facts his client gives him and proceeds to make of them a case, a thing of art and science that can stand up to outside tests. In this, indeed, the lawyer is not very different from the doctor, who takes a history of symptoms and orders it into a coherent diagnosis. But the lawyer, like the doctor, fails to meet the test of useful analogy, because once again the definition of the client's goal is too easily derived. The patient says, "These are my ailments." The lawyer's client says, "These are my deeds." The one asks to be made well, the other to be made free. The goals of the social system in which the architect must operate, and, indeed, the goals of the purchasers of architectural services, are unclear, poorly if at all articulated.

I consider briefly whether the real analogy might be to the beautician, but some of my best friends are architects, and I could not bear to trivialize them so. Nor would the artist do, although here the analogy carried me along some distance before I found its weakness. The architect, like the artist, has many patrons who ask only that their lives be graced by his vision, and, like the artist, he has more patrons still who specify broadly the medium and style but leave to the master all the rest. But the artist's is essentially a private product. If his work offends me, I can ignore it. It need please only its purchaser. Yet, if what I have written earlier is in any sense correct, then the architect's unseen client is almost always society itself. He who pays the piper calls the tune, but the tune, as performed by the architect, falls on all our ears.

196

Thus frustrated in my quest, I turned the problem on its head and asked what it is that the architect of whom I have spoken does, so that I too might specify the function first and only then the form. What an architect does, I should like to believe, is to take a client who often cannot articulate his own needs and tastes and, through an honest dialogue with his client, come to some approximation and some characterization of those needs. He then proceeds to show how the client's definitions may first be broadened, then interpreted. He is an unveiler of new options, a guide in new strategies. But the focus of his work is the client, and not his own vision. A new client is not an excuse for another chance to test one's own preferences but rather one more opportunity for genuine interaction. And the interaction, centered though it may be on the client's own position, nonetheless is rooted in society, the haunting and unseen client who does not pay the bill but bears the costs.

Thus stated, the analogy was clear. I speak of the architect as psychotherapist, of his task as akin to client-centered therapy. He is the informed interpreter, the guide through mysterious and unarticulated byways, the agent of change who abjures control in favor of providing his client with greater self-control.

No psychiatrist can survive without a working knowledge of the main currents of his society. The specific forms of social pathology in any time, in any place, affect most immediately the personal pathologies he is called upon to treat. The psychiatrist cannot enunciate the truth forever and for everywhere; there is no such psychiatric truth. There is, instead, the partial truth of a client seeking autonomy in a specific social context. So too the architectural truth is ephemeral, a truth not of nature but of human interaction. It is the truth of a situation, the truth of two men or twenty who come to know each other.

Typically, when people first enter therapy, they fear that they will no longer know themselves when they are done. They have some vague recognition of their need for therapy, but they do not know how it works, or what the therapist can do, or how he does it.

One might imagine that in such a situation the therapist would be inclined to overwhelm his client by confronting him with an elaborate and compelling diagnosis of his disorders. It is not uncommon for psychiatrists to have such diagnoses rather early in the therapeutic process. But the therapist knows that his diagnosis is an imposition on the client, that to understand fully one must first listen carefully, that to guide well one must guide step by step, that his role is partner in a process, not magician of the mind.

The same, I believe, is true of the architect. I am dazzled, as is any layman, by the splendid models, complete to the last detail, of tomorrow's buildings. I am dazzled, but unpersuaded, for the models are the architect's, not mine. They are not mine even when he has finished explaining all their virtues and conveniences. They are not mine because their virtues and conveniences are children of the architect's conception. They are, at best, a grafting of my groping hopes and the architectural wisdom. They are, as they are shown to me, an elaborate and compelling diagnosis, and they are, as well, an imposition.

Moreover, as I have suggested, there is always the unseen client. Society, if it is to be accounted for, must be accounted to. The models must therefore expose not only physical qualities but human relationships as well. I do not know which pattern fits here best, but I am inclined to think that some adaptation of the principle of "maximum feasible participation of the residents of the area and the members of the groups affected" might not be far off the mark.

The Community Action Program has taught us much about the capacities, as well as the limitations, of inexpert people in defining their own needs. Such a model is not easily applied, and it violates immediately the more comfortable assumption of lordly *expertise* which we all affect. Yet somehow it needs to be approached if the pluralistic mandate is to be fulfilled. Where the client is amorphous and cannot be himself involved, we must behave as if he were. He must walk side by side with us, even though he is unseen. Otherwise, we shall end up doing what we think is best, which will always mean what is best according to our own private perceptions of the public good. We shall fancy ourselves responsible, but we shall fail to be responsive. The pluralist commitment insists on partnership, not patronization.

What I have been talking about here are the scope and limits of *expertise*. The expert, whether he is an architect or engineer or social scientist, must know something of the social role of his profession. It is not enough that he is technically competent, for the task he is called upon to perform is not simply technical. Whether he wills it or not, he is engaged in social planning, and the function of his product has social implications. Though he might wish it otherwise, and though he might explicitly deny responsibility, the implications are still there. They are products not of his choice or will but of his task and role.

If the social implications of the architectural task point to a broadening in scope of the architectural wisdom, they also say something of the limits of that wisdom. There are aspects of our work which are not amenable to expert resolution. This is so whether or not we accept the pluralist commitment, since whatever our ideological convictions are, they are necessarily engaged as we participate in the social planning process.

Pluralism as an ideology differs not from other ideologies in this regard. But pluralism is not only ideology; it is also process. Not only must the architect be aware of pluralism, but he must himself be pluralist. He must, that is, be as aware of the process of his work as of his product, since it is largely in the process that the social meaning is embedded and only in the process that the social meaning of the product can be responsibly fixed.

There is, in short, no one social truth and hence no one architectural truth. The search for such a truth is doomed, hence wasteful. The recourse, however, is not to private intuition but to public participation. The balance between the chaos of total liberty and the oppression of total fraternity of which I have spoken can hardly be attained in any other way. That, I think, is both the analytic and the moral imperative of the pluralist commitment.

DISCUSSION

MAZLISH: I gather that you believe the architect and planner, himself, ought not to attempt to be interdisciplinary, which in any case is impossible today (though he should be aware of the various disciplines). Then you said that groups should have high internal cohesion, which is something like saying that they shouldn't be too interdisciplinary. How would you carry this out in practice? Specifically, if you have a group with certain ethnic and religious backgrounds who do not want Negroes in their neighborhood or in their schools, what are to be the guidelines for the planner in this matter, according to your pluralistic version?

FEIN: That is the obviously vulnerable point in my position. I come at it in this way. I am perfectly ready to settle for neighborhood segregation, since I think that thirty years hence most Negroes are going to be ready to settle for that too. I am not ready to settle for segregated schools, because I am too impressed with all the evidence that segregated schools are educationally unequal, and what I do is to disassociate the school district from the neighborhood.

I am convinced that the only plausible answer is in making absolutely sure that school district boundaries are not coterminous with residential neighborhood boundaries. Our evidence clearly shows that homogeneous neighborhoods, based commonly on class, race, and religion, are surviving, after all. Because they are unequal, I don't like homogeneous schools. So I think you must have the schools physically located at intersections of several neighborhoods. But I am ready to settle for some neighborhood self-segregation, if that is the price of community.

DAVIDOFF: Where public discussion is involved in location of new housing, what do you do? You say you'll accept neighborhood segregation — that is, where it is chosen by the neighbors. But where the public intervenes to decide whether the neighborhood should be maintained for one class only, what happens then?

FEIN: Given the weight of the ethnic factor in social life, which moves us toward segregation, I am prepared for the planner to use whatever autonomy he has as an antidote. I don't want to suggest that race, religion, and ethnicity are the only viable ties. I think they are the dominant ties. There are Greenwich Village, Harvard Square, as well as neighborhoods where people come together on the basis of taste, occupations, or other things. Since so much of our neighborhood structure today is based on race, religion, and ethnicity, I think that it is perfectly proper to plan for these other bases, and in time, I suspect, we will see what some of my friends — I am not at one with them — define as the irrational ties of race, religion, and ethnicity superseded by other kinds of organizational ties

All I am arguing against — and I grant you that in terms of the planning process it is a most difficult question — is that you can't just talk of communities and expect them to happen or expect people who move in next door to each other to be particularly fond of each other or even to learn to be particularly fond of each other.

TILLINGHAST: Are you claiming this neighbor can enforce *de facto* segregation? It is in violation of pluralism.

FEIN: I don't want enforcement; what I am suggesting is that, unless I miss my guess very widely, most people prefer to associate with others like themselves these days in America, and "like" usually means of the same race, religion, ethnic group.

TILLINGHAST: So the only pluralistic thing to do is to allow this.

FEIN: I think you allow it, but you don't permit people by law to keep the others out. I am suggesting that by sociological law the others will, by and large, stay out or will move to neighborhoods of equally rootless or differently rooted people. Yes, I think that is pluralism. Pluralism is not just heterogeneity; it is also order.

From the Floor: If you advocate pluralism, why do you think it is good for schools and bad for neighborhoods?

FEIN: I was speaking on the issue of balance. It is not that pluralism is good in one case and bad in another. What I was saying is that there is a balance and that policies of segregation or desegregation do not respond to that need for balance between some opportunity for self-segregation and some opportunity for genuine interaction. My prediction would be that if you had the schools at the intersecting points, in a couple of generations you would find new ways of determining preferred associational groupings; that is, many children would respond to the school setting more than to the family setting.

DYCKMAN: What is the definition of pluralism? Does it depend on separatism in space, or does it depend on the preservation of separate existence of separate culture?

FEIN: My own community, where I grew up, never had any interaction with other communities. Thus it was merely a segregated society; it was not pluralistic. If by "pluralistic" you mean what I mean — some balance between interaction and cohesiveness — we were cohesive, but we were not interactive. Our school and everything else was in our neighborhood. What I am arguing here is that one needs both and that most people should be exposed to both. If I were to include a sociometric map of my society as a child, it would have thick boundary lines beyond which no one ever walked. That is not pluralism. I think, by and large, the market mechanism is unaffected by the current dominant ideology and sociology, and thus it will result in high cohesion and low interaction. If the market mechanism is taken over by the sociological ideology, the result will be high interaction and low cohesion. That is why I am arguing that architects have to talk to people.

FRIEDEN: Do you have some thoughts on how "maximum feasible participation of the residents of the area" could be handled when you have several different sets of clients with different and possibly conflicting interests? Take the example of an architect designing a public housing project. Some of your clients are people who live there on the scene, others are people in the surrounding neighborhoods, and still others are those who see the project from a distance.

FEIN: I was afraid of that question. That is why I said, "Where the client is amorphous and cannot be himself involved, we must behave as if he were." You must gain access to what you would learn if you really could talk to him. I don't know how far I can carry the analogy. I beg off here on the grounds that I just don't know the kinds of relationships that architects typically have with the client.

BARNETT: Could you relate your discussion of pluralism to the growth of a public market sector? We have had a growth of economic decisions in government, though we once believed that we had an individualistic free-enterprise society. I don't know whether this is pluralistic.

FEIN: I think that currently pluralism tends to be defined very loosely and, I think, very unoperationally as "different." That is, if there are different ways of making decisions, that is called a pluralistic decision-making process. I would call that, perhaps, a multi-decision-making process. Possibly I ought to coin a new term. I want to make pluralism a very careful concept that applies only to those operations in which the central aspect of a balance between cohesion and interaction is maintained. And I think that problem, especially as it relates to the planning process, is central today because of the amount of investment in new towns, new neighborhoods, and urban planning for which we are really just beginning to organize.

The Triumph of Technology:
"Can" Implies "Ought"

HASAN OZBEKHAN[1]

I

Many of the speakers who have preceded me have, in one way or another, touched on the themes I intend to outline with reference to normative planning. This should make my task easier, as I feel somewhat exonerated from the necessity of dwelling at length on the preliminaries during which definitions are established, assumptions ordered, and semantic as well as logical clarifications provided so that the argument that follows can be glued together as tightly and neatly as possible. I shall deal with the subject from the somewhat special perspective of "planning" as intellectual work. I believe that such a perspective might help organize some of the points that were mentioned by other speakers in ways that are not always obvious and in terms of a frame of relationships that might lead to some interesting discussion.

II

The title I was assigned by Professor Stanford Anderson is almost a riddle. It needs, I believe, to be approached with some degree of indirection. Otherwise, its meaning may be hard to un-

[1] Mr. Ozbekhan is Director of Planning at System Development Corporation. Any views expressed in this paper are those of the author. They should not be interpreted as reflecting the views of the System Development Corporation or the official opinion or policy of any person or agency connected with it.

204

cover. This difficulty of approach affords me some freedom, which I intend to exploit.

The title describes a special conjuncture created by "technology," "can" and "ought." The situation that underlies this conjuncture is one in which we view technology as triumphant. It is with this situation that I want to begin.

There are, no doubt, many ways of judging what the advent of the technological age has done to — as well as for — mankind. Under our very eyes it has changed, and is changing, the face of the physical environment both in the technologically advanced and in the technologically backward countries, although the former are more visibly affected by this particular aspect of the direct application of science and engineering to our surroundings. More important by far, I believe, is what the age of technology has done to the geography of human outlook and expectations. In this field it would be wrong to make assessments that differentiate between countries and peoples. Here the effects of technology are universal, and by their very nature they represent a unifying force. They could perhaps be described as having led to a generalized phenomenon of expansion: expansion in numbers, expansion of possibilities, knowledge, information, ambitions, the boundaries of mobility, relationships, needs, requirements, and wants. What I am talking about is not so much a happening as an experience, an event of the mind. Nevertheless, the event is occurring throughout the world, affecting, moving and motivating, in various ways but strongly, the American, the European, the Asian, the African — whoever and wherever he might be.

Events of this magnitude have a price. The price of this particular event is, in all probability, that sense of strange and powerful disquiet we feel before the heaving horizon that confronts us. Old institutions, known ways of life, established relations, defined functions, well-traced frontiers of knowledge and feeling move and change as we go; we are constantly subjected to new configurations of perceived reality; we are constantly asked to adapt faster and faster to requirements generated by new information, by a narrowing yet always moving and always changing physical environment, by an increasingly confused yet proliferating set of goals, outlooks, and aspirations. It is as though the entire environment of man — his ecological, social, political, emotional, and physical space — were becoming less solid, less permanent, and less constant. It looks as if we were in the midst of a vast process of *liquefaction.*

Within this process, interlinked with it and activated by it, the old problems remain: famine in India, upheaval in China, lack of industrialization in all underdeveloped countries, a confused and confusing revival of nationalism in Europe, warring ideologies and interests in Vietnam, relative growth of poverty among the poor, relative growth of despair among the young — the multiple disequilibria of a world in full expansion and constant flux in which expectations and achievements fail to match.

As I said earlier, there are, no doubt, different judgments one can pass on our situation. However, the passing of a judgment is fruitful only insofar as it leads to decisions and to action. Yet in the case of the larger dynamics of our situation it would appear that there is not much we can do any longer — it is, by now, probably beyond our control. As Pascal has said, "You are embarked" — and once we are embarked, *"Il faut parier. . . ."* We have to wager. There is no choice. What counts are the ends we shall put our bets on.

III

But these ends I speak of, these goals as we would rather say in our epoch, what are they? How are they revealed, implemented, attained? To answer these questions, we must look more closely at the situation, at how we came to it, and at what we brought into it.

When our situation is viewed in its current immediacy, its most striking aspect is complexity. When we try to imagine it in terms of the future, what strikes us most are the uncertainties it unfolds in the mind. Thus we stand, perhaps more consciously and knowingly than ever before, in the grip of present world-wide complexities and future uncertainties trying to define those modes of action which best will order the one and reduce the other.

The organizing principles of these modes of action are what we have recently become reconciled to calling "planning." I say reconciled because I want to emphasize some feeling of reluctance. The notion of planning did not come easily to us. It did not come easily because we did not arrive in total innocence to this pass in our affairs. Actually, we reached it armed to the teeth with traditions, institutions, philosophies, self-images, achievements, failures, hypocrisies, prejudices, languages, values, and a world view — with everything which ultimately adds up to that state of mind we call Western Civilization.

Western Civilization, namely the ground and essence of technological civilization, is, however, the very complicated result of very complicated forces which were set in motion partly during the Renaissance by Galileo and partly during the eighteenth century — the Age of Enlightenment. Like other civilizations, ours is (or used to be) a way of life in which uncertainty is reduced by means of stable and dependable continuities while complexity is organized into those routines and rituals we call institutions.

However, in its long history Western Civilization also developed certain characteristic features with regard to freedom and the individual's decision-making role which permitted it to accommodate a great deal of loosely controlled initiative and even of venturesomeness. In fact, it could be said that our civilization nurtured two of its contrary inner tendencies with astonishing care and insistence: one was a deep commitment to detailed disorder, which it cherished as the stepchild of liberty; the other was an almost superstitious belief in the idea of automatism (as exemplified by Adam Smith's "hidden hand" or by the extraordinary notion of laissez-faire equilibrium), which it viewed as capable of regulating the disorder into a livable environment. This commitment to microcosmic disorder and this trust in the automatism of macro-processes — including social processes — are, in some truly nontrivial ways, the progenitors of our present situation.

Planning, in the sense that we are beginning to understand it, namely, in the sense of informed decision and calculated action, refutes and rejects both these parents. That is why we came to it late; that is why we came to it with reluctance; that is why we are still quite halfhearted about it. Clearly, we are not yet convinced that a reduction in social or political randomness will not necessarily signify a grievous narrowing of acquired freedoms, although it will necessarily be accompanied by major alterations of their institutional structure; and despite our having learned at great cost (the last major settling of accounts and paying of bills being the Great Depression) that what we took to be automatism in social processes was nothing but a myth, we are still not wholly reconciled to the proposition that conscious and rational decision making at the sources of power might be effective in reducing the uncertainties that the future has erected within us.

Of our two basic tendencies, the long-run effects of automatism have undoubtedly been the more disastrous insofar as the current state of planning is concerned. The cast of mind that was able to rationalize it into a jealously protected belief was also the kind of mind that, almost unconsciously, shaped our initial conception of planning.

This occurred when it seemed natural to take as our basic model one of the enduring and, no doubt, fruitful traits of classical Western thought: a pragmatic commitment to determinism in various forms. The deterministic model of planning is both simple and elegant. It tells us that there is sequentiality and linearity in events and that what we call the "future" descends in direct line from the past and can be explained in the same way. The fundamental tool of deterministic planning is extrapolation. The fundamental result of extrapolation is a single outcome, or future. In such a model the decision variables yield a single future for each decision. Among such parallel futures, issued from parallel decisions, one can then choose in accordance with a pre-established system of values. Some outcomes are good, while some are bad, if one knows what good and bad are. Consequently, one plans in terms of the decision that is going to yield the good or, at any rate, the best outcome. Thus some futures are more advantageous than others, less painful than others, some more worth while than the rest combined. The choice is always clear as long as the value system that serves as frame of reference remains solidly and operationally grounded and as long as there are institutions to enforce it within a particular environment.

The great weaknesses of deterministic planning are obvious: first comes its inability to accept events that are exogenous to the single closed decision system, which is its main constituent;

second, and as we are only now discovering by far its most crippling feature, is that it postulates and requires a value system that is given and constant and outside both its conceptual boundaries and its operational jurisdiction.

Clearly, the choices such planning offers could never be concerned with *ends,* namely, with ethical alternatives that find expression in "oughts"; they are concerned instead with feasibility — "can" it be done? — namely, with techno-economic alternatives.

Since the end of the Second World War, the economic component of this equation has weakened considerably. Abundance, relative though it may be, has lifted a great many of the limitations that scarcity had imposed on the spectrum of open choices. With this occurrence, technological feasibility has tended increasingly to become the sole criterion of decisions and action. Thus technology, as many others in recent years have remarked with increasing shrillness and fear, has grown into the central, the all-pervasive, the governing experience of Western man today.

One of the results of this encroachment has been that we are now envisioning our future almost exclusively in relation to alternatives predicated on feasibility: that which in my title is represented by "can." And because the realm of what we actually can do has expanded almost beyond belief, feasibility tends to define our ends and to suggest the only goals we are willing to entertain. "Can" has almost unconsciously and insidiously begun to imply, and thereby replace, "ought."

This evolution has been strengthened, encouraged, abetted by the neglect with which, since the eighteenth century, we have treated our traditional values or "oughts." The confines to vision and action that they used to form have been pierced here, overcome there, erased in most places. As we continuously failed to develop an ethic commensurate with our technology, the old ethic lost much of its meaning and guiding power. It has become abstract — hence operationally invalid as a policy-making or planning tool.

Today, in the situation that surrounds and confronts us, to act in the light of old dicta that used to relate the "good" to events

— for example, population increase is good, or the extension of the benefits of modern medicine to all men is good, or individual high productivity and hard work and thrift are good, or education for everybody is good — means to act blindly and to contribute to a set of vast consequences whose risks or even value content (namely, whose goodness) we have no way of calculating or judging. None of these instances need to be bad; I am only noting that we can no longer be unquestioningly certain that they will have good results.

Having made these points, I might now attempt to clarify what the title of this paper really means in planning terms. It means that in a technology-dominated age such as ours and as a result of forces and attitudes that have brought about this dominance, "can," a conditional and neutral expression of feasibility, begins to be read as if it were written "ought," which is an ethical statement connoting an imperative. Thus feasibility, which is a strategic concept, is elevated into a normative concept, with the result that whatever technological reality indicates we can do is taken as implying that we must do it. The strategy dictates its own goal. The action defines its own *telos*. Aims no longer guide invention; inventions reveal aims. Or, in Marshall McLuhan's now fashionable slogan, "The medium is the message."

In sum, these developments have had two major effects on the deterministic planning model I mentioned earlier. First, the power and scope of strategies open to us have been enlarged and multiplied to the point where it is no longer possible to make sense of any method that derives a single outcome from a given decision. Second, the model has lost the independent frame of values that had made it operative. And when I say lost, I really mean that it has taken it over, swallowed it, ingested it. In spite of this, we have not developed a new operational model. Hence, we are no longer sure of the direction in which our momentum is taking us.

The recognition of this fact is at the source of the general disquiet most of us seem to share. And this disquiet can, I think, be reduced to the following question: Is feasibility a good enough end in pursuit of which one can reach decisions and calculate the human risks and consequences of action in these perilous, complex, and uncertain times?

Offhand, the answer seems to be "No." But this "No" needs to be probed, elaborated, and operationally understood; and if possible, some positive solutions need to be pointed out. I shall try to do this with reference to some emerging conceptions in planning theory, policy, and implementation.

IV

Today in all advanced industrial countries, including those of capitalist persuasion, something called "planning" is going on. In fact, it appears possible now to ascribe much of the unexpected success of Western economies to the systematic application of this particular type of economic calculus at the government level. Generally speaking, the attitudes that underlie this application have been derived from welfare economics, while most of the operational concepts and tools that have been adopted are Keynesian in origin.

This planning, although it involves great effort, is still relatively primitive. It is built on a number of inherited *desirables* such as government control of extreme fluctuations, international balances, investment trends, employment, etc. More recently, attempts to extend it to social fields such as housing, education, health, old age, and poverty have been made. For the moment, the results of these new attempts do not appear too impressive. There is a sense of floundering — a feeling that we don't know exactly where it is we want to end up or that we have not really understood the problems we are trying to solve. The words that guide us along these paths are a set of rationalizable clichés: some still talk in terms of Keynes' particular vision of the "civilized life," others prefer to stand by something they call the "dignity of man," others still find inspiration in the "fulfillment of the human being." In the United States we have even derived a number of National Goals from similar desirables which have since been costed out and priority-ordered in relation to expected economic growth through 1975.

Our approach to all of this has been unimpeachably orthodox: from old notions of the good we have selected a number of socioeconomic desirables and translated them into a set of socioeconomic problems. The criterion for translation was the feasible,

211

and the calculus of the feasible was mostly economic in character. So now we know that if the GNP grows as forecasted, by 1975 we shall be in a position of doing certain things. At this point we generally pass to the implementation phase.

What we have failed to do in all this is to ascribe operational meaning to the desirables that motivate us, to question their intrinsic worth, to assess the long-range consequences of our aspirations and actions, to wonder if the outcome we seem to be expecting does in fact correspond to that *quality of life* we say we are striving for or if our current actions will lead us there. In other words, in my conception of planning we are failing to plan.

One of the major causes of our failure to plan is that the human mind apparently finds it almost impossible to plan without a conceptual and philosophical framework made up of integrative principles — in short, without a generally accepted theory of planning. We have not, or have not yet, succeeded in developing such a theory.

Whenever this point is mentioned, the difficulties surrounding that undertaking (while at the same time explaining its lack) become crystal-clear, and the questions grow tense. In such a theory is one to deal with facts or with goals, with the present or with the future? Are we concerned with continuity or new departures? Should one write for planners or policy makers?

It seems to me that these very questions show how much our intellectual traditions stand in the way of the needs we feel, how much our positivist inheritance vitiates our ability to grapple with the normative requirements of policy generation. Yet, despite such obstacles, the foundations for a unifying or integrative theory of planning must be laid. Hence, I shall try to answer the questions I have just asked.

I think much of what I have said up to this point shows my own conception of planning to consist of three interrelated and interactive approaches, which could be formulated as three plans that unfold in conjunction with each other. These are: The "normative plan," which deals with the *oughts* and defines the goals on which all policy rests; the "strategic plan," which formulates what in the light of elected oughts, or chosen policies, we *can* actually do; and finally the "operational plan," which establishes how, when, and in what sequence of action we *will* implement the strategies that have been accepted as capable of satisfying the policies. Thus a planning-relevant framework needs, in this particular conception, always to reveal what *ought* to be done, what *can* be done, and what actually *will* be done.

Strategic planning and operational planning fit quite well into current practice. Normative planning, to my knowledge, is not seriously considered yet as an integral element of that same practice. Policy considerations still remain outside the planning process and enter into it as exogenous givens. In the system I have just outlined such a differentiation would not exist. Policy making, strategy definition, and the determination of implementing steps would be viewed as parts of a single integrated and iterative process.

Normative planning has interesting conceptual dimensions, which I shall note briefly. To begin with, it deals with the consequences of value dynamics, hence with the delineation of qualitative futures. In this sense, it abolishes the old distinction between goals and facts in favor of viewing goals as facts, thereby ascribing to them the necessary practical weights. Similarly, it is in the course of normative planning that some new approaches to temporal relationships and interactions between what we call the present and what we call the future are recognized and established. If I may be permitted a play on words, I should like to say that the future is the *subject* of normative planning, but the present is its *object*. A close analysis of the consequences of value dynamics reveals not a single future deducible from the parameters of a given decision but a multiplicity of discrete possible future states, which have to be delineated and explored. Any choice, under these circumstances, tends to apply to a spectrum of states thus enlarging the field of decisions. And again decisions made in the light of such future "images" initiate that backward chain of calculable events which when they reach the present can be translated into it in the form of calculated "change." The possibility to act upon present reality by starting from an imagined or anticipated future situation affords great freedoms to the decision maker while at the same time providing him with better controls with which to guide events. Thus planning becomes in the true sense "future-creative," and the very fact of anticipating becomes causative of action. It is at this point that the policy-maker–planner is able to free himself from what René Dubos has called the "logical future" and operate in the light of a "willed future."

It is the introduction of this element of conscious and informed *will* into the system which frees us from the remnants of automatism while at the same time allowing real policy considerations to enter the planning process.

It would be a mistake to believe that what I am trying to say represents some rather involuted way of making predictions. On the contrary, what I am actually asserting is that planning does not really *deal* with the future; it deals with the present, inasmuch as it concerns itself with possible consequences that action taken in the face of future uncertainties will have on the present. Planning is directed toward the future not so that one can predict what is there, for clearly there is nothing *there*. (The forecasts we make about things like population increase, resource availability, etc., are obviously not based on what is there, but on what is here in the present.) Planning is directed to the future to "invent" it (as Denis Gabor has said) or to "construct" it (as Pierre Massé has put it).[2] And this is done to reduce uncertainties that confront current decisions, by encapsulating them within a firm enough normative "image" so that it can provide the kind of information one needs to attain the kind of ends one wants.

The fundamental questions with which normative planning must be approached are: If this good, then what future situation? And: If that situation, then is it good? What this amounts to is to say: If we want full employment, education, health, housing, equality, etc., we must want them for certain calculable reasons that will be reflected in a new situation. Hence, we must determine the following: Full employment for what? Education for what? Health for what? Housing for what? Equality for what? Only as a result of such complex determinations can we define which possible outcome really corresponds to what today we keep

2 Cf. entries in the bibliography.

calling "the civilized life," "fulfillment of the human being," "dignity of man." If we don't plan in this manner, then we shall, in fact, continue to act in good faith but without knowing whether our actions can satisfy the ends we have in mind. Nor shall we obtain enough alternative solutions to achieve some workable (optimizing) conjunction. I make the latter stipulation because one of our problems consists in the requirement that we achieve several such goals simultaneously; we are no longer advancing step by step.

I believe that the major lesson to be derived from these very sketchy considerations is that in normative planning the important thing is not to be surpassed or overcome by current events. This always tends to happen. Whenever it happens, planning reverts to becoming mainly responsive to current situations rather than creative of futures, and as long as planning is not futures-creative, it must be an after-the-fact ordering exercise dominated by present events. Such an exercise is obviously not planning but something else.

The next phase of the planning effort is strategic planning. As I have repeatedly noted, strategic planning is grounded in the concept of feasibility. However, if feasibility is approached as a parameter rather than as a norm, then its nature changes. The major result of establishing norms and assessing feasibility in their light is the effect of freeing policy making from its traditional prison of "expediency" and beginning to understand it in terms of "relevance." Expediency is often confused with practicality, which is undoubtedly important, but in terms of the line of thought that I have tried to develop, it is clear that a multiplicity of goals based on a multiplicity of norms enlarges the traditional boundaries of the practical and thereby lengthens the spectrum of alternative policies among which we could choose. Thus in strategic planning that which can be done must always refer to a particular number of alternatives that have grown from work accomplished in the normative stage. There is, no doubt, a narrowing of vision at this point, but this narrowing results from elimination of conflicting alternative possibilities that, under the circumstances, have been found as either irrelevant or insoluble. What is eliminated is the open-ended perspective that paralyzes action. What is introduced is coherence, numbers, milestones that are relevant to the ends we have chosen. It is during this phase that one of the most difficult aspects of planning work is encountered. It consists in formulating objective action links between the norm, namely, the "ought" and the "can." It is at this point that the analysis of whether or not a particular goal is relevant to a particular situation and to a particular strategy is made. Here, again, the issue is not so much whether the earlier parts of the plan are feasible; it is rather the determination of whether or not the earlier parts of the plan are consonant with reality and whether such a consonance can be translated into the probable realization of the goals themselves. The issue to emphasize in this progression is that solutions to subsystemic problems are approached, not with reference to the subsystem itself, but to a predetermined meta-system that permits the encompassing and the ordering of the alternative strategies that such solutions define.

The last step, which I have termed operational planning, consists mainly in the determination of how to implement the adopted strategies. In some sense, it is the phase of the plan that delineates what *will* be done. It is during this phase of planning that a translation takes place from the plausible to the probable. The set of priority-ordered interlocking decisions, of course, must foresee, within the temporal framework, a continuity of action, and, in its turn, that continuity of action must be so conceived as to be able to overcome the momentary uncertainties, the immediate disjunctions that every act creates if, as it must, it creates change within a given system.

Taken together, the general outline of the planning methodology I have tried to develop in the preceding pages constitutes a continuum — a self-feeding application of intellective analysis and synthesis to events whereby the present processes of society and of organization can be constantly guided with reference to the future. It is in this sense that we must understand planning as representing a fundamental and uninterrupted activity whether it takes place in the corporation, the city, the nation, or international relations, or whatever we choose to call "environment."

Of the three phases of planning I have just described, we know more about strategic planning and about operational planning than we do about normative planning. For the former two we have developed certain methodologies, which I shall merely mention without going into them because all of you are entirely familiar with them. I have in mind such things as systems analysis, system design, operations research, and simulation. The introduction of the computer into our lives and the advances we are making in natural language processing — an advance that will permit nonprogrammers to deal directly with the computer — have greatly enlarged our ability to question a wide variety of facts and variables. Our main effort should therefore be directed to the development of methodologies and techniques having the same kind of power for the making of normative plans. In this area we are lagging behind. And in this area the question is not, as it is often purported to be, that we should make efforts to eliminate man and computerize the entire system but rather that we should develop a greater understanding of how to relate the computer to man in more efficient ways so that we can benefit from technology in our attempts to firm up a theory of normative planning.

V

Earlier I stated that what counted were the ends we shall put our bets on. That statement obviously leads to the question: What are those "ends," feasibility, by itself, being insufficient? I should like, in concluding, to review those portions of my analysis which may contain clues toward an answer to that question.

To begin with it is obvious to me that the goals of practical human action cannot be established as immutable truths and that each situation encompasses a conjuncture that, if anticipated, operationally defined, and caused to happen might satisfy whatever is generally considered as good in a particular civilization at a particular time. The problem, therefore, is not in reinventing the good but in being able to redefine it in terms of meanings that have the most value for us in our present state. The dynamics of our situation is such that we are no longer sure of being able automatically to derive consequences we can judge as good from actions we do judge as good. Somehow the ability to link the value of a present act to the value of its chosen consequences must be created and made operational. Only such a link will permit us to determine those ends we should be betting on.

I have tried to outline the idea of such a link in terms of a particular planning approach. In my formulation goal valuation is integrated into the planning process itself. For this manner of planning we lack two things: first, a worked-out theory and methodology; second, the required institutional setting. These, clearly, are very major shortcomings.

Insofar as theory and methodology are concerned, it is evident that our current economic calculus is not enough. We need something in the nature of a social accounting system as well as a value calculus to supplement it. Some work is being done in both these areas, but it is as yet at a very tentative stage. Insofar as the institutional setting is concerned, progress is very slow.

In this connection a still ill-defined symbiosis, or at least a symbiotic interaction, between technique, theory, and institutional setting appears to exist. The absence of theory inhibits our ability to extend our techniques to the field of norm definition and goal valuation. Theory building, in turn, is affected by our current institutions. This is visible mainly in the difficulty we experience in determining *who* is going to plan. This difficulty arises, among other things, from our political tradition, which often views solutions satisfying individual self-interest as the major expression of freedom in society. This tends to make us look upon any extensive planning — namely, integrated solutions — with grave misgivings and as being outside the mainstream of the concepts that underlie our political organization. This, of course, is frustrating, for it is indeed difficult to see how any alteration in our planning can be obtained without ultimately raising some basic questions about our current institutional arrangements. I do not know whether the answer to this dilemma lies in pluralistic, or advocate, or expert planning, which we talked about. Nor do I really know whether the "invisible colleges" that were mentioned are a step in the right direction. I feel that the latter, at least, represent a recognition and an impatience — hence that they deserve some investment of hope in them.

I say this because I have great confidence in the power of ideas. I cannot help feeling that what Keynes used to call the "primitive stage" of the argument is probably behind us. After this stage, many things become possible. There is some ground now on which we can stand. The European experiment in planning is a prodding example for us. In the United States we have, after all, concluded that massive unemployment ought not to be allowed. We have decided that economic fluctuations are onerous and that they ought to be controlled. We have committed ourselves to certain notions of equality with regard to the distribution of wealth, education, and civil rights, even though we have not been too successful in defining the "what for" of these commitments beyond the words the "Great Society." In short, we seem to have understood that these "oughts" will not occur by themselves, that there is no automatism in social processes transcending human will and calculated action. We should now be able to exert that will in developing the knowledge and information that will sustain it. Only by that means can we succeed in distinguishing the real problems from the false ones and choosing among real answers, by which I mean answers that have some degree of precision and are capable of showing us some direction in this present of ours which contains all the future we can ever hope to have.

DISCUSSION

BARNETT: I understand your point that a concern with the possibilities that can occur might by itself preoccupy, influence, or impair the amount of concern with the possibilities that ought to occur. I don't understand why the array of possibilities that can occur would dictate or inhibit the possibilities that ought to occur — which was something else you said. In what sense does this take place?

OZBEKHAN: Let me give you an example. Remember that I put this discussion within a framework of our technology. Our technology dictates what *can* be done, and my assertion was that by dictating what *can* be done, it is also now beginning to dictate — or at least strongly suggest — what *ought* to be done. Let us take the "cans." We are probably capable of going to the moon. The question is: Have we really questioned, exhaustively and intelligently, whether we ought to go to the moon? I am not saying that the resulting decision would necessarily have been not to go. What I am saying is that no large-scale discussion took place, because the very possibility of going somehow caused us to forget to ask whether, in fact, we should. There are other examples. Let's take the medical field, where Dr. René Dubos of the Rockefeller University is very eloquent. We have almost eradicated a great number of diseases. And because medical technology is easy to export, we are exporting it without really understanding the system-wide (or world-wide) consequences of doing this. According to our ethics, it is a good thing to save people from disease. We can do it; therefore we do it. Whether we are really serving humanity in so doing is a question that almost nobody seems to have asked. I think it is only recently that some misgivings have begun to be voiced by the medical theorists. Here again the "can" is clearly dictating the "ought" without any further probing.

Professor AARON FLEISHER: But they do say it is a good thing. They may be mistaken, but they are concerned with the normative.

OZBEKHAN: I am not saying they are not concerned with the good. I am saying we are not concerned sufficiently with what good means today. It is not enough to refer to the traditional value system and say automatically that disease is bad and therefore the eradication of disease is good. When you are planning, you have to be able to think about the consequences of many "oughts," of the whole value dynamics in great detail, and I do not know many people who do that.

DUHL: There are really thousands of examples. Probably the most obvious one has been the use of antibiotics. Because we were capable of killing the bugs, we did it, but in the process we have created for ourselves a large collection of viral disorders that may well result in an uncontrollable epidemic.

FLEISHER: That is true, but even though these terrible consequences flow from the use of antibiotics, the most you might be able to accuse people of is of not having foreseen this; but to accuse them of not having worried about it at all is slightly different. A certain kind of criticism of planning is irresponsible, and I think this is what you are involved in. Having the benefit of hindsight, we can say that no one considered all the consequences; to be sure, we can never do so.

OZBEKHAN: What I am proposing is that perhaps we could find means to get away from hindsight and act through foresight.

FLEISHER: Would you expect to be able to prove that out of a set of possible alternates, one was an optimum?

OZBEKHAN: In some cases, yes. In the case of the moon venture, it is possible to take a straight measurement of financial and resource expenditures and apply it to alternative courses of action.

MAZLISH: Surely the decision in the Soviet Union preceded ours, which came, in a sense, mainly as a response. Do you want to say, therefore, that the only grounds on which a decision should be made are necessarily financial?

OZBEKHAN: No; obviously that should have been considered, too. However, all these considerations ought to have been brought into some sort of balance and compared. Such an analysis might well have shown that we, in fact, ought to go to the moon and that by doing so we optimize the national welfare as defined in some accepted way.

MAZLISH: I want to know whether Dr. Ozbekhan really believes that in all cases of "can," we in fact "do." This is an old notion, that what the technicians can do they will do. While it is true that we can build supersonic planes and therefore we are building them (and I happen to think it is a ghastly idea), it is also true that we can technically eliminate slums and build safe cars, and we don't. Therefore how strong, in fact, is your generalization? If it doesn't really hold up, then it is clear that we are always making some sort of a choice.

OZBEKHAN: Yes, no doubt, there is choice involved. And the answer to your question seems to lie in what is easiest to do when alternatives exist. The first conclusion would therefore seem to be that building the supersonic transport is easier than clearing slums. This fact, however, has a great many implications and somewhat unclear connotations, which I should elaborate briefly.

The norm that governs decisions concerning the supersonic transport is clearly technological — it arises from the question "Can we do it?" Or, in other words, is our technology sufficiently advanced to permit us to do it?

On the other hand, we know we can clear slums. Technical feasibility does not really enter into the argument. Here the norm that governs the decision obviously arises from the consideration of "Ought we to do it?" In this particular case it is not really possible to translate the considerations surrounding this "ought" into technological ones.

Moreover, in the instance of slum clearance any decision to proceed has to overcome the twin structures of current institutions and vested interests. Hence, it becomes extremely difficult and complicated, much more so on the nontechnical level than building supersonic planes.

BAUER: I think the group is entitled to this piece of specific information. Late in 1962, the man in the Bureau of the Budget in charge of the space program, without prompting, told me: "Don't think for a minute that this administration wouldn't have wanted to spend this space money on education or two or three other things, but they couldn't get it through Congress." Now, I would like to question whether or not you have tried a particular procedure for answering normative questions with your planning techniques. It bears on the question of the optimal solution where, because of the diversity of values and interests of the parties in complex systems, it is practically impossible to *calculate* an optimal solution. However, are there any prospects of simulating it by feeding in the data on the values and interests of the parties and their decision rules, and then calculating what these people, if they had the opportunity to make a reasonable set of trade-offs, would choose. Is that in the works?

OZBEKHAN: Yes, although at a very elementary level. What I have in mind is research work going on in various types of simulation.

WARTOFSKY: There seems to be a strange tension between the

suggestions that, on the one hand, we act pluralistically in the plans and that, on the other hand, we come up with an optimal solution — as if the optimal solution were waiting somewhere in the wings. It seems to me if you take a pluralization of normative planning seriously, then an optimal solution is at best a hope, not a fact. And thus you know that risky decisions must be made, and you will be firm precisely *because* of the indeterminacy involved in making a choice and knowing its consequences. Suppose we had not gone ahead with antibiotics. Could we have known what the consequences would be? So the notion of an optimal solution, or of *the* optimal solution, is already a restrictive notion with respect to creative planning, or "pluralization." It tends toward a dogmatism of present conceptions, rather than toward an open-ended experimentalism.

OZBEKHAN: I do not think that under conditions of complexity and uncertainty we can plan for a single optimal solution. The thought I advanced was rather that if we introduce the definition and analysis of norms into the planning process, then we might at least stand a chance of understanding the directions in which we are advancing and the consequences we should expect from our actions. Such an understanding must permit the conception of at least some optimal strategies. Clearly, when we went ahead with antibiotics, we did not, to my knowledge, expect the magnitude of problems that Dr. Duhl referred to. Had we stopped long enough to ask ourselves whether we ought to proceed, then, conceivably, these problems might have come up to the surface at least as possibilities to be studied. Thus, we might have obtained a comparative view between different outcomes, from which several courses of action with different optimalities could have been derived. Hence, our choice spectrum might have been enlarged. However, I agree with you that no single optimal solution is achievable under pluralistic planning.

DYCKMAN: One question that really confounded me a little in the discussion of the "can" and "ought" is the problem of prediction, which, I think, you were close to at times. It seems to me the question of "can" and "ought" is less critical than the question of the implicit prediction, which exists in all moral choice. As philosophers, you are familiar with the ethical need to predict the consequences of a choice. That is, one choice is better than another when its consequences are better. Now, if this is a general or philosophical statement of the problem, what do you think is the state of prediction that now warrants our being so confident about moral choice? I think Fleisher's implication was that prediction is not so well advanced. What is your view?

OZBEKHAN: This is an interesting and important question. I believe that two answers, taken at different levels of discourse, need to be given. The first has to do with the notion of prediction. I agree that our predictive capabilities in this field are very limited, but I also believe that prediction per se may not be so fruitful an idea in this particular connection. Clearly, it is not possible to predict all the consequences of one's actions. Hence, the important thing is to be able to outline and analyze as many alternative consequences as one can. The analysis of such consequences requires not so much derivation by whatever means as a very clear idea of the outcome that one has committed oneself to. If that is sufficiently well delineated, then it should be possible to develop alternative strategies to get there and to rank or weight those strategies with reference to some accepted or acceptable norms.

The second point is perhaps more mundane. We are beginning, thanks to simulation, to be able to replicate certain human situations under highly structured conditions. Differing sets of rules permit us to observe human behavior or strategies or decision consequences relative to various situations. I hope that from such observations certain new understandings might arise. Moreover, sometimes a computer helps us to operate or, better, to conduct the experiments in real time; namely the results of particular acts, or the alternatives for decision making that it opens up, become visible immediately so that it is possible to compress the time element and to enlarge what Kenneth Boulding has called the "decision agenda." I believe that if we can make progress along these lines of thinking and experimentation, we will strengthen not so much what we understand by the word "prediction" but rather what the French call *prévision*, the best translation of which, I think, is "foresight."

DYCKMAN: Do you want to suggest there is some cutoff where we can safely move from private choice to public ethical choice, because of the size of the agenda?

OZBEKHAN: I wouldn't say yes or no, because I am not informed on the matter.

BARNETT: Let me ask a question about which I care greatly. Apparently, you do not distinguish between what you call normative planning and democratic political discourse, process and decisions. Is your definition of planning, which I seem to find identical with that, a legitimate one?

OZBEKHAN: Yes, except that throughout all this discussion I have tried to suggest that both our current institutions and the democratic process through which they and we operate in society might have become insufficient. The need, perhaps, is for finer, more detailed, more individual or granular decision processes in our planning. I also believe that in some sense Dr. Duhl had the same thing in mind when he referred to the growth of the "invisible colleges." These are new informal decision points that emerge within society as the existing institutions begin to prove inadequate. Maybe it all adds up to saying that our current institutions work well still in the macro sense but are no longer sufficient to meet the demands of a growing need for pluralism in social decision making.

BARNETT: When you are asking for improved normative planning, are you really saying: "Let us improve our democratic political processes in the nation"?

OZBEKHAN: Yes, among other things.

CAZES: The important word, the new thing, is planning.

OZBEKHAN: That is right. Let's not forget that planning is a very new word in a democracy, because a democracy is supposed to be unplanned.

DYCKMAN: I am not sure I agree that it is supposed to be unplanned. I agree that constitutional democracy defined away the problem of aggregation of values. But now, because of this normative component of planning, we have to raise the question again. However, I don't think anybody has made any satisfactory disposal of it. Open acknowledgment of the normative question does not solve the problem of moving from individual choice to collective choice.

OZBEKHAN: No, but the problem, at least the recognition of the problem in the terms of which we have spoken, is relatively new, and a full understanding is going to take a long time. In debates like this one at least we have the consolation of ascertaining that we may not be crazy. I am sure that all of you know that a few years ago discussions of this kind would have been considered esoteric at best and probably meaningless.

FRIEDEN: I think we passed over the subject of planning methods rather quickly. The feeling was presented that we have adequate techniques but that we are not focusing enough on normative questions. I am not sure we have adequate techniques. Many issues raised in the normative sense — in terms of long-range goals — can also be raised with regard to specific planning programs where we have made decisions to go ahead for urban renewal, highways, and so on. Many things we build now are built according to plans based on the technical studies you mentioned, including cost analysis and simulation techniques. I am not aware that these techniques really cope very adequately with questions of distribution or with which social groups get which benefits. It seems, on the contrary, that many of our techniques bury those questions.

OZBEKHAN: I agree with you. For the present all I have tried to do was to indicate that in this field some research is being designed and serious thought is beginning to be given both to substantive issues and to techniques and methodologies. I hope that in time we will be able to go beyond merely technical questions and be able to feed some normative questions into the system and get some answers.

BAUER: I think, in stressing the difficulties of finding optimum solutions, that we may have liquidated the concept too thoroughly. The first difficulty is that we never know for certain if a course of action was optimal since we couldn't have conducted all of the experiments of actually carrying out all of the courses of action that were available to us after the fact. We can, at best, make a guess. In that sense, we can't tell whether you took an optimal course of action. There is another place where optimality, I think, is practically impossible, and that is calculating the optimal policy for a large complex group. This is because of the diversity of values and interests and so forth.

But, this does not rule out the possibility of optimality for the individual decision unit, and the issue of uncertainty doesn't cloud the concept of optimality at all. We can look at the future possible states of affairs, assign the value of each of those, assess their uncertainty, and we come out, not with the best payoff, but with the best expected payoff. This is optimal from the point of view of the present looking to the future, and in that case a sensible man has no choice except to do it. I think in that sense the notion of the optimal solution still stands pretty firmly.

OZBEKHAN: Yes, but you are taking, of course, the case of the individual with a single set of values — as long as he is consistent.

BAUER: Yes.

Mr. MYRON B. BLOY: In the light of what you said, we have been discussing the question of values as if there were a set of inert values that you can somehow program or deal with. Last night I was reading Oscar Lewis' article in *Science* about the culture of poverty. The problem seems to be that what characterizes the culture of poverty is the lack of passionate commitments, something not in the generalizable sense at all but in the sense of destiny. A sense of purpose is needed to get people together and break through that fatalism and lack of will. I think that if we are going to discuss this question of norms and guides, this aspect should be a part of it.

WARTOFSKY: There is a classical question about optimization. I think Keynes put it most clearly in his *Treatise on Probability,* that is, in distinguishing between knowing whether something is *true* and knowing that which it is rational to believe on given evidence. If rational belief always depends on finite evidence, it is possible that so-called rational beliefs are false, or will be shown to be false on further test. Thus, we always risk our beliefs in experimental test, if we take rationality seriously.

I think the confusion comes when we mistake one for the other, or when we confuse rational beliefs with truth. Now, certainly when I am given evidence, I decide on this basis what might be optimal. I make a rational decision, which is the best we can come up with so far. But then my argument is against taking "optimal" in any further sense, as the definitive or "true" solution. You have to pluralize "optimization" in order to see whether alternatives, or different evidence, or different interpretations of the same evidence would give you alternative solutions which you may then regard as more optimal or less optimal when they are articulated.

BAUER: I think the spirit of this meeting indicates, too, that you can make that decision at one point in time.

WARTOFSKY: That is precisely the point about the dynamics of this kind of decision making, which is, at the root, *fallible*. It is fallible in the normative sense because it constantly requires that it be criticized and reviewed and that alternatives be offered.

Now, I have a question for Mr. Ozbekhan and possibly for others. To what extent is this kind of normative planning computable? To what extent can it be put into the form of program? To what extent, for example, are aesthetic norms or ethical norms at the present time capable of being formulated in such a way that a question can be asked, a data base presented, and an answer given that is *more* than an analytical working-out of the consequences of a decision already made? It seems to me that there is a bound beyond which such a program can't go unless you have some kind of meta-programming, something which goes beyond what is essentially curve-fitting.

OZBEKHAN: It seems to me you have asked several questions. Insofar as what you called meta-programming is concerned, we are able to conceive of meta-systems in relation to particular systems encompassed within them. The answer to the question of how far these problems are computable is that, clearly, everything cannot be computable if by that you mean quantifiable. Often what is not computable is simulatable. Also, there are questions of analogic translation; in other words, you can state certain problems that are not computable in terms of other problems that are. Then, probably, one of the dominant issues becomes cost. When you say aesthetics at one level will cost so much and aesthetics at another level will cost less, and if you want to base your decision on cost, then it is not very difficult to compute the various costs and to make the appropriate decision in the light of the results you obtain.

WARTOFSKY: But suppose we want something more, something like normative programming?

OZBEKHAN: In the case of problems that are not amenable to computation, simulation or even model building ought at least to be looked into.

228

CAZES: Do you mean that you simulate reactions of people?

OZBEKHAN: Yes, I believe that it is becoming increasingly possible to simulate the reactions of people within a given system — if by reaction we are agreed to mean behavior.

DAVIDOFF: I should like to ask Dyckman about the question he raised concerning the difficulty of aggregating different choices. How can you establish democratic practice in planning? What is the practice today? Where do you go from there?

DYCKMAN: This is like asking Barnett's question again: What is better than some representative governmental process for aggregating? We have a very strong belief in representative government, in the democratic tradition; but I have a lack of confidence in representation through the electoral process. This is one reason why I am interested in planning, even though that sounds fundamentally antidemocratic.

I think that the capacity of traditional elected representative methods of dealing with value aggregation is probably not very great. I also suspect that in the world today decisions are being made increasingly bureaucratically. It has been my position for a long time that the problem of our society, so far as political representation is concerned, is now to make the bureaucratic decisions accessible to political forces in some basically aggregating way that is not now possible. But how that can be done, I just don't know. Two kinds of implicit projections are involved here: First, one must project or have an image of the character of bureaucratic decisions. Are they so technical that they cannot be made accessible to the public? Second, are a democracy's functions efficient if they are subject to the review of populations of small or large groups?

JUNGK: I should like to give an answer to Davidoff. As I tried to say yesterday, I have felt that we lack in our society institutions dedicated to the discussion of "oughts," permanent centers where the purposes of individual and collective existence could be probed more deeply than is presently the case. Today the issues are usually brought up by different conflicting interest groups, rarely by thinkers able to see them in a detached manner. If we, "the intellectuals," do only "what we can," we will not have done enough, we will not have given enough thought to what we ought to do.

In the technological field, there is a permanent and very intensive effort toward creating new "oughts," new technological goals. Industry has mastered the art of "inventing on order." Nothing similar is being done in other fields. There are no places where the social, political, ethical, and aesthetic "oughts" of mankind are studied with the same amount of *expertise*. Democratic society lacks institutions with this specific function. Is this so utopian that no one will take it up? Is it just a crazy thought? I would like to have your opinion on that.

DAVIDOFF: Some of us proposed plural planning as a way to get a solution, as a way to get representation for ideas that now are not raised. One of the questions is: Can there be any group capable of looking at these interests in a detached way? You are not detached from the subject of peace — you are a firm believer and an advocate of it, I assume.

JUNGK: Yes, you are quite right, but if a scientist starts an experiment, he first has a model and a theory and constructs an experiment in order to test them. We constantly develop and test scientific and technological models to the best of our knowledge and with little or no prejudice. But we neglect to develop and test new societal models.

OZBEKHAN: Those are the institutions that we have been talking about.

DYCKMAN: There have been such institutions. In the past revolutionary parties were formed, and such parties were the means of carrying forth social revolution and presenting utopias. I would warn you that revolutionary parties have been imperfect carriers. Their great disability in the past has been that they became fixed on the solution. Therefore, when parts of it didn't work, they couldn't change it fast enough. They have been unable to mobilize this kind of energy and discussion at the preliminary stage before their bureaucracy was set up. To take a course of action is one thing, but then to make it flexible after you have carried it into the next period is a different question under revolutionary mobilization.

MYER: I would like to have a little more discussion about the obsolescence of the object. So far I think nobody has quite grasped it, perhaps, or has felt prepared to deal with it.

OZBEKHAN: I think you are referring to what I called the phenomenon of "liquefaction" in our environment. I will try to make my point clear, but on this subject I am in the realm of random observations that I have not thought through systematically.

Several aspects or dimensions of our environment appear to me to be losing their physical or concrete attributes, which are increasingly replaced by less tangible, more abstract, rather impermanent, or more symbolic attributes. Economists, I suppose, are more aware of this phenomenon; hence, in order to make my meaning clear, I shall offer a first example from that subject.

Resources and products, as objects, are the prime foundations of economic life and the embodiments of value. In the exchange process the introduction of money is a relatively late occurrence, and in its earlier forms money was viewed (as in the case of silver and gold) as an object possessing intrinsic value of its own. It is only recently that this intrinsic value grew into symbolic value, and through the development of abstract conventions such as "promise to pay the bearer" that something whose value was not objectifiable was accepted to command things. Here we see an initial liquefaction of the material thing into an abstract symbol. For example, if you carry one hundred dollars in your pocket, it's the same as saying that you carry a table, or a chair, or several pairs of shoes, etc., which are objects. Nowadays, you carry also services, which are intangible products for exchange. The important thing is that the piece of paper with no intrinsic value does embody an indeterminate number of things or combinations of things with which you don't need to come into direct contact until you actually want to use them.

What appears to be a similar process of increasing intangibility is going on all around us. Credit, and now credit cards, liquify objects further. Soon we shall have electronic currencies, which will abolish physical money completely — you won't need to carry a cent with you. The evolution of "bearer shares" and "stocks" has similarly liquified property as an object.

However, corresponding trends toward intangibility are beginning to be visible in other dimensions of the environment. Communications is probably one of the prime examples. The telephone has indeed disembodied direct objective person-to-person communication. It has also multiplied and enlarged the possibilities of alternative as well as simultaneous communication patterns between people. Television has clearly done the same thing. Also, if we foresee the possibilities inherent in computer-assisted instruction in our schools, then it becomes clear that this trend toward liquefaction in certain fundamental relationships and processes of our society will grow.

A similar development is possible to conceive with respect to work patterns and the worker's direct contact with the product. There are today certain studies being conducted to discover the cost benefits that might be derived in some fields, such as computer programming or, more generally, software design, if the professionals involved were to remain in their homes, and were given the necessary consoles and communication apparatus that tied them to their work place. Some preliminary results of these studies show that in the fields I have mentioned, which are particularly amenable to this kind of arrangement, there might be cost gains and higher productivity to be derived from keeping the worker at home. I cannot think offhand why similar arrangements cannot be made in the future for most industries that depend on automation.

It is becoming clear that trends of this kind, which in some sense divorce the object or the product from human contact while increasing man's control over it, will be a generalized experience for all of us in the not-too-distant future. Of course, this trend will probably be encouraged by population growth and the necessity of solving traffic problems in totally new ways. It may even dictate not only the shape of the new society but also the physical configuration of our new cities and of the whole ecological environment of the human being. The proliferation of communication networks, in my view, represents a much more liquified social setting than we have hitherto known, and, clearly, there is no reason not to push the argument to its logical conclusion and visualize the multiplication of this type of network through the world. I believe that such possibilities do represent problems which, although they may be distant at the present time, should attract the attention of architects, city planners, regional planners, and others. I should very much like to learn of your views with respect to this kind of potential development.

S. ANDERSON: I should simply like to suggest that Ozbekhan's argument can also be extended to the realm of physical objects. Inexpensive materials that are well adapted to efficient production (plastics and other synthetic materials, for example) are used to provide very serviceable and low-cost objects. Since so little personal, psychic, and economic value attaches to such objects, one does not possess them in the usual sense. They are retained only as long as they serve — and are then thrust out because it is more economical and less wearing to replace them in the next season or the next residence. Most delightfully, such a liquefaction of objects would "vaporize" insurance on their possession!

New Methodologies for Pluralistic Situations

One of the forces of resistance to planning in the United States has been the fear that planning entails centralized decision making devoid of adequate popular representation or authorization.

The tendencies in the direction of centralization and the fears associated with that phenomenon are evidenced in the discussion of Raymond Bauer's proposal for improved social statistics.

The sanguine attitude of "liberals" toward the centralizing tendency of planning, whether in New Deal days or at present, has usually been based on the urgency of some social need which, it was felt, could be met only by efficient administrative action.

In recent years, the civil rights movement and the riots among the urban poor have forced a recognition that centralized "planning for" has not solved the problems, nor will it any longer be accepted by that part of the populace which is directly involved. The oppressed now demand inclusion in the attempts at resolving the great problems that demand action. These conditions suggest the development of a decentralized "planning with."

As indicated by the contributions of Leonard Duhl and Paul Davidoff to this conference, the liberals are now in full support of local decision making. Current political exigencies are once again in step with an old American tradition of local rights. Consequently, proposals for plural planning, advocacy planning, and the like are attuned to both the current political situation and a prominent facet of our established political doctrine.

However, there are several reasons why our pragmatic and traditional openness to a concept such as "plural planning" ought to be tested and instructed by theoretical studies as well as practical application.

Each of the proposed new planning techniques needs theoretical clarification and development. Choosing among these techniques and relating them to problem types also requires study.

Then too, as Marx Wartofsky points out later, if the application of a new planning technique is to rise above intuitive or even brute application, we need to recognize the intellectual model inherent in the new proposal and then go on to improve such models. The whole man and our best men will not be fully engaged on the appeals of tradition and immediacy alone.

Wartofsky supplies an excellent discussion of the role of models "as modes of action." Paul Feyerabend goes on to provide a sketch of an epistemology that encompasses the freedom and proliferation of individual insights and positions as a positive good — not just psychologically and socially but also intellectually. His formulation proposes that the advancement of knowledge relies on the opportunity for individuals to hold tenaciously to unusual or even unpopular positions which then serve to test, and are tested by, other positions. This is not a model of a society basking in the harmonies of a Golden Age. It is the much more relevant and convincing model of a society in which knowledge, artistic endeavor, and social relations are not devoid of conflict, but where conflict has been channeled into humane forms that incorporate both the individualism inherent in proliferation and the collective achievement inherent in the advancement of knowledge, the arts, and social well-being.

Social Indicators: Or Working in a Society Which Has Better Social Statistics

RAYMOND A. BAUER

If we are to anticipate the future or attempt to shape that future by deliberate action to avoid unpleasant situations that might otherwise greet us, we ought to understand our present state and its relationship to the past as the basis for understanding the trends that are in effect. Yet data on many important aspects of the society are missing, inadequate, or misleading. As an example, if we assume that the statements about national goals made by the Eisenhower commission[1] refer to important features of our society, the major national statistical series have data relevant to only slightly more than half of these goals. If we insisted that they be *adequate* measures, the proportion would be even lower.

The gross inadequacy and flaws in the data we keep about our society have long been realized. It appears now that something of major proportions may be done about this. I should like to suggest what is likely to happen and stimulate thought about what it will mean for architects to live and work in a society with an improved informational system.

In the most general sense, the purpose of having more adequate information about man's state of affairs is to enable him to act more rationally. One manifestation of this ought to be that the actions of the various people would be more closely coordinated. For the architect this means that if he chooses to take the initiative, he will have the opportunity of meshing his actions to the

[1] President's Commission on National Goals, *Goals for Americans* (Englewood Cliffs, N.J.: Prentice-Hall, 1960).

needs of others and choosing courses of action that are facilitated rather than hindered by others. However, even if he does not choose to exercise this initiative, there will be increasing formal or informal pressure on him to relate what he does to various over-all schemes. Most of the parties with whom he has to deal, whether they are the individual client, the corporation, or the community, will feel increasingly compelled to have "a plan" or at least the appearance of a plan, no matter whether it is misconceived or not. This plan will also have a time dimension in the sense that it will assume that the future will not be a simple projection of the present. This may mean that he will be required to design a building that will have a long life but be convertible to multiple uses as one kind of demand replaces another. Or he may have to build "disposable" structures whose life span is believed to be predictable and not very long. Perhaps there will be a high premium on modular factories to permit flexible exploitation of new technology or even new organizational forms. Probably there will be thoughts of multiplicity of function — such as the combination of civil defense structures with community centers. In general there will be a richer and more complex picture of those needs which structures can serve. None of the preceding is a qualitatively new phenomenon; however, I expect some increase in intensity that might dictate a rather fundamental reorientation.

In making such suggestions as these, I trust that I am not violating the pact that I should not presume to prescribe how buildings should be designed. What I am trying to predict here is the demands that will be placed on the architect and the new opportunities that will be available.

We presently make many measurements: of the numbers, age, and sex of our population, of their education, health, employment, income, wealth, crime, accidents, and so on. These measures, some of which date back to the founding of the Republic, are the output of a highly competent and proud statistical establishment located mainly in the federal government. Any statement of the limitations of these statistics is no criticism of the people who gather them. As a matter of fact, if I have anything at all to fear from them, it might be the charge of plagiarism since they have, in general, been the first to suggest improvements in existing series and the addition of new measurements — given the funds and mandate with which to proceed.

The attitudes of professional statisticians toward our social statistics is at wide variance from that of the casual user of them, or the social critic who blithely tells us what is happening to our civilization on the basis of evidence that is, at best, dubious.

Many of our measures most taken for granted are no better than an indirect indication of what they purport to represent. Figures on the educational level of the population are one of the most instructive examples. Statistics on the educational level of the U.S. population reflect only formal schooling, whereas some estimates indicate that at the present time instruction in the armed forces, in industry, and in other settings outside the formal educational system accounts for almost as many man-hours of education and training as within the formal system. Next, a given number of years of education is counted as equal regardless of the school system in which it was obtained or how long the individual has been out of school. And we make no allowance for the quality of the human vessel into whom this education was poured. But I have not mentioned the most fundamental limitation of this measure. It is used to represent the level of skill, knowledge, and ability of the population when these attributes can be measured directly by the use of standardized measures on a sample of the population. Why use years of schooling as a substitute for what we are actually interested in? Simply because we become accustomed to using data which were collected administratively, such as records of numbers of persons graduating or dropping out of school in a given year, or which were developed before we had the technology of the sample survey and sophisticated means of measurement.

For a long time one of the worst examples of the use of administratively gathered statistics was in the records of the number of persons applying for unemployment relief as a measure of unemployment. After a person exhausted his benefits, he dropped out of the count! This error has been rectified in recent years, but it is an example of how recently moves have been made to correct blatantly inadequate measures.

Some measures, such as the index of serious crimes, may reflect the opposite of what they claim to represent. This index is weighted toward automobile thefts, which are no longer "serious crimes" but unauthorized joy rides (over 90 per cent of stolen autos are now recovered), and toward larceny, which is defined as the unauthorized removal of an object worth fifty dollars or more. The index of serious crimes may, in fact, be an index of affluence. It cannot help rising in a period of prosperity and inflation unless there is a compensating drastic drop in the criminal inclinations of the public.

As for the criminal state of crime statistics, as usually reported, these are not even corrected for age-specific rates. The juvenile population has been growing at a disproportionate rate. Competent authorities have reported regularly that a simple adjustment for this fact would in itself wipe out the reputed increases in crime, even if we did not look into the matters of definition that I hinted at just previously.

Other matters, such as the social values and the aspirations of our people, are apparently issues about which we care a great deal. There is certainly a plethora of comments on what is happening to our moral fiber. But there are simply no trend data that are reasonable approximations of being measures of such concerns.

Some things are measured rather well: the number, age, and sex of the population, for example. However, the ten-year interval between censuses can make such data useless for many purposes. The population of individual census tracts can change so rapidly that census data can be drastically misleading within a few years.

I have identified three deficiencies of our present social statistics. First, they may not mean what they pretend to mean. Second, there may simply be *no* data series for things we are concerned with. And, third, they may be out of date.

Now I want to mention a fourth and a fifth difficulty.

The fourth is that some statistics, such as the health survey, are not taken with large enough samples so that they give adequate information for planning or other action on any unit less than the nation. Many of these statistics cannot be broken down even to the state level.

Fifth is the fact that our present series of social statistics do not constitute in any meaningful sense a *system* of data designed to reflect some underlying social phenomena which are inter-related in a patterned fashion. This latter criticism is a rather stringent one, and not susceptible to easy remedy. However, the notion that we should have a *system* of social statistics is spurred by our system of economic indicators, which over the past twenty years have become a valuable tool in the guidance of our economy.

What makes it possible to speak of the economic indicators as constituting a meaningful system is, of course, the fact that econo-mists have been able to reach some reasonable consensus on a *model* of the economy and can thereby specify that set of inter-acting economic variables which they feel it is necessary to measure.

All, including economists, agree that there is a larger social system that extends beyond those considerations to which econo-mists habitually pay attention. (1) All benefits, for example, can-not be measured in direct monetary terms. (2) Many phenomena cannot be controlled by monetary incentives or constraints alone. The birth rate, for example, is a function of values and beliefs that operate independently of the economics of family size. (3) Noneconomic institutions, such as the family, are valued (or not valued) for their own sake. (4) In turn, they have serious conse-quences for the productivity of the economy because of the values transmitted to the new generation, the degree of mutual support between generations that ensures the training of one generation and the security of the other, the participation of the various members in the labor force, the levels and type of consumption of goods and services, and so on.

If we were interested only in the performance of the econ-omy, we should want measures of many of the phenomena that are not ordinarily considered to be "economic." But the issue be-comes more serious when we reflect on the fact that the perfor-mance of the economy should not be regarded in any sense as an end in itself but as a means to the serving of national goals and the personal values of the population.

Furthermore, we must freely grant that these noneconomic factors do themselves constitute a system in that they interact with each other in a determinate, patterned fashion. I shall not, however, pretend that there is any one model of the society on which we might expect rapid consensus.

All of the foregoing matters are in no sense new, with the one exception that we have had a system of economic indicators in effect in recent decades. Aside from that the cry for systematic social statistics has been raised for many centuries. Historically, the word "statistics" is derived from the Latin *ratio status*, which might be translated as "state of the nation." *Webster's Third New International Dictionary* gives the New Latin *statisticus*, meaning "state of affairs." From a very early time it was contemplated that one might have a societal informational system to enable one to judge "How are we doing?"

What is importantly new is that this issue, which has been the concern of professional statisticians, some social scientists, and some administrators, has very recently become a matter of lively concern in wider circles. A directive from the President instructing the Secretary of Health, Education, and Welfare to look into this matter is probably the most important evidence of this concern. Professor Daniel Bell is chairman of the group that has been assembled to guide this effort.

My own perspective on these developments is conditioned by an experience beginning about three years ago. At that time I was directing a research program for the American Academy of Arts and Sciences on the social impact of space exploration. I became aroused by the fact that most of the phenomena about which there was speculation — the values and aspirations of our people, phenomena such as anomie and alienation, grand abstractions such as "dignity of the individual" — are ones on which we haven't the slightest trace of direct historical data. Because this gap existed, I encouraged several people to write essays, which have appeared recently in the form of a book entitled *Social Indicators*.[2]

At the time we started this work, a subpanel of the President's Science Advisory Committee had just recommended that we gather better social statistics. But this had become almost a ritual.

[2] Raymond A. Bauer, ed., *Social Indicators* (Cambridge, Mass.: The M.I.T. Press, 1966).

For decades almost every recommendation for progress in the social sciences had included such a recommendation. In the intervening years, however, there has been a perceptible acceleration of interest. One Presidential commission (Technology, Automation, and Economic Progress) recommended the development of such series. The Russell Sage Foundation has launched a major effort to improve our ability to measure social change. Throughout the federal statistical establishment there is increasing interest and a general feeling that things are about to move. New and imaginative developments are already taking place in the Bureau of Census, the Department of Health, Education, and Welfare, the Department of Labor, and other places. The Crime Commission is even supporting the re-examination of our means of measuring crime. Throughout the nation there is interest in "data banks" on the federal, state, and local levels. (Such data banks involve the storage and retrieval of information rather than its gathering. However, they reflect the common concern with having more adequate information for planning and action.) In addition to the Presidential directive I mentioned, there is the apparent active interest of members of the White House staff. Finally, it appears that persons recently engaged in reviewing the federal statistical effort are ready to recommend that this effort be doubled or tripled *rapidly*.

In brief, there is already stepped-up activity in the establishment of more and better social statistics, and there are signs pointing toward further acceleration in the future.

We are engaged in "inventing the future," and one of the strongest arguments for having better data about the past and present is that they aid us in anticipating what will come. Hence, we might well consider the basis on which to judge whether or not this particular anticipation of the future of social statistics is warranted.

Let us consider the forces that will act against the expanded development of a system of social indicators. The most serious negative consideration is the issue of personal privacy. There is very widespread serious concern over whether certain types of personal questions should be asked of people, and whether observation and recording of their behavior — such as clandestine pictures of women shopping — are not an invasion of the individual's privacy. Added to this is the concern that the central accumulation of data about individuals may make it possible to control and harm them. These are serious issues; I believe they must be handled, can be handled, and will be handled. The most likely effect of these concerns for the privacy and rights of the individual is not that they will stop an over-all growth of social statistics. They may slow up the trend somewhat, but they are more likely to have a selective impact on the gathering and assembling of specific types of data.

Unfortunately, one of the most sensitive types of data is longitudinal information tracing an individual through the cycles of his life. For some purposes it is also essential. Aggregate data on the types of housing people of various ages live in cannot tell us what the various sequences of housing needs and uses are in the life of an individual. The latter can be obtained only through the life histories of individuals. My guess is that sufficient protection can be built into the handling of these data so that people's anxieties will be allayed.

Data, however, are not neutral and therefore may be used against the interests of some individuals. We may expect that there will be interested opposition to certain data series, such as those showing that some person or agency was not doing a very good job. Here, again, I should expect the effect to be selective.

Then there are great technical difficulties. Take some grand abstraction such as "the dignity of the individual." We can all be in favor of this without knowing just what it is we favor. If it includes decent housing and also concern for both one's privacy and some degree of self-expression in his surroundings, such a concept has obvious implications for the architect. Perhaps it could be extended to specify the degree of privacy to which a sick person is entitled in a hospital. You may say that a good architect is already concerned about "the dignity of the individual." Unfortunately, it will take some time to work out a reasonable consensus on what is meant by such a concept — for example, whether it includes freedom of economic activity (the Republican version) or economic security (the Democratic version). Once agreement on the concept is reached, there is the additional problem of deciding what phenomenon in the real world is to represent this abstraction. For example, is "economic security" a subjective state of feeling secure regardless of reality, or is it represented by an uninterrupted job history or by funds available at the age of retirement? Even when such an issue is decided, there are still measurement problems left. I mentioned an "uninterrupted job history." Is time off for retraining an interruption? Does this depend on whether one took the time off because he saw an opportunity for advancement or because he felt threatened with displacement? How threatened? Do we take his word for it?

Such technical problems will obviously slow things up. Again, they will probably have a selective effect, since some concepts are more difficult to make operational and some phenomena more difficult to observe.

All in all, there are such factors, which stand in the way of developing more adequate statistical series. Only if the issue of the privacy and rights of the individual is badly handled can I see the trend for expansion of our social indicators stopped or reversed. My own exposure to persons in the relevant professions and in the government indicates that there is great awareness of the importance of the privacy issue, and I expect it will not be mishandled.

What, then, are the factors favoring the development of better social indicators? As a precondition there is the growing gross national product. I did not mention cost as an inhibiting factor because, though the issue will certainly be raised, the growing GNP will make the matter of cost minor. Statistics gathered on a sample basis, as they are increasingly, cost no more for a large population and large economy than for a small one. Hence, the relative cost of any data series — except the population census, to which we are bound in any event — will decline.

For positive motivation and facilitation we find a whole set of interacting factors. The growing affluence of the society makes it possible, and to some extent imperative, to attend to phenomena which we once ignored. If technological growth creates structural unemployment, urban renewal and highway location displace people, industry and automobiles pollute the environment, it is no longer acceptable to shrug off these second-order consequences of our actions as "the price of progress." We believe that we can and must redress those parties injured by actions that are beneficial to the larger society or economy. Furthermore, as we become more sophisticated about the ramifications of our actions, we not only think in more complex terms but try to act that way.

Planning is increasingly a part of our way of doing things. Unquestionably, our relative success with the control of our economy has been a spur to expand our efforts in this direction. Added to this are the newer techniques of decision making. The spread of the McNamara-sponsored cost-benefit analysis to the regions of the government beyond the Pentagon has been a stimulus to which much of the recent interest in better statistics can be traced directly. While enthusiasm for this particular planning tool may wane, and we may even have cycles of disillusion with formal planning and decision-making tools, it is hard to conclude that there is not and will not continue to be a secular trend toward greater rationalization of our way of conducting our lives. And such planning and decision making demands information — particularly information about benefits that cannot be measured in straight dollars and cents and about the things that our people value and want.

I have mentioned the system of economic indicators several times. They appear to play two roles in the trends I am discussing. First, they serve as an example of what can be done. Second, as people use them, their limitations become more apparent, thereby creating a demand for supplemental data to fill in the gaps.

Our ability to make relevant measurements and handle a great volume of complex data is developing rapidly. This is a result of our increased experience with measuring social phenomena, as well as our increased ability to store and retrieve data with the use of computers.

For all these reasons, I feel certain that over the next couple of decades we shall have much more information about the society in which we live and the people who are part of it. These data will include increasingly direct measures of people's capacities, of their wishes and aspirations, of their relations to each other, and of the sequence of stages that they pass through in their life cycle. Such information will be used increasingly as a guide to social action, with an increasing concern for a wider range of consequences over a longer time span. We shall develop more elaborate and explicit models of the sort of society we have, and we shall use these models for predicting and planning. Since any modern notion of planning incorporates the assumption that our intentions will be imperfectly realized, we shall provide for more rapid and precise feedback of the consequences of our actions. For better or worse, we shall be aware of our mistakes more rapidly and therefore, I hope, be able to correct them more nearly in time.

I have talked about the "society" as though it were a unit and as though all statistics will be collected on a federal level. This impression must now be modified. It is about as certain as anything can be that there will be a trend toward making data available for increasingly smaller units, whether they are geographical units, smaller political units, types of institutions, or what have you. At this very moment the word "disaggregation" is a very popular one in discussions of social statistics. "Disaggregation" means — if jargon doesn't come naturally to you — breaking the data into smaller units. Some plans for computer storage and retrieval of various sorts of data would permit them to be stored by individuals. (This would be necessary if longitudinal data are gathered.) This would make it possible to combine the data according to any units that were of interest.

The sole difficulty, and far from a trivial one, in providing data for smaller units of the society is that for these purposes data gathered on a sample basis will have to use either larger samples or more samples. This is a matter of cost and effort, and these considerations will certainly have an influence on the extent to which data for units smaller than the nation will be developed.

What will it mean for the architect to work in such an environment? I asked this question of a nonarchitect, who replied: "The biggest complaint about architects is that they don't pay attention to the users, but just build to impress other architects." I choose to regard this as a not very constructive basis for our deliberations.

I also regard the specter of Big Brother as not a very useful point of departure *for us in this context*. It is very true that a great potential for social ills lies in the collection and assemblage of a great deal of information about a great number of people. This issue, however, should be discussed in some other context.

The fruitful assumption for us is that such expanded series of data exist, that we are all generally more sophisticated in using them, that they are intended for primarily beneficial purposes. Then we should consider what this would mean for the architect. Here are *some* suggestions.

We may anticipate that the behavioral scientist's way of looking at some problems will become pervasive. It is probable that the family will be looked on not solely as a social unit but as an economic resource and/or a generator of economic resources. The rural family has been assumed to be a producing unit of the economy. But the type of organization of the family, the pattern of interpersonal relations, and the values communicated within the family determine which members of the family will be involved in the labor force at a given time, what the consumption needs of the family will be, the level and quality of the motivation of its younger members, the functions the house will serve for it, and so on.

The amount and arrangement of housing space can certainly affect the number of persons who inhabit a unit and the nature of their interaction. Conversely, the small nuclear family and the large extended family may demand different types of housing. The family whose members exhibit high "need achievement," a motivational pattern associated with economic growth, ought to be less inclined to spend its resources on display and immediate gratification than a family of equal affluence but different motivational pattern.

It is possible to imagine a variety of ways in which the nature of the family unit would interact with its housing. And, as I have indicated, behavioral scientists have been concerned with the interaction of the family structure and functioning with other vital features of the society such as the economy. However, it is only very recently that really serious attention has been turned to the possibility of making trend measurements of the nature of the American family. If we may assume that this will take place, the projection of the trends can give the architect an idea of the housing requirements that the family of the future will pose. Or social policy may suggest that certain family forms — such as having retired people live or not live with the younger generations — may be inherently desirable or undesirable, or may serve or inhibit some other value of the society. Once we understand these matters better, then we may evolve a policy of subsidizing or penalizing some forms or sizes of housing units.

I have spoken of the possibility of gathering longitudinal data about people. At this time our understanding of patterns of social mobility in American society is badly handicapped by the lack of such data. Presumably, the architect could be as interested in how people move around the social structure as in how they move around the landscape. In addition, we have thought of man's passage through life in terms of one continuous variable — age. Newer studies indicate that the concept of life cycle, which takes into account one's marital status, whether or not he or she has children, and whether or not the children are still living in the household is more clearly related to some (but not all) important behavior such as the consumption of goods than is the matter of age alone. The use of the life cycle concept in the gathering and analysis of social data in the future seems certain.

Aside from the fact that having data on many of these phenomena will have direct implications on the markets for housing and other structures, we must assume that if the sorts of study that have been discussed are carried out, our understanding of the role of the family in the society and of the individual in the family will be expanded in ways that we cannot presently anticipate. This, in turn, should be a stimulus for extending our thinking about the role of housing.

The foregoing examples of types of data that directly or indirectly will impinge on the architect's activities are, of course, illustrative at best.

However, the methods used to make continuous measurements on the parameters of the society will also be available for *ad hoc* measurements. And it may be assumed that the atmosphere of planning and rationalization will place a premium on closer studies of the needs of clients. Furthermore, any up-to-date notion of planning is based on the premise that nothing ever turns out exactly as intended. Therefore, feedback mechanisms to detect errors and permit their correction will become a more integral part of life. I do not see how architecture will be able to escape such a general phenomenon, but, on the other hand, I have difficulty in imagining a concrete example of what actually might happen. It *could* be, for example, that some project such as a shopping center might be required to provide for an alternative use of a portion of its structures if the traffic generated by the center at critical times passed some prescribed limit.

It is probably as obvious to you as it is to me that, as certain as my intuition is that all these things will matter to the architect, I am not prepared to give a long list of specifics. But perhaps that is proper, since I do not know your business, and the burden is better left on your shoulders. It seems to me, in any event, that the task of architectural education involves getting the student to think of the relationship of his actions to the society at large. If this step were not already deeply implanted in your minds, we should not be here today. The problem is to discover what sorts of knowledge one will require in order to do this. It is almost with a sense of embarrassment that I suggest: a little sociology, a little statistics, a lot of brains.

DISCUSSION

GEDDES: Which social indicators are in good shape?

BAUER: Except for the infrequency of their collection, data gathered by the census are quite good, if they are used for what they are supposed to represent. The big improvement has been in the use of sample statistics, because with sample surveys you can get data from people which may be more appropriate than the information you were getting from records.

A look at the health data would be the most instructive because there you have had changing and more relevant criteria. Originally the basic index of health was the death rate, that is, mortality. Then it became morbidity, that is, how many people are sick. In recent times it has become whether or not people are functioning in their social role, whether they can go to work, whether they can get around the house, and so on — something that, by and large, you can get only by asking the person involved.

It is with the health statistics, I suppose, that the advantages and limitations of the sample survey method show up most concretely because comparisons have been made of what people tell us in that situation and what doctors find if they examine a comparable group of people. My own judgment is that each has advantages and limitations. For example, doctors examining people will pick up more cardiac cases than people will report. This is not surprising, because most people wouldn't know they had heart trouble unless a doctor told them, some hypochondriacs excepted.

On the other hand, people report more colds and allergies than the doctors detect, and this is not any surprise either, because the doctor examines persons at one point in time and they may have had the cold or allergy the day or week before.

The employment statistics are again vastly improved, and that has been accomplished by a monthly survey of a sample of real people. We are no longer dependent on vagaries of records such that a person ceased to be "unemployed" simply because he had been out of work so long that he had exhausted his unemployment benefits and his name was dropped from the records.

There are a couple of regularities that we deduced. For example, the statements of national goals made during the Hoover period in about 1930 now have a fairly good representation in our statistical series. It looks as if up to now there has been a one-generation time lag between the nation becoming interested in phenomena and our starting to gather measurements on them. Many things having to do with technology, for example, are very badly represented, and the higher abstractions of quality of life are even more poorly represented. While this shouldn't be so, it is no surprise either.

FRIEDEN: You mentioned the problem of time lag in the census series, which is a serious one for urban studies. What, do you think, are the prospects for getting a census every five years?

BAUER: I wouldn't be at all surprised if we got one every five years. However, I think there is going to be a real struggle over whether we have more frequent censuses or more data series and special studies. There was a recent prospect of a five-year census, but it was shot down this time around because it was felt that other types of information that could be gathered on a sample basis for even less cost were more urgent. When that is taken care of, we will get the census on a five-year basis. What is more urgent is to get more frequent data in various local areas.

DYCKMAN: In some subclassifications of the basic data categories, you are going to make the partitioning of that set which really is decisive. I think there remains a continuing conflict in all data systems between the needs of time series and the requirements of stocktaking, or assessing the state of the system. Now, in response to some immediate policy need, cross-sectional information is obviously as powerful as it is with the Census Bureau personnel. At the point where you need long-range planning, where you need to do projections, time series become very important and would go much higher in the scale of priorities. And when you are dealing with time series, obviously it is advantageous to have these data reported frequently so that you get a sufficient number of observations to obtain statistical significance without having the observation spread over a period of time in which the institution changes.

BAUER: I want to acknowledge that. You mentioned one important consideration, the fact that definitions will change. They inevitably will. If you start measuring one thing and keep measuring it, it is going to be something else simply because you will be operating on a different population. Even the meanings of questions, for example, change over time.

One way of dealing with this is to overlap your series for a while. If you feel that you want to improve your instrument, you ought to use the old instrument while you are breaking in the new instrument and get a calibration so that you can then make translations back to the old one.

DYCKMAN: If I may put on the economist's hat for the moment and look at the data, I would say that we could make very excellent time studies of employment and wages, and we could do it in monthly and quarterly series. The definitions haven't changed very much in the last seven or eight years, and we could get observations on the nature of coefficients and reliability measures for our estimates, and so on.

What you said about the American society is true, that there

252

have been changing institutions from one generation to the next; but in some ways we are very fortunate. The economic institutions haven't changed much in American life: a corporation is still a corporation. I know some countries in the world where the basic enterprise has changed since last year.

FLEISHER: I would like to address a remark to Dr. Dyckman. If you take the series more seriously, you can make a better prediction. If the series is five years long, you can make a prediction of only two and one-half years.

DYCKMAN: That is right. The state of California wants estimates of personal income next year for tax purposes. They want a kind of short-run projection with a high degree of accuracy, for which, it seems to me, the time series is still necessary.

FLEISHER: It is not going to help the man who wants to make a twenty-five-year prediction.

DUHL: Almost all of us find that welfare data are not comparable with housing data and not comparable with health data. I was involved for several years with the mental health data collections. It took us about five years before we got eleven states to agree on what we meant by first admissions to a hospital. The definition of how long a patient was in a hospital also varied. Once you cut across all the fields, you suddenly find yourself with a great organizational problem. How do you plan for the strategy of really getting this process under way?

BAUER: I have some very great difficulties in envisioning how one would get series instituted. My coauthor Albert Biderman, in his essay,[3] presents a jaundiced view of the whole thing and doubts whether it is sensible to expect to introduce a whole new system of social statistics. My posture is that whether you could do it or not, I want to conceive what it would be like if we could get it done. I can't answer your question except to agree it is a difficult job.

S. ANDERSON: First of all, was the word you used "disaggregation"?

BAUER: Yes. It is a terrible word, but it refers to something quite meaningful. It means breaking the data down into measure-

---

[3] Albert Biderman in Bauer, ed., *op. cit.*, pp. 68–153.

ments of smaller units, on a state or local basis, or even smaller units.

S. ANDERSON: I would like to ask about that in relation to Fein's paper, which evidenced a concern for rather small blocs within the society. To what degree might your social indicators be of assistance in such matters? Or might the existence of social indicators tend to blur the conditions at a small scale?

BAUER: The census, of course, because it refers to everybody, can be broken down infinitely fine. But sample series, even if they are based on a very large sample of 50,000 or 100,000 cannot be broken down on a state basis, except perhaps for California or New York. With the inauguration of sample surveys for gathering many of these data, the samples aren't large enough. There is much agitation on this score. It is a matter of cost and a matter of how much muscle can be put into it by the people who want those statistics. All the problems are practical ones. In principle, anything that can be gathered on the national basis can be gathered on any small unit, but it just costs a lot.

There are all sorts of data series in existence now that aren't even being gathered by the Bureau of Census. The Health, Education, and Welfare and the Labor Departments both have monthly censuses of the state of the population on many of these variables.

However, there is a real problem. People legitimately say that with the federal government gathering all these data, we will get an undesirable centralization of decision making. I agree very strongly; many decisions should be made in a decentralized fashion. But how are you going to do this with respect to the gathering of data? I doubt that we want too much local autonomy in the gathering of regular data series for the reasons that Leonard Duhl was mentioning. It is a big job getting comparability.

DUHL: Actually, it has already happened; the local data banks sponsored by the Department of Housing and Urban Development can't talk to each other.

S. ANDERSON: So either way we can get a data system that relates poorly to a concern for the individual or specific small groups.

BAUER: You could get local data for local purposes that would be noncomparable to other data that would be gathered in other localities and be suited to these other localities. Such local data cannot be grouped together for the study of larger units.

S. ANDERSON: If you had local information and learned to use it well, you would, nevertheless, have to start all over again in a new location. The first experience yields lessons in method rather than in generalizable programs.

BAUER: Yes.

JUNGK: I wonder if some of the best features of the journalistic method of information gathering could be built into a system of statistical research? I can offer an example. In 1946–1947, as a refugee from Germany, I had little difficulty in making contact with former Germans who had been brought to the United States to work on the space program. Relatively early I could see that the space industry would sooner or later be of great interest to the national economy. The newspaperman goes out and looks for new developments and sees them before they have been categorized. Now, I wonder if any social statisticians studying the impact of the space industry could have arrived at a similar forecast at such an early date.

BAUER: In my book we have one chapter, also written by Biderman, which is a proposal for an anticipatory study.[4] An effort should be made to sense possible future events for which it would be of importance to gather baseline data at appropriate intervals.

The interesting thing about Biderman's insight is that if any prospective event is important enough to catch our attention, we would be just as interested in knowing what the result would be if it did not happen. If it doesn't happen, there will be a lot of people who have been expecting it to happen, and the violation of these expectations will be a matter of importance. So the arguments for anticipatory studies of this sort are even stronger than when we first began thinking about them. There is some prospect that at least one department of the government will begin working on this problem.

JUNGK: The other thing I want to say is that the forecasting

4 Biderman in *ibid.*, pp. 272–301.

ability of the journalist is probably related to a special mode of perception. The journalist as an individual usually sees a much more complex picture than any analyst of statistical data. Can you build something of that specifically human capacity into an official data-gathering system? Wouldn't that be a very important thing to do?

BAUER: I don't know what my answer should be. I know we said definitely that no data series can of themselves make the inferences that have to be made in order to understand what is happening.

We considered it to be our job, not to suggest how one should make such inferences, but merely to point out that the inferences still had to be made. You might see two things varying concurrently, but in most instances one can't say why they are varying concurrently. Generally, one would have to make specific studies designed to choose among alternate explanations.

S. ANDERSON: You have data that are gathered in relation to a model; if you decide the model isn't really an operative one, the whole system of collection must change.

BAUER: This is one reason why I wouldn't press very rapidly for a model, because it would mean commitment.

S. ANDERSON: Isn't there a model implicit in data that are being collected?

BAUER: Everybody knows there is a model implicit in everything you do. But the question is how to gather some data that are obviously going to be useful, and that don't commit you to *too specific a model.* I don't know if we can come away with a better answer than to say we ought to start with data whose usefulness is widely accepted and then keep refining the model as we go along.

WARTOFSKY: This past year I have watched psychologists gathering data, and the mood seems to be as you describe. They have, in a sense, abandoned all the classical systematic models because these either were too restrictive or committed them in directions that were too definitive. Now the psychologists are sticking to their lasts, so to speak, working in a very *ad hoc* way, and do not want to be constrained by a definitive model of what they are looking for. I think it is probably a matter of style and development here. At certain stages in a science, this *ad hoc* approach evidently becomes desirable. At another stage, such an approach may be a diffusion of energies in too many directions at once. The present guide seems to be to accept something like a consensus of what is useful.

The question I wanted to ask is this: To what extent are the data locked into decision procedures? For example, cost-of-living increases and things of that type are automatically dependent on data of a certain sort. The decision is data-determined. How much of this data gathering is locked into procedures of that sort?

BAUER: Your question doesn't surprise me. I was ready for it. But all I can do is plead guilty of ignorance. I don't think anybody has done a decent analysis of the full scope of the decisions for which the data are used.

Biderman discussed this question, and one of my colleagues is working on the marketing information systems. Logically, there is no difference between that and what I have been talking about. The problem in designing marketing information systems is that one can't get the executives in an organization to sit down and tell what sorts of decisions they want to use the information for, and in what way. There you are dealing with a much simpler system, for one company, and yet you can get relative chaos just because you don't know precisely enough for what purposes to gather and package the data.

On a societal level, at this point I don't even know what questions to ask, except some very obvious ones. The criteria ought to be the decisions for which the information is to be used. But the scope of the problem just escapes me.

DAVIDOFF: May I ask two questions of Professor Bauer? First, what indices will we have for so-called antisocial behavior? Second, somebody mentioned abortion rates. We may need to legalize abortions; what do we know about them? Is this information, or information on drug usage, to be publicized regularly?

BAUER: We don't know.

DAVIDOFF: Is this something that the reporters have to do for us?

BAUER: I would like to keep their hands off. I think they have done enough damage. These things have been very badly handled. We have tough detection problems there. I wouldn't immediately propose any standard reporting series on things like this. What we need is good hard work on finding out how to detect these phenomena. Then we can begin thinking of what to build in the way of data series.

DUHL: There is a good example on statistics of homosexuality that Evelyn Hooker collected in Los Angeles.[5] She spent five years beginning to understand the entire network of the homosexual, what gets reported, and how and what are the contacts. Now you finally get to the point where you have indices of the up-and-down changes without doing the extensive studies she did. In the areas you asked about, we haven't even done any of the preliminary work.

DAVIDOFF: My other question has to do in part with the "can" and "ought." Do we report only what we are capable of measuring but not those things for which we only have crude measures but which may be important? Are these normative activities?

BAUER: You have more than one point. To start with, does something get measured because it can be measured? Yes, worse than that, something that is measured gets attention. If your observations are representing previously unrepresented interests, you would be expected to pay attention to their wants. It is a very serious decision as to whether or not to make the measurement to start with. Many of these discussions are being taken up initially by technicians who, in turn, are interacting with the people in a policy position and probably interacting with some people outside the government. I doubt that they have any intention of hiding such discussions. The assumption is that they have to get these matters worked out before they can present them to anybody. There is a regular conference of users of federal statistics, about which I confess I don't know as much as I should, where potential users express their opinions. There was a regular conference on the users of census tract statistics where the Bureau of Census sent material to all sorts of people. I got several notices to appear and complain about the census tract statistics if I had any complaints to make.

---

[5] Dr. Evelyn Hooker is the principal investigator in a series of social psychological studies of male homosexuals, being conducted under a National Institute of Mental Health grant in Los Angeles, California.

Telos and Technique: Models as Modes of Action

MARX WARTOFSKY

There is something hopelessly desperate about attempting to find a radically new departure for talking or thinking about the future. At times, it seems a phantasmagorical task, fit for Sisyphus, of finding the key for a lock whose shape is itself vague and indeterminate. We are burdened with the consciousness of our vast achievements, of our apparently limitless technological prospects, of the grim optimism assuring us that whatever we undertake will somehow and at some time be effected. Together with this, we are haunted by the history of moral and political failure, by that vision of the servant become master or of a technology blind and soulless which works us to its own dialectic processes and whose rationales we are expedient enough to parade as if these were our own choices and our own ideologies.

So our *Angst* is compounded, on the one hand, of a power and dominion that commits us to what it *can* achieve, because what it can achieve is just what we had intended it to achieve — the control of a recalcitrant nature, to fit it to our needs — and, on the other, of the conviction that we are thus somehow the captives of our own past intentions. Thus our ingenuity, our creativity, the openness of free invention, all seem bound to what we once thought — or what was thought for us — to constitute rational goals and moral ends.

Now I do not propose to moralize about the dead hand of the past or about the limitations on our creative invention of the future, for at its worst this degenerates into pious confessions of impotence or the whining assertion that we are lost, alone, and fallen from the grace of an earlier golden age.

Rather, I would like to attempt something modestly hopeful and not at all desperate — that is, to characterize the normal process of creating the future, by bringing it down from the scale of cosmic crisis to that of daily and local necessity. I do not think there is a millennial solution to the future; but I do think that the pattern of our ordinary planning and striving prefigures whatever larger structures there are in terms of which long-range creation of the future can take place.

Perhaps some truisms may not be amiss here. The first is that man creates his future in the present; the second is that the present is more than a simple summation of the past, for it includes, at least at the level of conscious human activity, the element of anticipation. The epistemological aspect of this resides in our capacity to envision the future.

Unfortunately, in the context of much of epistemology, including that common-sense kind which traditionally conceives of thinking as an intellectual activity "in the mind," so to speak, envisioning the future comes to mean thinking about it or imagining it in some private mental space. Since, clearly, it cannot exist in the present as such, since it is the future, the future is assigned a merely ideational status, as an object of thought or imagination. I would argue that this is a false view and that adherence to it leads to passivity and practical impotence, because the future becomes the toy of imagination, the fantasy life of the inadequate present, the realm of unenacted wish, or if enacted at all, then only in imagination.

That this is false even of what is purely intellectual about thinking of the future is something that such diverse thinkers as Aristotle, Descartes, Kant, Marx, Peirce, and Dewey have shown. For them, in various interpretations, thinking is an activity that results in action in the world. Moreover, it is broadly conceived of as that activity which is unique to human beings and is characterized by conscious purpose. Therefore, it is not simply some object held up before the mind within the confines of one's own thoughts.

The prototype of such future-directed action — in which the future is more than the blindly inevitable fact of succession in time and includes some envisioned goal as its content — I would call a model.

Now this is surely perverse, for "models" in our ordinary sense are imitations, diagrams, scale versions, or pictures of something already existing. However, they can be more than this, as in prototypes, plans, hypothetical constructions of various sorts which serve as guides to action. But I mean more than this by "model." Initially, let me suggest that models are the highly specialized part of our technological equipment whose specific function it is to create the future. I cannot mean by model, then, anything quite as narrow as either an imitative version of something already existing, as in scale models, or simply a prototype or plan for some future embodiment. At best, these are what models may look like but not what they function as. To stretch the term "model" even further, let me suggest that what I mean by model is not simply the *entity* we take as a model but rather the *mode of action* that such an entity itself represents. In this sense, models are embodiments of purpose and, at the same time, instruments for carrying out such purposes.

Let me attempt to clarify this idea. No entity is a model of anything simply by virtue of looking like, or being like, that thing. Anything is like anything else in an infinite number of respects and certainly in some specifiable respect; thus, if I like, I may take anything as a model of anything else, as long as I can specify the respect in which I take it. There is no restriction on this. Thus an array of teacups, for example, may be taken as a model of the deployment of infantry battalions, and matchsticks as models of mu-mesons, there being some properties that any of these things share with the others. But when we choose something to be a model, we choose it with some end in view, even if that end in view is simply to aid the imagination or the understanding. In the most trivial cases, then, the model is already normative and telic. It is normative in that it is chosen to represent abstractively only certain features of the thing we model, not everything all at once, but those features taken to be important or significant or valuable. The model is telic in that such significance and value can exist only with respect to some end in view or purpose that the model serves.

Let us go one step further. Even in the weakest sense, the model is an aid to the achievement of something in the future which is as yet unachieved. If this is no more than intellectual enlightenment, or a clear understanding, then it is no small gain if we value these as goods. So even in the case where we say the model is only an aid to the imagination or that it only helps us to envision or picture or understand what is happening — for example, when we make a schematic model of some complex organism, or make a proto-typical model of something we intend to produce — this in itself is an achievement. In a sense, it is a creation of something working toward the future, something which, at the point of making the model or contemplating it, has not yet been achieved. Of course, that is a very weak sense. But now let us turn to the stronger sense in which the model is an achievement of something in the future. I have claimed that the models are not merely part of the technology for creating the future, that is, they are not merely instruments to be used but are themselves modes of action that, in fact, create the future.

Perhaps, then, we had better unpack the metaphorical term "creating the future," or "inventing the future." We mean by it, I think, *acting* in such a way as to make the future conform to some present vision of it. In a trivial and uninteresting sense, any action whatever "creates the future." If I raise my hand now, I have changed, in some way, what the future will be. However, "crea-tion" and, still more, "invention" carry the connotation of conscious and purposive action (if not also of rational action), as well as that sort of conscious and purposive action which has the highest values set upon it, whatever these are taken to be.

Now let me turn Kantian for a moment. That action or mode of action which I take the model to be is a model action. If I may be forgiven the pun here, I mean to say that it is a model action in the sense that it sets up a normative prototype whose function is not simply descriptive but imperative. It is an action or mode of action that one could rationally will to be universally emulated. Thus, it is more than an action; it is at the same time a *call* to ac-tion. It functions (in the way of this paraphrase of the categorical imperative of Kant) as an exemplary model with a claim on us to share in its purpose and in its mode of action to achieve this pur-pose.

What seems queer here is that our usual wire and paper-clip models or our plaster mock-ups seem more modest than this. It is hard to attach this resounding phrase "call to action" to something as simple, for example, as a scale model or some string-and-wire model. But this is a matter of scale and scope rather than of function. The values of a proper construction, in architecture or in logic, seem small compared to that larger human future which our large-scale social and technological models envision. But the demand of the normative construction of a logical proof or of model building is still: "This is how it ought to be done; this is what needs to be understood; this is how one ought to operate." Thus alternative models, as embodiments of purpose, present choices among alternative purposes. But, furthermore, models as embodiments of one or another kind of belief are, as C. S. Peirce would have pointed out, exemplifications of readiness to act in a certain way. To believe something, according to Peirce, is to be prepared to act in such and such a way. Therefore, we may say that the belief is already part of the action, and not something that stands "behind" the action and "waits" for the action to take place. The action, as it is considered here, is not just something that begins at point A and ends at point B but is rather something already embodied in the tacit or explicit "beliefs" that the model represents, which precede the overt activity itself.

Authors of ideal imitation theories in aesthetics, drawing on Aristotle's profound ideas, talk of *emulating* the divine way or Nature's way of working — not copying God's or Nature's handiwork, but rather emulating the mode of operation, of which the handiwork is only the exemplification. The master stands in the same relation to the apprentice: the teacher is the model not simply of this or that but of a *way* of work, a technique of inquiry, a kind of commitment. The emphasis is on the mode of action which the model represents, that is, a mode of action with respect to some end in view. So it is two-sided: on the one hand, it is an embodiment of a purpose; on the other hand, it is also, dynamically, the means of realization of the purpose. The purposes here are, at the same time, *entertained and undertaken* in the model.

So far, I have said that a model is an aid to the understanding or to the imagination. It is also a call to action in the sense of presenting some exemplary form of how things ought to be done or what ought to be done. This normative claim of the model is strongest when the model goes beyond the exemplary function. Even in the exemplary function of models the future is to be patterned after some present version, even if this is presently an ideal version. But in being "ideal," this present version is taken to be good and, therefore, bears the claim that one *ought* to emulate it. The limits of conception here delimit the present ideal. But some models do more than serve in the creation of a future in terms of some present ideal; they transform the total vision of those who involve themselves in the model. They are radical and revolutionary in their effect. They are modes of action which act by infection upon an age and its consciousness, and they help release energies and possibilities of the imagination and mind beyond anything that the model itself exemplifies. That is, the model produces more than it contains. It is a nonconservative model in this sense. It is perhaps hard to think of what such a model would be like unless one gives some examples, which broaden the concept of "model" still further.

I think poetry, at its best, works such a transformation of vision. Similarly, ethical and religious and political ideas have triggered such effects. That is, they have produced more than they were taken to contain in any dated version or interpretation of them, as have the not-so-exemplary lives of great men — for often the life of a great man may be all but exemplary in the ordinary sense. The point of emulating a great man is not merely to live as he lived but to create as he created — not to emulate his life in any other respect than to be able to achieve the kind of creativity, or the mode of activity, which he represents.

The purposes that such a model presents, the goals and ideals to which it summons commitment, are not simply "in it," as lessons to be learned or as raisins in a cake. They are read out of it by the interpretive and creative genius, the inventiveness of those who respond to it. The model thus generates creative action. How it does this, I think, has not been investigated and is not clearly known.

If one were to examine the theological and religious version of this sort of model, it would be instructive. We are told that "God is made great by belief," which we may choose to translate (after

264

the fashion of Ludwig Feuerbach) as meaning that "God's greatness is nothing but the greatness of the belief in God." We may paraphrase *this* paraphrase in our own context: "The greatness of the future is nothing but the greatness of our vision of the future." There is nothing "great" about the future. In a sense it doesn't have any character at all which we can ascertain, except in our present vision of it. The future may be very different from our present models of it. But it will not come about randomly. If it is a human future at all, if human actions have some part in shaping it, it will be different from the present models because different and alternative models have been created, each in its way coming to constitute the future in the ongoing process of "present" actions. There is no other place where real work is done, except in the present, and work without a model is brute work, not action at all in the sense of consciously purposed activity; it is not human action at all but at best a dehumanized and brute activity. What we should thus characterize as distinctively human action is that technique which is governed by *telos*, by conscious purpose; and a "model," in this broad sense, is the embodiment of that kind of action, that is, the embodiment of creative human purpose.

In this sense, the creative model is not simply one that exemplifies the creativity of whoever proposes or enacts it. "Creative" here should be taken to apply to a model that calls forth the creativity of men, releases their energies from the present, and serves to transform it radically.

The features of such a model are, then, that it is necessarily critical of the present, and not simply an envisioning of the future. Thus, such a model has to be both a vision and a creation of the future that is not simply "more of the same," or that simply represents the present at a later time. The future here has to be one that destroys the present, preserving only those elements of it which are future-now, those which represent radical innovation in the present.

There are therefore things that are *presently* "future," to use this paradoxical locution. Since they ought to be preserved, they are not "obsolescibles." There are things that are "past-now," which are "obsolescibles." Which to preserve and which to eliminate is a choice but not a choice that is made merely in theory.

It is a choice which has to be made in practice. But even this is a false division because the theoretical choice, if it is a real choice, is one that will terminate in an action of some sort, or is already the inception of an action of some sort. In this context, the broad sense in which I am using the term "model" is one involving such choices and actions, whether these choices or actions are embodied in some visible or tangible form or whether they are in the more fluid form that Mr. Ozbekhan discussed previously. Parenthetically, I should say that it struck me that there is a certain conformity between this conception of the model and Mr. Ozbekhan's analysis of so-called operational models, strategic ones and normative ones. He called them "plans," but I think we mean the same thing.

What I had intended to call *technical* models are what Ozbekhan calls operational and strategic ones. What I call an *ideal* model in the exemplary sense is the normative model — that is, what we take to be a proposive model of what ought to be. But beyond this, there is needed something like the last conception of model which I propose: a revolutionary model, which goes beyond the presentation of norms and which is creative and critical in the sense of a criticism of "oughts," a criticism of these norms themselves. Such a model may be embodied in a number of forms.

It has been mentioned here that revolutionary political parties may represent such a "model." I shall add that there are all sorts of revolutionary models in the world; some of them are political parties, some of them are works of art, some are environments; some of them are persons and lives lived.[1] Each of these presents here what I regard as a revolutionary proposal: not simply "This is how these specific things ought to be done," but "This is how one ought to approach the doing of things; this is the mode of operation one ought to adopt."

---

[1] It is striking that biography is perhaps one of the most revolutionary of the arts in this respect. How many world leaders in history have been molded, in their aims and modes of action (for better or worse), by biographical works such as Plutarch's *Lives* . . . ? This is an essential feature, too, of the creative models that history and literature present. A superficial and simplistic version of this view is to consider such works simply as didactic. This reduces the creative model to a trivial parable.

Because of the abstractness of this presentation, I ought to give some examples, which flow from our present experience. Perhaps one example of this extended sense of "model" would be this conference itself. It is a mode of action. Simply described, of course, it is a conference of people called for such and such a purpose. Also, it is a model in the sense of proposing some exemplar of how things ought to be done. Whether we accept this exemplary model or not is a matter of criticism and evaluation. But it proposes that this is how, in this particular case, one ought to go about talking about or inventing the future environment.

There are, clearly, alternative ways of going about this same task, and either one may propose, "Let's get the best man and let him decide and go ahead" or one may say, "After all, we are architects, and though it may be enlightening to hear what others have to say, they are not addressing themselves to 'our thing,' and their problems are not the same as ours." There are, thus, alternative ways in which this meeting could have been called or this purpose served. These are the alternative models. But *criticism* of the alternatives is something that goes beyond the actual modes of action involved in such alternatives. Rather it takes such alternatives as objects of criticism; that is, it is critical reflection on action or on alternative modes of action.

Professor Tillinghast's paper presented alternative models of work; that is, the "work" model was used to represent other things. Sex was presented under the "work" model. Leisure was presented under the "work" model. Here, then, is a particular way of envisioning these activities. In the peculiar case here, a model was presented as something to arouse our critical opposition, to reveal to us that when things are presented under this aspect, they are clearly not acceptable. That is a normative approach, somewhat akin to the art of caricature, which focuses on features and qualities of physiognomy that give striking insight into character and appearance.

There is one other homely example that I would like to take from the discussion following Fein's paper. It is interesting to me that architects talk about their "clients." Think for a moment about the professions that take clients (such as law and architecture). By contrast, medical practice takes "patients." Much is revealed in this difference. A patient is someone who is *passive*, upon whom an agent acts. The psychiatrist or clinical psychologist talks about his "patient" as a "client" sometimes, as in the phrase "client-centered therapy." What is the difference? A *client* presumably has something to say about what he wants or needs; a *patient* does not. Most doctors are upset by patients who act like clients, since, as everyone knows, "The doctor knows best." What I am suggesting is that these are *alternative* models *as modes of action*. Each entails some complex union of *telos* and technique, some distinctive projection of ends and choice of means, that we may represent abstractly in a conceptual model.

In all of these cases what I am proposing is that the model here is not simply our way of entertaining a hypothesis or of bringing things before our view in order to consider alternatives. This is rather too passive an account of the interaction of ideas and action. The model is rather a tentative commitment, already the initiation of an action. The function of a model is not simply to entertain an action but to undertake it. Or to put it differently, to entertain an action is, in this sense, already to undertake it in some degree.

The argument here is that models are more than abstract ideas. They are technological means for conceptual exploration leading to experimentation. But an experiment is something that has to be performed and not merely conceived to be useful. In this sense, models are experimental probes, essential parts of the human technique for confronting the future — but not as a passive encounter with something already formed. Rather, in that unique way in which human action is creative, such an encounter shapes the future. Thus, we may suggest that models constitute the distinctive technology of purpose.

DISCUSSION

TILLINGHAST: You said the future has destroyed the present, that other things are obsolete already. How do you react to these without having seen the future?

WARTOFSKY: Either you force the future to conform to your model of it, or you don't do anything about it.

TILLINGHAST: I thought you were against forcing the future on your model.

WARTOFSKY: What I am saying is we shouldn't try to force *more of the same*. Any model which is a model of what presently exists is not a telic model at all. It is simply a duplicate of what already exists. It has no normative content whatsoever. A model has to pick out certain things as being important relevant characteristics. If it is not selective, in terms of relevance, it is not a model. I can certainly re-create the present in the future, but that is an empty sense of "future." In the sense in which I am using the notion of model here, it entails that kind of future which is the outcome of combined *telos* and *technique*, which is an embodiment of some purpose. If the future-directed purpose is to retain the present — and one can find good arguments for this — then I would have to go along with the notion that such a future is simply more of the present. But I can't see that this option is serious. I can't even think of a period in history when this would have been true. But certainly even if it were so (supposing there were people who believed that the future is already here, that the millennium has arrived), there would always be others whose vision of the future required abolition of the present, or of specific features of it.

MAZLISH: Let me comment on the last point you made. Aren't you running roughshod with experimentation in human affairs, as distinct from experimentation in the natural sciences, when you talk about the proliferation of the former? You are talking about the ongoing system, and the problem is that you can do one thing, but you are not going to be able to go back and do the other. My first question is: Is there more to this than what you said?

My second question concerns your typology of models. Would you include models of the past, such as the Garden of Eden, which cannot be realized again? Where do you work this in?

WARTOFSKY: These are both good questions. The first one I will begin to answer, although I haven't thought it through fully: I don't like to sound apocalyptic about this kind of social experimentation. I believe that one should never *force* anyone to experiment, but one should permit any experiment that anyone wants to make. In this sense, one can say that the serious responsibility for undertaking the experiment is inherent in the precariousness of present human experience, in the depth of its present ills. This obliges us to undertake to shape a future different from the present.

MAZLISH: At what level are you talking? We could experiment with different ways of living, and with different types of families. Furthermore, what happens when you get into the large-scale social processes?

OZBEKHAN: Technology is beginning to permit us to make these experiments off-line; that is, through various types of simulation, social experiments are becoming more and more feasible.

MAZLISH: That is proliferation of experiment.

WARTOFSKY: Yes, with no risks.

TILLINGHAST: Did you say that any experiment ought to be done?

OZBEKHAN: As long as it is off-line and doesn't hurt anyone.

WARTOFSKY: That, of course, is a big qualification. Furthermore, unless we had a way of knowing that any experiment we allowed would end up with a *less* optimal solution, in the long run, than if we did not allow it, then our deciding not to allow it is a presumption.

TILLINGHAST: But the Nazi doctors tried a number of experiments.

WARTOFSKY: I wouldn't call these experiments. The doctors in the extermination camps did not do experiments. There was nothing they were trying to discover about the future. These were perversions of the experimental process. It is a real and a serious problem, and the question of costs in human lives of an experiment going wrong or haywire is very difficult. I think this is why Kant argued so hard for a criterion of morality independent of consequences of actions. He said that since we can't possibly know what all the consequences of any act are, our decision that an act is good can't depend on what its consequences are but has to depend on something else, namely, on whether it is in accordance with some imperative that any rational person could will to be obeyed by every other person.

In answer to your second question, I don't think that the Garden of Eden myth is the re-creation of a Paradise lost, of what once was and can't be again. Whatever the historical or anthropological sources of such myths may be, I think they are essentially interpretations of the future. I can't see them as meaningful in any other sense, except perhaps with respect to notions of lost innocence. It is interesting that in all the versions of the future, as in the versions of the lost past or of the Golden Age, you end up with a kind of unity between nature and man, and man and man, which is supposed to have existed ideally before Eve tempted Adam. Any sense in which such myths are meaningful as models, or as normative or ethical or psychological insights, interprets them as visions of the future. There may be a much more profound interpretation of them, of course. But I think this much is true of them. They are not simply symbolic representations of a historical past, or records of racial memory. There is one other sense in which I think this is interesting. Many of our models are models of the past, so they would not, at first glance, seem to be envisioning the future. But I think that, even here, conceiving or reconstructing the past in a certain way is already the expression of a belief in how things ought to be or ought not to be. Thus, the historical reconstruction of the characteristics of a past age — that is, a purportedly descriptive account of the past as far as we can reconstruct it — is normative, in the sense that any historical reconstruction is selective. Certain things are regarded as important by the person who does the reconstruction. So, in a sense, even such historical models mirror present interests. But it is precisely such present interests and their vectorial character that enter into models of the future.

JUNGK: I would like to ask you once more: Are there any places where such models are being built? I mentioned earlier in my presentation of "Mankind 2000" that, in Germany, I started a series of books devoted to the "building" of societal models. I would like to have other conferences and books grow out of them and to cooperate with similar enterprises in other countries, but I have not yet found any place where new models or new visions are actually being produced. If we really think seriously about model building, we might make a distinction between pure social imagination and applied social imagination. The first would concern itself with very "far out" visions — not something that has to be done right away. You have pure model building, pure visionary construction, so that you might also have practical model building derived from actual, and pressing, necessities.

The visionary or the prophet, who was a very important person in former ages, will somehow have to be brought back into our society and into our context of things; and he must not be regarded as a fool or as a useless dreamer. We certainly should have institutions where models of desirable futures can be built; then we should not only construct models answering pressing needs but go beyond that and try to embody in a future-oriented society the visionary tradition from which philosophy, the arts, and most of our creativity spring.

WARTOFSKY: I agree, but aren't we missing the fact that we have an enormous source of that kind of thing available to us already which we are not utilizing fully? If we can say that any model, whenever it is constructed, is a model of the future if it carries this kind of heuristic function with it, then we have an untapped source of such models in any number of areas of thought. Certainly this is true in philosophy. Thus, even Aristotle's and Plato's works contain models for the future (not simply in their time but now) in the sense that there is more in them than they could have foreseen. In this sense, these are creative models, as I described them in my paper.

I have argued in another context[2] that metaphysics is a heuristic for science, a source of models for science. I will also argue that in many contexts, there are things that we do not take to be models which function in this way, heuristically.

We spoke earlier of revolutionary political parties. There is much revolutionary activity in the world today which represents this kind of model building, but perhaps not in the specific theoretical sense of having formulated an ideology or plan, or anything of this sort. I think students in the university are creating models right and left, that is, experimenting with modes of action, proliferating them in a way that hasn't been characteristic of university life for a long time. In this extended sense of "model" there is this kind of model building going on all about us.

[2] "Metaphysics as Heuristic for Science," in R. S. Cohen and M. W. Wartofsky, eds., *Boston Studies in the Philosophy of Science*, Vol. III (New York: Humanities Press–Dordrecht: Reidel, 1967).

The need here is for conscious realization, utilization, and a readiness to face the risks of it. Now, the explicit articulation of these things in some systematic way is necessary. One doesn't just sit down to think up models, just as one doesn't simply *decide* to become a prophet. Furthermore, if there were a prophet who was not thought to be crazy or a dreamer by a large section of present society, then he would actually be a very ineffectual prophet, because his message wouldn't be at all revolutionary. He would be a "social worker" in the worst sense, and certainly not a prophet. (I am not against social workers; I am talking about them in a metaphorical way.)

OzBEKHAN: Several of the points you have made are now finding an operational description, especially in the strategic and operating planning area, by something I have called "causative anticipation" — the calculated anticipations that are causative of action. These are decision modes that a real plan, a futures-creative plan, ought to contain.

WARTOFSKY: I would like very much to see the material on that. There is a very subtle consideration of this (in *The Critique of Pure Reason,* of all places) in Kant's notion of one of the types of causality — the relation of community, or so-called reciprocal or functional causality.

JUNGK: I think you are right when you say that the prophet has to go against the grain of society, but the tremendous difficulty of the prophet nowadays is that he is not taken seriously by the intellectual community. In former ages there existed a number of people who were ready to see the prophet as a saint, even if they did not understand what he said. Today a prophet is almost automatically classified as a charlatan by his community. I wonder if this does not betray a certain attitude of the academic community that is directed against the radically new, against the unusual, against the future. Hasn't the elite become too narrow-minded, too fact-bound to accept or even welcome the prophet?

WARTOFSKY: In the case you describe, I would say he is not the right prophet for his time. I mean that he is not effective. He would have to be effective within *this* context, able to transform this present. He can't cry "foul" on the grounds that if he had existed in another age, he would have had a following. A prophet, by definition, is a prophet in his own time, and not simply a forecaster.

From the Floor: Mr. Wartofsky, I don't understand what you meant when you spoke of this conference as a model for the future. Would you clarify that for me?

WARTOFSKY: It is a model in the special sense I described, namely a model of the kind of thing one does when one wants to talk about inventing the future. The model itself becomes an instrument for *creating* the future environment in the very process as you begin organizing and talking about this, whether successfully or not. That is what I think I had in mind in the subtitle of my paper, "Models as Modes of Action."

Outline of a Pluralistic Theory of Knowledge and Action

PAUL K. FEYERABEND

HISTORICAL SKETCH

It is a commonplace — and a very ancient one — that man, when growing up, must put aside childish things and must adapt to reality. The dreams of his childhood, the aspirations of his youthful years, the many fanciful ways of looking at the world which made it such an interesting and mysterious place — all these must be abandoned if the aim is to achieve knowledge and a mastery of nature. The way to knowledge and to the conquest of nature consists in increasingly restricting the range of possible ideas until a close fit is established between behavior and thinking, on the one side, and "reality," on the other. The aim is reached as soon as a single point of view is established beyond doubt as the one correct picture of the world.

It is interesting to see how many different phases in the history of mankind are united by this commonplace idea. The initiation rites that in a primitive society accentuate the transition to manhood all have the same consequence: they make it almost impossible for the initiate ever again to think along lines essentially different from the ideology of the tribe. Plato, who was well aware of the psychological mechanisms creating a state of firm and unwavering belief, gives an extremely perceptive account of such rites and backs them by arguments to show the absolute truth of the story that *he* would have liked to be believed forever. This double machinery of psychological manipulation and philosophical argument was then developed to perfection by the church fathers. Never again was there to be such a deep understanding of human nature; and never again was this understanding used with such fatal effect for the physical and conceptual propagation of ideologies. The new philosophy of the sixteenth and seventeenth centuries differs from its ancestor in only two respects. The content of the doctrines defended differs from that of the preceding ideologies. And the psychological manipulation is left to each individual — it is not institutionalized. Otherwise, the situation is exactly the same: there is only one correct point of view; the correct philosophical method aims at proving its truth; and the correct psychological procedure aims at establishing unanimity as well as steadfastness in the pursuit of truth. There is no doubt at all that the founders of modern philosophy, Descartes and Bacon, were interested in the psychology of belief. Both develop a theory of idols and try to explain why man is so frequently deceived. Both devise methods for undeceiving him. And both recognize that the transition to the new philosophy involves perhaps a rather lengthy period of training that creates a mind capable of understanding the arguments and prepared to cling unwaveringly to their results.

The characteristic just mentioned applies even to the founders of modern science. Galileo especially recognizes the need to prepare the mind of the reader so that he will be able to understand the new astronomy and to remain loyal to it even in the face of difficulties. But while Bacon and Descartes are quite explicit about their enterprise and while they oppose common sense from the outset, Galileo uses parts of common sense and the psychological hold it has upon the individual to destroy the rest. Newton, who is quite different in this respect, restricts himself to experiment and philosophical argument; but his theories soon become the basis for new and institutionalized means of creating unanimity. This is how modern science, or "mature" science (Kuhn), comes into being. It is no exaggeration to say that it shares many properties with the primitive ideologies outlined earlier. There is, however, one important difference.

The basic doctrine of a closed society determines all the aspects of the life in this society. The arts, or those activities which we today characterize as artistic, have the function of either creating

276

or reinforcing the belief in the basic myth. Dances, burial cere-monies, statutes, sacred buildings — all these things are repeti-tions, in different media, of the basic myth. It is therefore possible, on the one hand, to give a rational explanation of their structure and of the particular rules that the artists use at their trade. On the other hand, there is not a single avenue left open to those who might want to think along different lines. Even dreams conform to the basic pattern. The restriction of the individual is complete.

It is different with the more "modern" manifestations of con-formity. While the modern theories of knowledge are still largely hostile to a proliferation of ideas and while contemporary philos-ophers and scientists (with an increasing number of exceptions, to be sure) regard it as their main task to delimit the number of alternative views, such a restriction is no longer demanded in the arts. We have here — side by side with more conservative theories — the principle that it is the task of the artist to express himself, and to follow up any idea, any emotion, however peculiar, that might strike his fancy. The dreams of childhood and the aspirations of youth are no longer pushed aside. One may retain them. But although externalized they remain dreams as they are confined to the private sphere of a single individual, or of a school. They are not allowed to develop in the face of resistance, and they do not contribute to the understanding of the material universe in which we live. The impression of mystery that they convey is no guide whatever in these matters. Is this all that can be expected from them? Or is it perhaps possible to ascribe to them a more substantial function? Is it possible to retain what one might call the freedom of artistic creation and yet to utilize it in the improvement of our knowledge? This is the question to which I want to address myself.

REASONS FOR HOPE

There are various reasons why one may hope that this question has an affirmative answer. First of all, let us remember that the development of animal species is the result of a process of prolif-eration that goes on even if the existing species happen to be well adapted to their surroundings. The limits of their ability and

the limits of their degree of adaptation are usually revealed only
by the succeeding forms. The criterion is the survival of the
variants in situations in which their predecessors fail. Many
thinkers have assumed that the same process of proliferation might
be useful also in the case of theories (ideologies or plans for the
anticipation or the formation of the future). They have pointed
out — and this brings me to the second hopeful point — that the
faults of the apparently most perfect theory can often be discovered only with the help of alternatives that, while retaining
and explaining its success, also explain why it must nevertheless
be abandoned. The most striking demonstration of this feature
of our knowledge is found in the courtroom procedure. Who does
not remember trials where the point of view of the prosecution
is supported by the evidence to an extent that makes doubt not
only impossible but simply irrational? And who does not remember his surprise at the way in which a clever and resourceful
counsel for the defense can develop an alternative interpretation
which first provides reasons for seeing the evidence differently
and then shows that the alternative is supported by the newly
arranged evidence as firmly as was the original view of the
prosecution? The starting point of such a procedure is always
an idea that is inconsistent with the theory to be criticized and
that is therefore initially incompatible with evidence of the most
convincing kind. The starting point is therefore what one might
call a foolish and absurd conjecture. But such a foolish and
absurd conjecture may make one look at the evidence in a new
and different light and may lead to the discovery of facts that
are fatal for the "well-established" position.

It is the glory of the judiciary system of most civilized countries
that this possibility is fully recognized and is made part of the
legal procedure: there must be counsel for the defense even in
the most "obvious" cases. He must be able to challenge not only
the legal aspects of the proceedings but any point, even if it is
made by the highest "authority" and by the most qualified
"expert." We also see how in many trials the assurance of the
expert turns out to be without foundation and that he may not
know what he is talking about. And, mind you, these faults are
uncovered, not by a still bigger expert, *but by a clever layman,* by

a lawyer who has taken the trouble to study the point in question for two or three weeks and who has the advantage of not being bound by the prejudices of some profession.

This now brings me to the final point. The restrictions that the guardians of knowledge — be they scientists or philosophers — want to impose upon us are usually defined by the latest fashion, by the most popular theory in their own field. They are defined by what some rather clever men have arrived at after long study and patient investigation. They merit serious attention. But these restrictions, this concentration upon a narrow domain of theories indicates also that the scientists have come to the end of their rope, that they can no longer think of any decisive objection (or of any decisive reason for defending an alternative) and that they have therefore, for the time being, agreed to accept a single point of view to the exclusion of everything else. Of course, the situation is hardly ever presented in that way. Instead of admitting that their ingenuity has given out and that they are no longer able to advance knowledge, scientists are usually in the habit of saying that they have finally arrived at the truth. But we, looking at the situation from the point of view of a lawyer dealing with an obstinate and conceited expert, cannot permit ourselves to be so easily impressed. A brief look at certain features of what some people are pleased to call the "scientific method" shows that this attitude is supported not only by general considerations, such as those just given, but also by a more detailed study.

ARGUMENTS FOR PROLIFERATION

It would be imprudent to give up a theory that either is inconsistent with observational results or suffers from internal difficulties. Theories can be developed and improved, and their relation to observation is also capable of modification. It took considerable time until the relation of the kinetic theory to the "fact" of irreversibility was properly understood, and research in this direction still proceeds. Moreover, it would be a complete surprise if it turned out that all the available experimental results support a certain theory, even if the theory were true. Different observers using different experimental equipment and different methods of interpretation introduce idiosyncrasies and errors of their own, and it takes a long time until all these differences are brought to a common denominator. Considerations like these make us accept a *principle of tenacity*, which suggests, first, that we select from a number of theories the one that has the most attractive features and that promises to lead to the most fruitful results; and, second, that we stick to this theory despite considerable difficulties.

After tenacity is accepted, a theory T can no longer be removed by discordant experiments. One might now be inclined to specify a limit of disagreement beyond which one is not prepared to go. But it is not easy to see how such a limit can be fixed in a non-arbitrary fashion. The most overwhelming difficulties have been overcome, and minor disturbances have proved fatal (just compare the initial difficulties of the heliocentric system with the initial attitude toward the experiment of Michelson and Morley). But it *is* rational to withdraw T if there exists another theory T' that accentuates the difficulties of T (and which is therefore inconsistent with T) while at the same time promising means for their removal and opening up new avenues of research. In this case the principle of tenacity itself urges us to remove T. Such a method of refutation, of course, works only if one is permitted to consider theories inconsistent with T: alternatives of T. The result is that a science that is prepared to develop its theories despite difficulties needs a *principle of proliferation* for the effective criticism of the tenaciously held theories.

So far, we have assumed that the facts endangering T are already available, and we have asked how T can be eliminated if one is prepared to retain it despite their existence. But the situation is frequently much more complex than that. There may exist facts that endanger T but that can be revealed with the help of alternatives only. Assume, for that purpose, that T entails C, that C' is what actually happens, that C', but not C, triggers a macroscopic process M that can be seen by all, and assume further that C and C' are indistinguishable not only because our measuring instruments are too crude but because the laws of nature prohibit the distinction by any physical means. In this case M refutes T, but we can never ascertain that this is so. Only

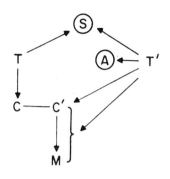

the Good Lord, who stands above all laws of nature and is not bound by them, is able to point out that T is refuted by M — unless the erring mortals are allowed to proliferate and to invent alternatives of T. For if one of these alternatives, say T', predicts C' and the connection between C' and M, and if it approximately repeats the successful predictions S of T and makes in addition some other predictions A, then we shall trust T' more than T and accept the assertion, following from it, that T has been refuted by M. In this case the alternative has not just accentuated an already existing difficulty; it has actually created it. In the light of this possibility, the use of alternatives is recommended even if the theory that stands in the center of attention should happen to be without blemish. The refutation of the phenomenological second law of thermodynamics is a case in point.[1]

There is another reason in favor of proliferation which is even more subtle and which has been put forth, quite recently, by Dr. Imre Lakatos.[2] This reason is concerned with what one might call the metaphysical components of observation.

Observational terms, as it has been frequently assumed, can be defined without reference to theories, simply by exhibiting the phenomena to which they refer. On the other hand, it was also pointed out that observations are always guided by more general ideas. Kant especially emphasized that experience, as conceived by scientists, contains theoretical elements and that observational reports lacking these elements are not admitted into the body of

[1] For a more detailed discussion, see Section vi of my "Problems of Empiricism" in Robert G. Colodny, ed., *Beyond the Edge of Certainty* (Englewood Cliffs, N.J.: Prentice-Hall, 1965).

[2] See I. Lakatos, "Criticism and the Methodology of Scientific Research Programmes," in Lakatos and Musgrave, eds., *Criticism and the Growth of Knowledge*, in press.

scientific knowledge. It is now generally agreed that a sense data language is useless for the purpose of science and that useful observation reports must go beyond what is immediately seen. However, the sense data position is still far from abandoned, as is revealed by the tendency to *minimize* the additional, hypothetical element. It is still believed that actual observational reports are hypothetical only to a very small degree.

It is not difficult to show that this assumption is erroneous. Every ordinary statement about medium-sized objects such as "this table is brown" or, to use more technical terms, every statement of what Rudolf Carnap has called the physical-thing-language contains the idea of observer independence (which entails, among other things, that a fast motion of the observer in the neighborhood of Sirius will leave tables unaffected). This idea is not only highly hypothetical but also metaphysical (as was already noted by Berkeley); it is metaphysical because it is not possible to specify an experimental result that would endanger it and that might force us to give it up. Ordinary observation statements, therefore, have metaphysical components.

Now Dr. Lakatos has shown that one can arrive at the same result in a different and much more interesting manner. Consider a theory T. According to Karl Popper, whose procedure most adequately reflects what is going on in the sciences, T is scientific only if it has potential falsifiers, that is, only if there exist observational statements S_i such that S_iT is a contradiction (we omit mentioning the conditions that must be imposed in order to eliminate trivial cases). Now in determining the truth value of the S_i, one usually refers to auxiliary theories T' (the test of Newton's celestial mechanics involves optical theory, theory of elasticity, physiology, chemistry, and so on). These auxiliary theories help us to test the S_i, and they also have an influence upon the terms of S_i. It is clear that the strength of the tests of T which are provided by the S_i will be the greater as the number of potential falsifiers of T' becomes greater. These potential falsifiers involve further auxiliary theories T'', and so on. But $T^i \neq T^k$ for any $i \neq k$ as circularity must be avoided. The result is that we are involved in an infinite regress unless we admit that there is some T^i without potential falsifiers. And as tests are carried out, this is not only a possibility but a fact of scientific procedure: every test involves metaphysical auxiliary assumptions.

A look at the history of science convinces one that this abstract scheme corresponds quite closely to reality. Thus some of Galileo's arguments against his opponents were based upon what was seen through the telescope. At the time in question the auxiliary theory involved, namely optics (physical and physiological), was nonexistent and a fortiori metaphysical. Similarly, cosmological hypotheses are often measured by their agreement or nonagreement with the red shift of distant galaxies interpreted as a Doppler effect. This interpretation is again without potential falsifiers. Both abstract considerations and historical inquiry teach us that many tests involve metaphysical assumptions.

Turning the argument around, we now realize that we can increase the strength of experimental refutations by replacing these metaphysical assumptions with scientific theories, that is, by again developing alternatives to the theories under test: decisive refutation is impossible without proliferation (this is one of the features which distinguish Popper's criterion of falsifiability from such anticipations as may be found in Peirce, Dubislav, and others).

To sum up, proliferation is required both in order to strengthen our tests and in order to bring to light refuting facts that would otherwise remain inaccessible. The progress of science is unthinkable without it.

OUTLINE OF A HUMANITARIAN SCIENCE

We can now answer the question we asked before: Is it possible to retain our childhood dreams, to develop them in a pleasing and fruitful fashion without losing touch with reality? The reply is clearly affirmative. Proliferation means that there is no need to suppress even the most outlandish product of the human brain, and science, far from giving comfort to the doctrinaire, will profit from such an activity and is unthinkable without it. Tenacity means that one is encouraged not just to follow one's inclinations but to develop them further, to raise them, with the help of criticism (which involves a comparison with other existing alternatives), to a higher level of articulation and thereby to raise oneself to a higher level of consciousness. The interplay between proliferation and tenacity also amounts to the continuation, on a new level, of the biological development of the species, and it may even increase the tendency for useful *biological* mutations. It may be the only possible means of preventing our species from stagnation. This I regard as the final and most important argument against the traditional theories of knowledge. Such theories are not only ill conceived and ill fitted to the task of conquering nature, but their defense is also incompatible with a humanitarian outlook.

Response from the Architects

Dean LAWRENCE B. ANDERSON: This conference has shown, I think, in looking into the future, that the design professions will have to prepare for a collaboration with their colleagues in the social sciences. And now we are going to initiate an assessment of what the impact of these ideas should be and what the implications should be in relation to the professional education of architects and planners.

One suggestion, which has already been made, was to introduce a course into the curriculum dealing with the sociology of the profession. This could be valuable, certainly. But most of us are aware that curricula tend to grow by such a process, of adding something here and something there, until any further possibility of venture on the part of the student is gone.

I suspect that somewhat more fundamental reorientation will be needed in order to take account of the factors we have been discussing. Our London observer, Cedric Price, will initiate the discussion.

INITIATION OF THE DISCUSSION

Mr. CEDRIC PRICE: In 1935 Professor Ritchie Calder wrote some articles in the *News Chronicle* about how the world would be in thirty years' time. In commenting on H. G. Wells and his capacity for prediction, he suggested that while Wells achieved some interesting predictions, he always forgot to remove his bicycle clips. Calder has, since then, suggested that the only man, in fact, who had any idea of what might possibly be the future was George

285

Orwell. He suggested Orwell because Orwell pointed out that the first change, which was essential, would be the change in language. There is no hiding the fact that language is continually changing, profession by profession and nation by nation.

And I have been interested in hearing new words, which I shall probably misuse. But the title of the conference worries me a little. I find "Inventing the Future Environment" a little too capable of whiz-kid redefinition. And I think that if one could concern oneself more with the conscious design of the immediate future, then I would be happier in my tight professional way.

When I use the word "planners," I shall use it purely in the sense of physical planning related to architecture. Architects and planners are loath to look too far into the future because they are extremely frightened that they won't find themselves there.

They are second only to politicians in not concerning themselves with the future. Politicians, of course, would be extremely dangerous if they did. And in the discussions so far the extremely beneficial content for me, as a practitioner, has been the very avoidance of any prediction, any crystal gazing. It is the superficial utopian attitude that I find extremely dangerous. In fact, the avoidance of prediction for the future might, from the architectural planning point of view, be the very key issue for operation from now on.

I am not suggesting that fumbling expediency is the order of the day, but I am suggesting that one of our main tools is calculated uncertainty. In fact, we are concerned not with negative "Utopia" but with "No-town," with an order that we establish for progress that doesn't have, and never wants, a particular goal in any physical terms.

Another interesting point is that the comments have been extremely national. Some of the issues we talked about, such as the difficulties of governmental procedure and decision making, have been literally quite foreign to me, but extremely interesting.

Allied to that has been, in a great number of cases, the concern with policy. Policy has been directed toward the question of ghetto slums and the Negro poor and the white poor. Therefore, it has a kind of a national orientation. This type of consideration is vital to Western countries. But, of course, it does or should remind us that maintenance of peace is probably our prime planning aim. So we should also remember that most of the world is becoming poorer and is likely to continue to do so in the tragically short period that leads us to the year 2000.

At the moment the prediction of increasing world poverty and illiteracy has no particular solution attached to it. And there has been a rather frightening avoidance of the fact that in 1900 it was estimated that the accumulated knowledge of the world would double in fifty years' time. In 1955 this figure had been dropped to ten years, and it is calculated again that by 1975 the world store of retrievable knowledge would double every five years.

This is one of the major resources that we have over and above the natural resources that have been so well noted in relation to this country; and this resource of accumulated knowledge is at the moment not used to sufficient advantage as far as the poor are concerned, whether they are our poor, your poor, or collective world poor. These figures are ones on which architects and planners should base some of their attitudes as to just what their task is, and this attempt will not have any beneficial end effect until the attitude toward architects and planners is basically altered by architects and planners — never mind the client. In *The Oxford English Dictionary* one of the definitions of "client" is someone who comes to you in a state of distress. While clothes, motorcars, forms of government, and wives are increasingly becoming objects of limited periods of predilection, we are still prepared to accept buildings and towns, not for the benefit of the user or for us, but for posterity; and we live in New York or London in spite of the buildings, not because of them. If, in fact, the generative force of architecture should be calculated change, then the question of planned obsolescence employed in the artifactual act is primary to what I am suggesting. Therefore, I am convinced that the valid social life of the activity that one is asked to shelter or encourage is the governing factor of whatever is produced; and that need not always be a building. It might be a free telephone service, in preference to a community center. Again in the architectural profession and certainly for those who use the architectural profession, there seems to be necessity for a redefinition of terms. Too often words such as "town center," "house," and "window" are unquestioned, and those preconceptions too often result in form before any particular questioning has been made of the relevant use. This is even more unhealthy when it is related to the conglomeration of artifacts such as a town.

No one now needs to see City Hall. Few vote for its occupants. So I would suggest that the profession has to do a lot of leapfrogging because if, in fact, we have anything to offer, it is to avoid the rate of progression of development that we are at the moment achieving through our own concern in looking over our shoulder. That is, there is too much step-by-step progression. And when this is, in fact, offered as a solution to emergent nations, then our negligence becomes criminal.

What I am suggesting is that when the increasing invisible servicing now available in the advanced technological countries (and soon to be available elsewhere) becomes totally independent of position, then the importance attached to the actual location of any activity disappears, and one is enabled to imbalance the development.

Let us assume a town is not a balanced community or even a balanced activity. In fact, as has been pointed out, to a large extent the nature of community and society has no important relation to the built environment. The physical requirements of society can be increasingly uneven both in their disposition and in their content.

With reference to Ozbekhan's paper I suggest that the word "must" must replace "ought" and must come before the word "can." In "ought" I find an implication of moral blackmail. Bad architectural planning is the result of bad architects and planners, not bad clients. The "can" is thus at fault, not the "ought." However, society in general must make far more demands on architects and planners and not be so content with feeble and totally irrelevant efforts of image making and mood creating. It is encouraging in a way that in this country only 10 per cent of your built environment is controlled by architects. In the United Kingdom, we control a larger portion. Finally, I must come back to that loaded question, the question of beauty related to artifactual remains. It does not concern me that the human delight in visual imagery has moved from the Acropolis to Cape Kennedy via

Detroit — architects have still to increase the range of human activities by artifactual means.

GENERAL DISCUSSION

DUHL: One of the most interesting things that should take place on the last day of a conference is the attempted synthesis of many separate and apparently disconnected thoughts. I was interested that you [Price] began by talking about some of the most important issues — language and communication — because I have a sneaking suspicion that we are not at the point where we have really communicated and we can really synthesize.

The attempt to talk about the training of an architect demands that we find out what objective we are trying to reach with this training at this particular moment.

All the professions are struggling with the concept of whether they should change their whole self-concept and identity and how they should link up their own specialized activities with people from a host of other fields. I think the critical issue here is that it is impossible to plan any kind of future as a separate profession. It is required of all of us to join forces and make a kind of synthesis.

One of the important themes that has been discussed here is the primacy of goal determination, and what we ought to be doing. So I think that the critical aspect of training anybody, whether he is an architect or planner or psychiatrist or physician, is really what we ought to be doing in directing society and discussing the direction that society will take despite anything we actually do. We must also consider the alternatives — what we should try to do to divert inadvisable changes.

There are many ways to immerse oneself in developing this kind of thought. One way is to persuade people like ourselves, who have had varied experiences, to try to share experiences and opinions. Another is actually to take on a common project with people from other professions. I would like to recommend, as one of the highest-priority items for any kind of training program that we take on, as a laboratory, a *community*. Instead of looking at it in an architectural or physical planning way, let us take on

289

the real job — let's adopt a community and participate with the people who are really involved in that particular community for the development of the community of the future.

Such a project would mean the deep involvement and services of the sort that no profession has had as part of its training. It means involvement in politics in the questions we have been discussing, and it would involve confrontation of the poor by the professions and the interaction of a pluralistic society. I think we must become aware that some of the things we have been talking about (and this is where I disagree with you) are not American at all and not nationalistic but rather world-wide phenomena. There are the great changes occurring as a result of fantastically rapid communication. The great amount and scope of communication are forcing everybody — institutions, cities, communities, and governments — to deal with the problem of identity, of who and what they are and what they want to be. All this requires a model; the models that have been discussed here are models that are not usual in either architecture or other professional fields. They are either systems models or ecological models.

I think we have to be conversant not only with the word but also with the cold notion of *process*. We must become involved with that which is not static but ever changing, so ever changing that, as each second passes, the whole world is altered. With this as a background, I think what we do with physical aspects is entirely different than when time has a very different meaning.

Therefore, I suggest that in training there be an involvement and participation in community. I propose that the concept of change and change in organizations and institutions be central to the kind of planning we ought to learn about. I also suggest, as I did at the opening session, that there are two parts of training to be considered. One part is very specific. A psychiatrist has to be a psychiatrist, and an architect has to be an architect, and both should know their respective skills very well. The other part is that we have to know something about the questions of policy, of interchange and interaction, and of all that we have been discussing. The critical question is going to be the linkage of these two parts. It seems to me that this is the challenge for any university today.

Finally, I think we have said something here which is very important, which I don't think any profession has fully realized. Where in the past George Bernard Shaw could be right in stating that every profession is a conspiracy against the laity, right now the laity will no longer let us conspire. Today they demand deep involvement in the way in which every profession is going to practice. This means that from the very moment we start working in our profession, we are going to have to become deeply immersed, deeply conscious of consumer confrontation about our every operation.

I suggest that our ivory towers of training have disconnected us from this confrontation. The best way to begin psychiatric training might very well be to put the young psychiatrist in a psychiatric ward or in a family to see what life is really like before he starts treating patients. Training cannot be achieved just by immersion in a lovely house like Endicott, but it can by immersion in the real world. The real world is not just slums and poverty but the politics of Congress, the politics of City Hall, and the interchange on a political and social and professional level.

If I were to leave you with one thought, it would probably be that of change, of process, and of time. These are really the most critical words in any kind of training program that you are going to develop.

DAVIDOFF: I agree with what Leonard Duhl has said. It is a very interesting statement, but I don't think it goes quite far enough. I shall return to my politicking. We have all spoken of "change" and "great change" and "tremendous technological advance"; but there is constancy in the world too. The social justice of the world is the same as it has always been; it hasn't improved greatly over time. If we shy away from substantive issues, we shall be preserving what has always been. What we are preserving is a highly corrupt society — corrupt because it permits very few to share what Endicott House has, and it deprives far more of any opportunity at all. That has to be the primary focus of our concern with change.

PRICE: This is, in fact, why I was implying a certain amount of criticism as to the national content of what has been said. There seemed to be an inconsistency in the rate of change required in general compared with the rate of change that was being suggested in this country. In fact, I was extremely concerned because it appeared that to some extent you [Duhl] were quite happy to operate within the system as found if, in fact, the system could be sufficiently manipulated in a sort of expanding beneficial way.

I found that some of your suggestions were extremely conservative so far as global relevance goes, and this is instanced by your just stating the need to be involved in various arenas, including political arenas. The quantitative difference in the results of such involvement in one part of the world and another — in this country, say, compared to India — is so great that there is, in fact, a qualitative difference in the end.

DUHL: I am very pleased to be called a conservative because this is not very usual. What I think is essential, and may have given you the idea of conservatism, is that if you are concerned with the process of change, you must start with what you can do with already established systems, values, attitudes, and so on, and gradually change them.

What Paul Davidoff is talking about here, despite the fact that it may sound as though he is defending a position of people who want a radical change, is that just to ask for radical change and expect it overnight is impossible. What you can and do expect are small gains and gradual progress. If you can use my analogy, and the analogy of Professor Fein earlier, the process of change in the therapeutic situation has to be a slow evolutionary process. Similarly, the process of involving people in the very values that Davidoff was talking about is a gradual one. We have to speed it up, but we can't start with something that is too far in the future.

PRICE: I agree with that. What I was saying was that there is a differential between rates of change, and what concerns me is the social do-goodery, say, of the Peace Corps or the architectural Schweitzer movement. Colleagues show me with delight how they construct Fuller domes in Africa out of the bamboos and twine. This, I think, is an extremely overcontented liberal attitude on our part toward emergent countries, and eventually anything good we have given them will be thrown out with the bath water.

DUHL: I think you are making a false point. You can't give things to people. You really have to involve people in getting what they want, whether they are underdeveloped countries or developed countries.

PRICE: This is where we might disagree. I feel that a certain amount of leapfrogging must be done, and this is where I am doubtful about your proposal for architectural education in physical terms, although you didn't necessarily mean it only in physical terms. You talk about being involved in the community and its problems and understanding its demands. Possibly because architectural planning is so far behind the disciplines that have been described in the last two days — and I doubt that you realize this — I claim that it must leapfrog.

When architects think of getting into an area and involving themselves with the people, they take things too literally. Because it is easier to record and delineate the obvious problems in a step-by-step way, these are very often the problems that are dealt with, and ill-defined desires to change or move are ignored. Thus I consider your suggestion slightly folksy in an architectural context.

DAVIDOFF: I think Leonard Duhl is correct in predicting that the change will come slowly. I don't think there is any question about that. But the urgency of the commitment is quite a different matter.

Dean ANDERSON: It seems to me that although there are complaints that we don't build for the future in the sense that the cathedrals were built, still, as we build better, the buildings last longer. Moreover, it takes longer to design and build, and industrialization requires that all decisions be made earlier in the process than in the old days. So, in this sense, there is a greater inertia about the process of getting things made and changed than before.

BAUER: I think that some of us will want to address ourselves to that: What can be changed as we go along, and how much planning ahead can we do as we look at the time perspective involved?

FRIEDEN: I don't think the process of adaptation has received enough study. Some elements of it are included in planning education. There is a body of knowledge that concerns such things as the movement of people through the city and the way in which physical structures are adapted. And if you look at any old part of an American city, you will see many examples of adaptation. I think we ought to know more of what has been done and what is happening now in the cities. We have a home repair and renovation industry that absorbs something like seven billion dollars a year. A considerable amount of money is also spent for change at the neighborhood level, for public facilities, and for schools. And I think we are missing out on a great deal by not incorporating what is already known.

MYER: Our great problem is that we can't test what life and the environment ought to be, because there are so many variables. For now, the best we can do is work with the wholes, build or find full-scale models, observe people living in them all at once, and then change and try another.

I don't yet know enough about simulation techniques of the computer to be convinced that they really work; I still have a suspicion that we will need to watch the organism in process in a number of alternative full-scale situations. In part, I think Bernie Frieden was saying that there are a large number of existing natural models that we could watch, but nobody is watching at all. If you go about, for example, attempting to develop criteria for the design of housing right now, you find that there is little information that can be gained from any source. Nobody has watched and reported the existing conditions.

Little work has been done at the microsociological scale, without which we are hamstrung. There is beginning to be some input about special groups that are in particular need now, like the aged. Also there begins to be some material on the poor. But you can't find anything, for example, about the bachelor male with a normal income or about the problems of the husband and wife and children living in their isolated suburban house and the kind of emotional and cultural thinness of their life.

It interests me that this conference has spent very little time discussing the center of gravity of our culture and has been concerned with poverty and the peripheral estranged minorities. This is fine, but there is a problem with the heart of our society too. And it interests me that we should not tackle that and not heed it because all of our attention is focused on some extreme condition like poverty. As I mentioned before, in many ways our life in this country is emotionally thin. It is, of course, a function of a number of things. There is little adult life for the male who is raising children because either he has to work or he has to help his wife, who is desperately behind by the end of the day, because machines don't do the same things that the nursemaid did. We are anxious, tense, and without real freedom in our affluence; we have to move around constantly in this group of two grownups and a bunch of kids.

Part of the problem here is that there are no models. Nobody is talking about the holistic characteristic of our life or suggesting models that would be attractive to us. In our literature we have a great deal of criticism and commentary about our life, but usually it is analytic, tending to break down the whole so we can be aware of it, perhaps, but it is not a whole model that is suggested.

CAZES: What you have just said impels me to ask you and all the architects here for information about the impact — if any — made by the pioneering work by the Goodman brothers, *Communitas*,[1] which tried to bring together in an interesting fashion economic values and town and city planning. Has it had any influence, or was it a one-shot essay? I ask because what you have just been saying about a holistic view of existence was fundamental to this very original book.

MYERS: Yes, that is true. It was quite a while ago. As the only study, we have a rather meager national effort in this field. Furthermore, I think it tended to be somewhat opaque and mystical for many American readers.

FLEISHER: Professor Myer complains that there is no holistic view of the world, and he is perfectly right. And the reason is that it is too difficult. I suggest, Dean Anderson, that we have gone as far as we can possibly go in this direction. We have heard the lists of relevancies these people have made, and it was already too large after the first day. What we ought to do is to cut down the list and see what part of it is really workable and what the priorities are. I think the priorities to a large extent must be developed

---

[1] Paul and Percival Goodman, *Communitas* (2nd ed. rev., New York: Vintage, 1960).

from what you can do right now, and not from what is possible to do ten years or fifty years from now. Therefore, the present circumstances are very important.

DUHL: My immediate response is that everything becomes everything else and that any one thing you do really has to involve all sorts of other things. You can't think of a building any more in only physical terms. You have to talk about it in social terms and in terms of meaning to people, and so on.

May I give you just one example from my own profession? In creating a community mental health center, if one started with the notion that it was a "psychiatric center," in the usual sense, and the architect had come in and said, "I will therefore design offices, waiting rooms, certain kinds of hospital facilities, and so on," he probably would have created mental health centers as they existed in the past. However, in the example I am citing the planner was very aware that today's mental health program is interrelated with other agencies and other dynamics, and he came up with a mental health center as an integrated part of the society.

FLEISHER: I think this is exactly what the architect has been doing on one scale or another all along. The contribution that you can make is to suggest that certain considerations have been omitted in the past as, for example, in designing mental health centers. And that is a valuable suggestion. But merely to increase the number of things the architect must take into account without either contact or any limit as to what he can manipulate at one time, I think, is trivial.

What you want is the holistic view. The holistic view is a mistake not because it's wrong but because it's not possible to implement. You ought to be concerned with intelligent ways of limiting yourself.

PRICE: In the field of architectural planning, architects should concern themselves with trying to make order out of calculated uncertainty.

And Dean Anderson's point with regard to the time factors involved in erecting some buildings means that architects must be very careful before they recommend a large permanent building or a large permanent city. The situation is more critical now.

MILLON: The major problem with the forms we have left around

and with which we have to cope is that they reflect a social structure that is no longer applicable. This is where the friction is
occurring. There is no reason why architects before us should
have understood our requirements. The inability of their buildings to adapt to change has put us in this bind, and that is why
those buildings no longer reflect our social needs or our social
structure.

Now, if the buildings that house other than planned activities
have a capacity to respond to change, then they are always going
to reflect the nature of the social structure. Indeed, that is the
only way that the building can be functionally important in terms
of enhancing the quality of life lived in it. Otherwise, its inflexi-
bility makes the process of change more difficult.

DYCKMAN: Certain insights that we were offered earlier have
been surprisingly dropped. I have the uncomfortable feeling that
the speculation about change has gone on here without taking
off the bicycle clips. It's very interesting that the discussion of
change is all in terms of the life of a building. I am impressed that
in the architectural field the attention is focused so much on this
product, this outcome of the activity, and so little on the character
of the people doing it. To me the most interesting speculation is
what will happen to the architect himself in this process, how the
profession will change, and how the education of the architect
will change. It's marvelous to think that we will always be calling
the tunes, but if buildings are to become such transitory things,
why would we need to have such an investment in architecture?

PRICE: Your question clearly relates to what I believe is the
changing role of the architect, which is probably, if not a reduced
role, a far more diverse one.

If you consider the variable room, this in fact provides flexibility
only within one unit. The architect's concern now, I suggest, is
that the sort of flexibility provided by physical units has largely
been taken out of his hands. The capacity for mobility of family
units is an example. In the case of a private house, demands by a
client for immense flexibility in the event that his children live
differently from him are quite unnecessary because the children
would move out long before they would move a wall.

If the buildings that contain inbuilt flexibility are in themselves permanent, then their grouping, which we might call a town or a suburb, has a disciplining factor and permanence that in many instances acts in an adverse way almost through the omission of consideration by the architects and the planner.

HURST: Jack Dyckman has put a question to us that deserves response. Those of us who have some responsibility for education are going to see the profession leap, crawl, or be dragged into the future in terms of its own competence and contribution. I think we might discuss the question of how we are going to prepare students in terms of some very significant things that have been said and questions that have been raised.

I would like to make four suggestions. The first one has to do with the question of *distribution of the architect's services in our society*. Dr. Duhl put the question very clearly, as did others, in talking about normative values. We have to look at the profession as one which has grown up serving a very limited segment of society. Today we have been challenged to change that situation. The question is how. Who pays for the services in this kind of context?

In our city, the Watts riots have raised this question. After the riots we saw the architects move in, often in consort with city-planning agencies to try to do something in the area. As a result, the question of social responsibility has been brought before the profession.

My second point concerns the question of *separateness and wholeness*. I believe that we have to look at the profession of architecture to some extent as still separate from planning, although we have often tended to talk about them together — and we want to see them act together. In the ultimate sense the architect has the unique responsibility in our society to deal with buildings as objects and to do this at the highest level of quality — call it art if you will — and in our concern to move toward the planner, toward the social sciences, and toward an expanding responsibility for social concerns, we can't give up that kind of unique responsibility.

Many of the proposals being made in education today appear extremely permissive regarding the extent to which they train people for this continuing responsibility to build and produce objects that are of a very high order of value.

298

However much respect we pay to social purposes and human functions, finally the architect has to materialize these things. This is his almost unique responsibility, one that is least shared with others. In doing this he has to produce objects, and these objects do indeed have a long-range value. However much we might construct a rationale for some obsolescence, the architects' creations have a relatively long-term function in our society, and I would hate to see that value discounted.

There is a kind of nihilism in current attitudes toward object making. Perhaps this is expressed in a description of a recent building in California by one of its architects, who called it a "a no-nonsense building." I think this is going too far in discounting instrinsic value in the object. While we need to be more responsive to social purpose and to democratic processes and pluralistic values, this act of object making does have to be authoritarian to a substantial degree. One has to face the alternative choices and make decisions that may be called authoritarian.

Third, there is the question of *our ability or inability to meet the social sciences* and to get from them or accomplish with them the kind of working relationships that we want. I am interested in how much dichotomy there has been in this conference between the hard, analytical, objective, respectably scientific approach, on the one hand, and what seems to be a softer, more normative, value-laden approach, on the other. This is a problem that we have to acknowledge; the architect has been trained to make very large conceptual leaps and oftentimes without a sufficient basis in rigorous analysis to make those leaps intelligently.

The problem is how to get the inputs from the hard-science fields and, particularly now, from the social science fields to allow the architect to conceptualize with more reliability, to move from intuitive judgments to more rational judgments. I think the *time-scale problem* compounds the difficulty. In California we see this dramatically demonstrated when new campuses are built in five years for very large numbers of students. The general dynamics of change is so great that anyone who is active is being forced constantly to make decisions and make them too rapidly.

An interesting ownership change has emerged, which Mr. Ozbekhan has included in his question concerning the liquidity of things today. Architecture is being produced as a *commodity* in our society today, and we are not really equipped to deal with this unfamiliar situation. Buildings are being produced for clients who are, in effect, buying and selling to other clients. These buildings are frequently designed before the site is selected, and they are turned over as soon as they are built. They have no permanent owner in the sense that someone uses and keeps them. This situation poses a great many questions as to how the architect approaches such a client.

We could discuss further the question of values that has been raised. I was particularly interested in the "can-ought" dichotomy, and I will ask if we ought not to acknowledge that there have been many architectural achievements in our history that seem to be in the "can" category. I think the Eiffel Tower and the Crystal Palace are examples — the ability to build was the thing to be demonstrated, not the fact this ought to serve any particular purpose. I suspect we will continue to give considerable value to this kind of thing, for there is need to work at the extreme limits of our technology even though we may not immediately see its relevance.

Fourth, in the value area, I am very anxious to reflect on the possible meaning of the suggestion that obsolescence was the real wave of the future, and also on the meaning of the problems of leisure in ethical terms. I wish we had more time to hear from philosophers and theologians in this session, because the problem of values is very largely in their hands. Perhaps our concerns here reflect a kind of equivocal status of these areas in our society today insofar as their institutionalization is concerned. By that I mean that the philosopher is too hidden in academic institutions and the theologian is too hidden in the orthodoxy of the church.

I think they should have more to say on this whole question of what we ought to be doing. I have had some interesting meetings and discussions with a theologian, Robert Lee, who was a professor at Union Seminary in New York and has written on leisure. The question of the *ethics of responsibility* is raised. To what extent do urbanization and impersonalization in our society contribute to a decline of responsibility?

Dean ANDERSON: This is a very thoughtful summary. Reflecting on your first point regarding the distribution of professional services, I am tempted to see a parallel with the legal profession. The means for simultaneous advocacy of opposing causes, including resolution at the hands of the jurist, seem to be contained within the one professional arena. Perhaps this suggests an approach to the question of pluralism that planning and architecture have not sufficiently developed.

DAVIDOFF: In the law schools during the last few years there has been tremendous concern about the nature of legal training for aid to the poor. The law is beginning to recognize that it hasn't been fulfilling its responsibilities, hasn't been distributing the services of well-trained lawyers throughout society. The planners and the doctors are also beginning to recognize this.

What kind of neighborhood architectural offices and services are available in Watts? Is it possible to establish some type of neighborhood architectural service to provide help for the design of a community center or for other things in which the architect can play a role?

GOODMAN: I think one of the real problems is the professional ethics of the architect. Very often he is not allowed to "peddle his wares" — to borrow Mr. Barnett's term. He is supposed to wait in his office until someone decides he should be given a project to design.

I think if we are going to argue, as I would, that the architect should have normative concerns, we have to readjust the role of the architect to fit that view. The architect should advertise the kinds of values that he would promote in society and the way he proposes to do this. His practice should be based more on problems with which he is concerned rather than left to the chance coincidence that a project may fit his value system.

BAUER: In response to the question of setting priorities, I would like to think of this as input into this meeting and into the architectural profession. I know there is much activity that won't be *referred* to when we set priorities. But one of the goals in selecting priority topics is that they enable you to deal with almost all the other issues involved. There are three inputs that I believe we need. First, what has obviously been implicit in what we have been saying is that the desirable future is to be conjured up by whatever means we may. Argument on that or on a range of desirable states would establish the basis for priorities in all other areas of our concern.

The second is a very wide-gauge look at the functions and role of the architect and planner in this society and the society of the future. This examination should be as broad as possible in terms of identifying the real functions to be served, the duties of the planner or architect, and what changes must be made.

And the third input is a systematic coverage and continuing empirical investigation of the types of activities that are alleged to occur within the structures that we build.

S. ANDERSON: I would like to say that a statement such as Dean Hurst's is very helpful in trying to pull together some of the ideas that have been presented in the conference. On the other hand, at least on two matters, he was reading another point of view into the conference; that is good, but then it shouldn't be taken as a summary.

For example, the question of the separateness of architecture and dealing with buildings as objects is something that most of the discussion here has tended to resist. Similarly, the comment about a need for authoritarianism is perhaps not intended to be as strong as it sounds; but even the inclination to accept rather than to question authoritarianism is different from the general tenor of the discussion.

I would like to summarize one small part and then raise a question about Duhl's statement. I suppose that much of the conference has been generated by the happenstance of the Princeton Project. But, in addition, much of the conference has been generated by a concern for the future, even if we decide to opt for more of the same thing. This is an implicit image of the future, too — we are saying that what exists is good enough or that more of it is either the same or better than the current state.

There is reason to question such acquiescence. So we have asked people to come and speak to us about the way they are trying to generate images of the future, whether in a general or a more particular sense. Out of this has come the recognition that there certainly can be no single image — that people coming from different areas, trained in different ways, and concerned with different things are going to want to work toward different images of the future. Consequently, it is reasonable that even those people who are clearest about what they would like to see would not try to build or make or do that which can be seen only with reference to their total image — an image that they recognize would never come to be.

In other words, process rather than image has indeed become the most important concern. It is the question of how to deal with such a situation that I had hoped some of the methodological papers would help to answer; but obviously it is a very complicated question to which we can expect no easy answers.

Both in the practical examples and in the philosophical discussions I think there have been some recurrent points. One of these is the need for the architect to learn about the social context in which he is working; another is to learn how to build for change — if not for all the buildings in our society, at least for a great many of them. This tends to put the architect in the position of having to get out and learn about some things that occur in what Duhl called the real world. It does seem to me that his suggestion of field work, of taking on projects that involve us with other disciplines and with people in society, is very well taken.

The only reservation that I have concerning his suggestion is that we are talking about university education — and the university is a very important part of the real world too. In fact, we know very well that much of what we call the real world today has taken that form because universities have made basic contributions to what has changed the so-called real world. So, while it may be that we ought to go out and involve ourselves in society, there is also a necessity for research and studies in the schools of architecture in order to discover not only the ecological patterns of society but also the patterns of the thoughts of intellectuals. We are dealing with situations from some level of *expertise,* and it won't do any good to try to deny that. Perhaps we can become more effective in a humble situation only if we are as aware as we can be of the possibilities before us.

MILLON: Architects and planners have become increasingly aware of their own place within the social structure. They are also more aware of some of the problems of the social environment. We have become, perhaps, oversensitive to our weaknesses and have not looked sharply enough at our preconceptions. We hold uncritically many middle-class values that cause us to respond in ways that are strange when examined from a somewhat different perspective.

We may take comfort in the fact that, as we have discovered at this conference, lack of perspective doesn't apply only to architects. We share it with members of other disciplines represented. If we have anything to say to them, it is that there seems also to be a very clear need, for example, on the part of all social planners, economists, and those involved in the planning process, to look at their assumptions (social and other) much more critically than in the past. Stan Anderson was implying this. I am stating it.

Summary: Planning for Fullness

STANFORD ANDERSON

Among Ian Jarvie's contributions was a taxonomy of futurists. This catalogue of orientations toward, or away from, the future not only was well discussed within a critical theory of knowledge but also proved to be a fine field guide to the participants in the conference.

However, despite the diversity of the participants, it became clear that most of those who were familiar with architecture and planning had been impressed by the recent political and social criticism of modern architectural and planning practice. There was a consensus that physical or formal order alone incorporates only a single dimension of the human environment. Dr. Leonard Duhl quoted George Bernard Shaw as saying that every profession is a conspiracy against the laity. Duhl went on to say that the laity will no longer permit this conspiracy; the professionals have been confronted by the consumers. A general agreement that the environment must provide for the individual and social well-being of an intensely diverse world led to much discussion of such concepts as pluralism, diversity, choice, opportunity, and distribution.

After a policy of planning for the fullness of life was embraced, there was little professional hand-wringing over the possibility that the architect had lost all demand for his formal *expertise*. It was not a question of the survival of the profession, but rather a question of how the area of *expertise* should be enlarged or changed as well as a question of the emerging role of professionals in society.

CHANGING *EXPERTISE*

It was Duhl once again who spoke of the architect and planner working within a highly complex ecological system in which there are many unexpected consequences of every action. The importance of those unexpected consequences shifts the emphasis from the product to the on-going process of which the product is only a part. Hasan Ozbekhan emphasized the process of planning that seeks to bring control to the societal processes. Planning is conceived to be a continuing process that refers to past states and future possibilities but always operates on a dynamic present.

It surely is fair to say that modern architecture has placed virtually the whole of its concern on the architectural product — on the physical, spatial, and visual experience without reference to those experiences which are extended in time. What is visually well organized may yet be so poorly organized as to be disruptive of process. The use of the word "environment," now popular in architectural circles, is a way of enlarging the traditional meaning of architecture and planning so as to include social, temporal, and other nonvisual, nonmaterial concerns. Once the well-formed human and social process is seen as the problem domain for architects as well as other professionals, it ceases to be obvious that a thing or a construction is the appropriate response for every need. A place of work may be replaced by a communications network, for example. Both Ozbekhan and Cedric Price spoke of the increasing evidence of the dematerialization or "liquefaction" of our environment.

Processes such as those just discussed suggest that the psychological disorientation caused by change is becoming less prevalent. Duhl claimed that the adolescent is the great predictor of the future and that one characteristic of today's adolescents is a decreasing concern with material things and with phenomena such as obsolescence. Gratification of needs or desires is less allied with possession than with availability of things — or even just with action. Bruce Mazlish's study suggested that a changing attitude toward change, and more techniques for dealing with change, could bring many processes under our control and thus into the range of individual or social choice.

Studies of demography by Herbert Moller and of resources by Harold Barnett were extremely optimistic for the United States. The implications of their studies for world patterns of resources and demographic conditions were also encouraging, though this was not stressed. Nature is not the limitation for either man himself or his material needs. This optimism is, of course, predicated on the assumption that man will choose wisely among the rapidly increasing opportunities before him.

POLICY AND DECISION IN AN OPEN, PLURALISTIC SITUATION

These very advantages of the possibility to constantly re-evaluate and alter processes and to choose among numerous alternatives pose very difficult problems. On the one hand, these are complex issues seeming to call for a highly developed *expertise*. On the other hand, the vastness of the possibilities and the freedom of choice strongly suggest both the desirability and the possibility of involving the community and each individual in the decision-making process.

The claim for the expert is that he is capable of setting out alternatives within his area of *expertise*. These alternatives can be on a policy level (goals, values) or on a technical level (means). In either case, the implications at the other level ought to be explored too. Since this does take place within a complex ecological situation, many competing proposals, representing different policies and professional orientations, will be brought out. Planning, according to Duhl, is largely a matter of comparing, judging, choosing, and initiating the implementation of certain of these proposals. Under the current situations such a planning process is most effectively carried out by what may be termed "non-institutionalized colleges." That is, experts and concerned people from many different fields (especially in the universities, research organizations, and in government) develop common concerns and informal means for confronting these issues. While there is no question about the existence of such invisible colleges and of the good that has come from some of them, this procedure does raise questions about the dictation of an elite — the establishment of what has been called a "meritocracy."

In contrast to this elitism — what Dr. Robert Jungk called "our expert-ridden society" — there was support for a truly operative participatory democracy. The views, the goals, and the proposals of the public should be discovered and implemented. Duhl and Paul Davidoff spoke for the distribution of decision making to the entire population, but perhaps Dr. Jungk was most ardent in this desire. The study of social indicators by Raymond Bauer suggested some methods for increasingly democratized decision procedures. However, despite such new methods and techniques and despite the claims for an organic sensibility that could be termed "the intelligence of democracy," there remained doubts about the adequacy of this near-populism. Would the best possible range of possibilities emerge without the active participation of experts? Similarly, would the most advantageous choice among alternatives be made without the critical judgment of experts? These questions arise relative to policy issues; they become even more obvious in terms of technical or other detailed decisions that nevertheless have wide implications.

PLURAL PLANNING, ADVOCACY, AND CRITICISM

While both the elitist and the populist poles emerged in the discussions, most attention was given to the ways in which the advantages and interests of all parts of society could be maximized. It seemed clear that a "forum" for the confrontation of competing values, policies, and proposals has to be created. Such a forum implies new institutions, the encouragement of reasoned criticism, the improvement of public debate, and the representation of currently unrepresented groups.

I. C. Jarvie opened the conference with a paper in which proposals of all kinds and from all sources were encouraged; the control over this proliferation of programs would result from intense criticism of the proposals. He termed this "critical utopianism." Davidoff acknowledged the emergence of "alternative planning" but pointed out limitations inherent in a situation where the alternatives are developed and criticized within the value structure of a single agency.

Several of the participants encouraged the exploration of "plural planning" in which many groups with varying degrees of *expertise* and immediate involvement would participate in policy determination. One of the techniques for making plural planning operative is "advocacy," which was represented most strongly by Davidoff and Robert Goodman. Traditionally, advocates are, of course, lawyers. "Advocacy planners" now exist in a number of American cities; there could be advocates drawn from other professions, including architecture. The advocate is, then, a professional who uses his *expertise* to represent the interests of a group in a forum of policy determination. In this way, advocacy is very effective in bridging the elitist-populist gap both intellectually and practically.

The advocacy program appears very promising, but it was also clear that both the theory and practice of advocacy need much study. Presently there is no satisfactory structure to the "forum of policy determination." For the moment, this can mean only some highly involved arena that includes legislative bodies, the governmental executive, administrative agencies, organized interest groups, the courts, the press, etc. The model for the theory and practice of advocacy is not clear. In addition to the lawyer, there is something to be learned from representational legislative bodies, labor negotiators, ombudsmen, psychotherapists, and others.

In many fields, especially in architecture, there is also the need to learn to present proposals in such a way that they are criticizable and then to learn from the criticism. This requires a study of the theory and pratice of the field and of the criticism of that field.

THE THEORY OF PLURALISM

The conference tended to emphasize the desirability of a society that is highly articulated socially, physically, and experientially. And the decisions that bring about that articulation should result from the pluralism of the decision-making process, not from an arbitrarily imposed diversity. Such an advocacy of pluralism raises a whole series of issues from the highest abstractions of epistemology to the techniques of statistical sampling.

The studies by Ozbekhan, Bauer, Wartofsky, and Feyerabend all suggest that there are means for handling these complex situations and, still further, that these conditions of diversity and proliferation are contributive to social development and well-being. Feyerabend's "Outline" sketches a theory that encompasses many of the issues of the conference.

Finally, I shall attempt to construct at least one interpretation of the conference. The meritocracy-democracy problem has been inflated. Democracy is more concerned with equal opportunity for full development of the individual than with identity of social condition. To repress diversity of talent and meaningful *expertise* would not be a contribution to pluralistic democracy. The resolution of divergent values, policies, and proposals within such a pluralistic democracy calls for the invention of new methods and institutions and for the constant study and adjustment of the processes that are thus initiated. The enlightenment which the experts may come to offer is that we can enjoy more freedom and use it better if we plan our organizations and processes well.

The planning theories suggested by this conference, and the environment that would emerge from their application, might well be highly articulated. However, the form-function relationship is not unique. Provision for the full diversity of people and actions does not imply equal complexity in either the planning theory or the resultant environment.

Postscript

In the spring 1967 issue of *Landscape,* Melvin Charney, a young Canadian architect, published an essay that seems appropriate for inclusion here. His essay makes reference to specific environmental projects as well as themes relevant to those of the Endicott House conference.

Charney does not present the illustrated works as *the* models or prototypes for a new urbanism. Nor should these works be understood to be the culmination or implication of problems discussed in this book.

The shared viewpoint that has led to the inclusion of Charney's essay is the following. In the best of the innovative environmental projects, the "hardware," as prominent as it may appear to be, is less important than the implicit changes of societal organization.

Cedric Price's "Thinkbelt" project for a dispersed and mobile university in the English Midlands may be taken as an example. "Thinkbelt" employs well-established technologies; such prominent aspects of the project as railroads, traveling cranes, and certain structural systems are nineteenth-century technological innovations.

If one looked at the hardware alone, it would appear that Price could be criticized as a futurist "who forgot to take off his bycicle clips." On the contrary, Price welcomes technological innovation; but the important point is that existing technology can be implemented in such a way as to effect complete institutional change. "Thinkbelt" would generate a new type of faculty and a student body from a new sector of the population. The interrelationships of work, study, and research, and of student and community would change. Neither the institution of higher learning nor its products would be as we now know them.

311

New patterns of organization are constantly generated within society; other patterns can be invented as in "Thinkbelt." Hardware will have its influence on these patterns; indeed, one of our pleasures is to recognize and feel the relationship of our physical surroundings to our activities. But coercive situations will arise, or opportunities will be missed, if there is not discussion and decision concerning alternative patterns of human activity.

Environmental Conjecture:
In the Jungle of the Grand Prediction*

MELVIN CHARNEY

These remarks are occasioned by the recent surfeit of plug-ins-ville architectures, of walking cities, computer cities, helicoidal and cubed infrastructures, *villes spatiales*, *villes ponts*, and *villes flottantes* — the superarchitectures predicting the inevitable "urblands" in which it is said we will all live — as well as by a letter from *Landscape* magazine asking how do we get there from here.

The prediction of the unknown was once the art of augury and divination; if it was considered to be scientific, it was based upon the recognition of regular patterns traced through history. The unknown is always worrisome, and when prediction is framed in apocalyptic stimuli and couched in parascientific phrases, it generates responsive chords.

At the beginning of this century, the impact of technology and the changing fabric of social institutions inspired visions of soaring social edifices rendered in a hard (metal) or soft (concrete) edge geometry, depending on the disposition of its designer. A vision of technology was used in the design of buildings and new urban centers—for example, the paratechnology of the "international style." The public responded to these excursions into the shape of things to come (from Sant'Elia to Flash Gordon) with enthusiasm; they were on their way to a new world of plenty, a technological rebirth into an urban Garden of Eden.

---

* Reprinted, with minor editorial changes, by permission from *Landscape*, Spring 1967, pp. 21–24, where it appeared as "Predictions for Design."

313

It is now a commonplace idea that planning has become imperative for our times, and what used to be for the most part a diverting excursion into the future is now part of the decision-making apparatus of the technologically advanced nations. Looking ahead has become an indispensable tool; every design of environmental equipment — a road or a school — involves a prognostication of future patterns. Complex and detailed anticipation is now needed in order to deal with current problems. As Nigel Calder, the editor of *The World in 1984*, has pointed out, we are getting them, but unfortunately in a disjointed way.[1] Planning groups in government, in industry, and in the universities are at work making "models" of possible worlds to come. These planning techniques involve the extrapolation of existing trends, the use of computers to organize and digest data, and what Daniel Bell has called "intellectual technology" — linear programming, simulation, and game theory.[2] Prediction, like other informally conceived spheres of human activity, has now assumed a formalized (i.e., scientific) role.

At the same time the optimism, the sense of wonder, and the fantasy are gone from prediction. Conclusions generally tend to be pessimistic. There is still a lingering fear of the future, which is coupled with what seems to be a latent paranoia. The probable scarcity of educated manpower, the decline in national intelligence, the control of mass behavior, and the smooth plastic intestines in which we shall all have to live — these predictions have conjured up a world of lost sensibilities. We have learned that science and technology can efficiently serve any master and any set of goals. The magnificent electronic computers that are used to simulate future patterns reason according to the determinate logic of their bit memories, and the present distortion in the indeterminate relationships between social and political man and machines is all too evident in the kind of sensibly insensible output that surrounds us, such as "kill, kill for peace." The Garden of Eden was found, furthermore, to have plastic flowers and

1 Nigel Calder, "Wells and the Future," *New Statesman*, September 23, 1966.

2 Daniel Bell, "The Future as Zeitgeist," *New Leader*, October 28, 1963.

polyvinylchloride grass (Astro-turf, in the trade) in a spongy polyurethane landscape.

George Lichtheim pointed out that of those who are trying to sketch future trends, even the most empiricist are obliged to make projections that are not simply enumerations of abstract possibilities.[3] In environmental design, prediction is not only a question of the extrapolation of existing trends and countertrends but also the demonstration of the environmental and symbolic potential inherent in the fantastic display of technologic capability current in other fields.

It is no less commonplace to say that the present development of aerospace and armament technologies is far ahead of the development of any of the environmental technologies. Several agencies in the United States responsible for the research and development of the aerospace program have, in anticipation of the post-Apollo lag, turned their systems know-how to environmental problems. In developing the weapons he biologically lacks, the human animal has invented, as a by-product, the processes that have made his life better. Computers and human engineering, important to current environmental design techniques, are World War II developments. We now know about defoliating sprays. How soon, then, will someone start to work on a re-foliating spray?

The environmental equipment that is being projected for the years to come must draw on present developments in armament and aerospace. It is, however, of less technical interest, less radical in its implications and less self-assured in its goals. So much is now technologically possible that one can, by simply making a photomontage of an aircraft carrier sitting in a wheatfield (as Hans Hollein has done) or by drawing people in on a photograph of a cross section of an air conditioning machine, predict the texture of a new place. We are so concerned with the total industrialization of our environment that any illustration of a machine to live in says something to which we are predisposed (Fig. 1).

---

[3] See George Lichtheim, "Idea of the Future," *Partisan Review*, Vol. 33, No. 3 (1966).

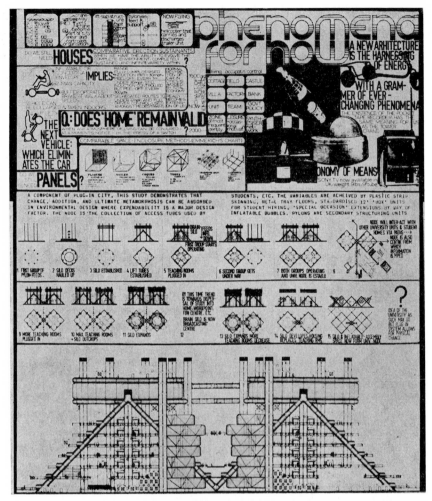

Figure 1   A typical slice of plug-in polemic; an assemblage of industrial, aerospace, and computer hardware and verbiage, designed in the image of a new technologic life style; from *Archigram*, No. 6.

Among the British experimental architects, *Archigram's* Warren Chalk claims the ack-ack forts in the Thames Estuary, dating from the early years of World War II, as the respectable ancestors of their plug-insville projects; Arthur Quarmby's plug-in plastic capsule dwelling tower can be seen as a stacked, polyester version of the trailer home; and Cedric Price's "Fun Palace" installation uses the physical planning of a steel mill–cum–department store of about 1930 (Fig. 2).

Predicted environmental hardware is also far less radical than many systems now operative. A common example, but one worth mentioning, is the system of mobile homes that can be plugged into service lines like family toasters — a system much more technically sophisticated than that of the conventional home-building industry. Thin lightweight metal and plastic capsules travel the highways behind a Ford "Galaxie" power unit like some tandem module in orbit. The figures for mobile homes are now well known: one out of every six single-family dwellings in the United States in 1965 was mobile. The attractions are low initial cost, low maintenance, and, since the mobile home is not classed as real estate, a tax-free existence. High-rise mobile home parks are being projected to provide docking facilities for these capsules close to the urban cores of several cities.[4] Here the dwelling capsules are driven up a ramp, backed into a concrete pigeonhole and plugged into a service core. Regardless of the slumlike "mobile ghettos" that do exist, and the fact that some of the mobile units make only one trip from the plant to their site because of road restrictions, the mobile homes show us a raw but operating model of predicted plug-insvilles.[5]

The current projects predicting the future environment, unlike the supercity architecture that was proposed earlier in this century, are generally uninterested in the ultimate shape of things. I suggest that their main interest lies in the possible new organizations of the physical environment that they imply. The plug-insvilles present the new human environment implied by technology,

[4] David F. Lyon, "High rise mobile home parks," *Trailer Life*, October 1964.

[5] See "The Evolving Strip," *Landscape*, Vol. 16, No. 1 (1966); and a recent study published by Cornell University (*New York Times*, April 11, 1967) that reports: "At their present rate of growth, mobile homes could dominate the low-cost housing market by 1970, despite the fact that the mobile homes have as yet to be recognized as houses by many government agencies. Contrary to popular conception, the mobile home owners stayed in one place about as long as other home owners do, and the largest group of dwellers are young, lower middle class families."

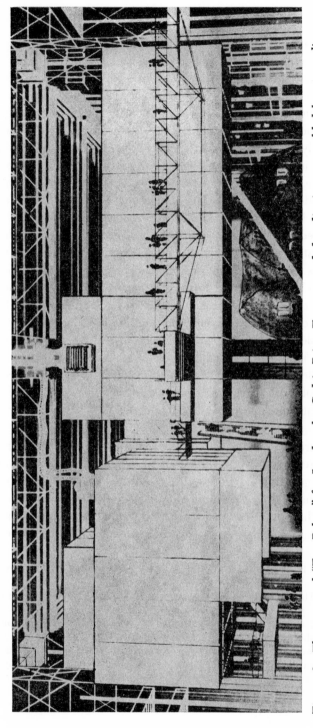

Figure 2 The proposed "Fun Palace" for London, by Cedric Price. Two suspended auditoriums assembled by a traveling gantry crane that could later take them apart. The system clearly distinguished the transient potential of a technological environmental machine.

which, in turn, predisposes the physical environment to further technological development. In this light, these projects stand between our present technological know-how and our inability to know what to do with the urban environment.

This gap can be illustrated by the attitude of a corporation which developed aerospace equipment — nose cones and thrust chambers of rocket units and space module shells. These elements are constructed out of filament-wound, fiber-glass-reinforced plastics, with the complex stress conditions of each component preprogrammed into the winding process. The same company that produced this hardware designed a house of the future: a typical suburban dwelling was recast in the filament-wound shells. Who needs filament-wound bungalows? What form of housing do we really need, and can it effectively use these stressed-skin components? Another large corporation — General Electric — has been looking for a site on which to build the first of several new cities with a population of 100,000. The company already makes much of the equipment needed to build and maintain a city, from nuclear power plants through heating and cooling equipment and electric cars down to toasters. Big-city building for large corporations has evidently become simply a method of creating markets for new products.

In the current environmental design establishment, this gap is seen as the distance between its method and its products and the environmental processes involved. We now know that change, adaptation, obsolescence, and renewal affect any physical plan, and we are learning that these characteristics are not simple mechanisms but relationships with varying rates and reversible conditions. The professional design worriers have argued for the last fifteen years that environmental products are unforeseeable results of a process. If one looks at the plan of any town or building in use for several years, these remarks become self-evident. The form of any segment of the physical human environment is not fixed in time but molded by life processes. Even though change has now become a fashionable word, the projects of several experimental architects, such as Yona Friedman and Cedric Price, are actually based on hard-core realities, far less fanciful than most current building and urban design (Fig. 3).

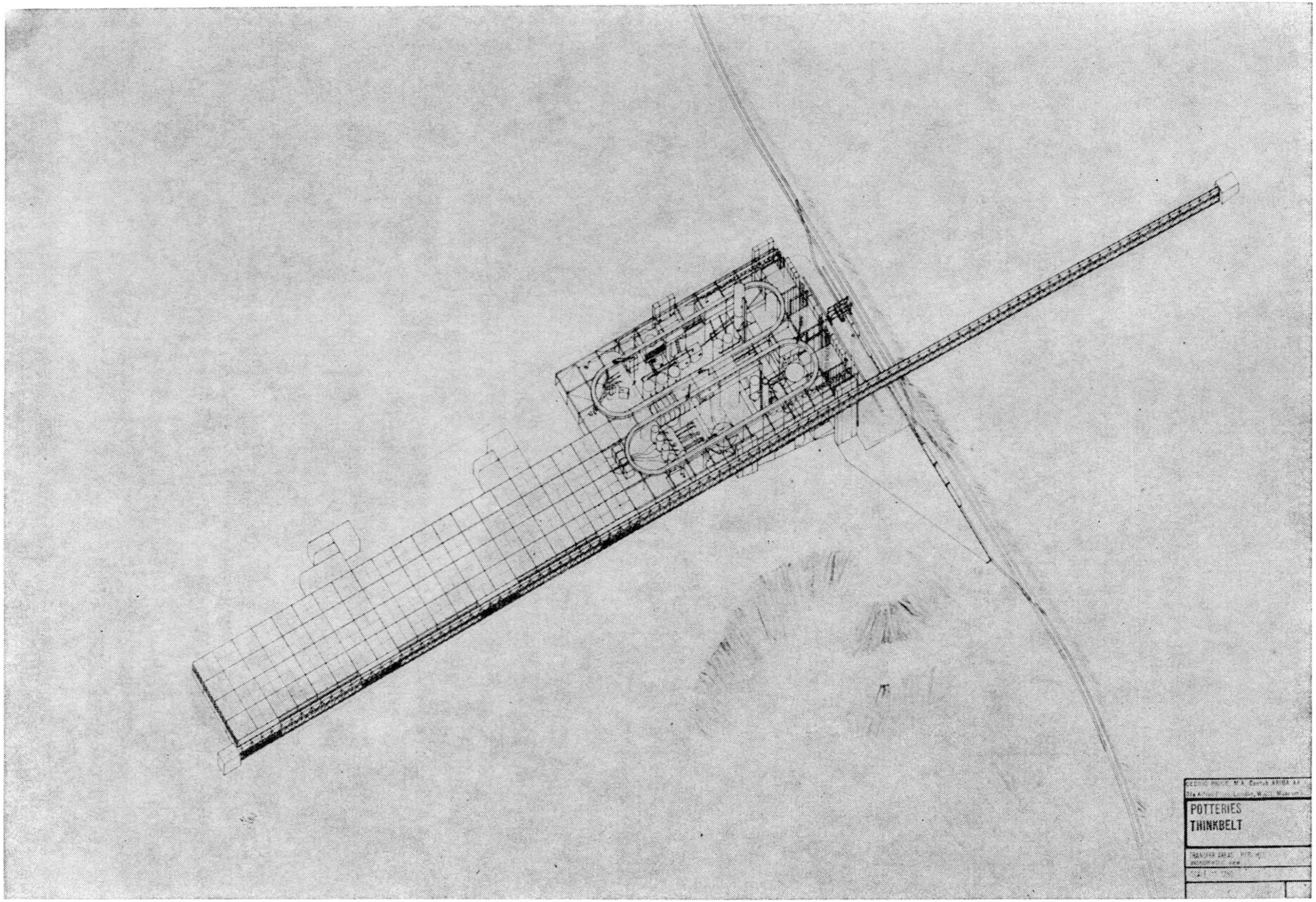

Figure 3 "Potteries Thinkbelt," by Cedric Price, a proposal for a university using a mobile and dispersed organization; from print of original drawing

Environmental design has now become technologically complex social hardware design. Engineered and electronically designed microenvironments have begun to appear in the form of quasi buildings such as bus shelters, telephone booths, and hamburger stands, fitted and molded to specific needs using mass-produced, interchangeable components. The promotion by the American Institute of Architects of "performance concept" — the operative feedback of materials and material systems performance data — and research in architecture indicate at least some involvement of the established design profession.

The opened rear end of an electronic computer (Fig. 4) can be used to illustrate the mechanical base of most current environmental projection: a firmly grounded superstructure carrying the

Figure 4   Monolithic Integrated Circuits in the RCA Spectra 70 Series Logic Boards; courtesy of RCA.

trunk lines into which are plugged clusters of thousands of specific, parasitic microcircuits.

The microenvironments (microcircuits) of most designs utilize, with disarming ease, pods of fiber-glass-reinforced plastics, expandable, inflatable, and disposable materials derived from current aerospace innovation.

At the scale of cluster and the supercluster of microenvironments we are no longer dealing with a strictly physical structure but with a process involving social and behavioral prediction. At this scale, the proposed future urban infrastructures are often brave visions of multidimensional networks containing many levels of response. However, urban organization involves extensive sequences of data and complex relationships, and the current masterminding of the complexities of this dimension result, all too often, in oversimplifications.

Since many of the experimental projects are at ease with technology and are models of new ways of organizing, operating, and redefining the objectives of urban structure, they can tell us more about current problems than much of the current planning work. These models suggest probable patterns with probability itself acting as a variable. This built-in hesitation is indeed the saving grace of most of this experimental work.

Modern technology is feared as a force that is arranging the world in such a way that it will be unnecessary to experience it in a personal manner. Norman Mailer sees in the contemporary world a totalitarian impulse that not only washes away distinctions but also looks for a style in buildings and in daily objects which diminishes one's sense of reality. If one important point is to be drawn from the work of Yona Friedman, the *Archigram* group, and Cedric Price, it is their involvement with a physical organization that acknowledges human action, and a new scale of individualization.[6] In their work there is a redefinition of distinctions.

These projects design situations where the inhabitants will be able to participate in the specific place making of the micro-

[6] See Warren Chalk, "Plug-in and After," in "Urbland 2000," edited by M. Charney, *Parallel*, No. 6 (1967).

environments. The British architect Cedric Price's "Fun Palace," which was prepared under the direction of Joan Littlewood, is an "area of probability" where spectators can come to interact with one another and with the machinery of the palace, an area capable of producing different spectacles. The "Potteries Thinkbelt," also by Cedric Price, is a university for 20,000 students, to be built around an existing rail and road network, conceived as a highly flexible physical plant that can be assembled and reconstituted as readily as a freight train. Universities should initiate progress and change rather than attempt to catch up with progress; in "Thinkbelt" the environmental hardware is geared to initiating change. Price's design is an important commentary on university planning in a country that needs to increase its facilities in a time when the process of education is changing; in "Thinkbelt" there is a commitment not to permanent buildings but only to a serviceable installation that can be easily fabricated out of current technology. If there is anyone in the environmental field who is clairvoyant today, it is the man who can tell us what is possible with existing technologies.

The engagement of the users of buildings in the active modification of the physical surroundings — as citizen architects — is evident in some current work. In many primary and secondary schools now under construction sliding walls are being installed; the internal spaces can be varied for different learning activities, and the teacher can thus generate a form of instant architecture. Place making becomes, in this way, an activity shared with the pupils and hence part of a learning process.

The design of adaptive equipment programmed to respond to varying conditions has been well advanced in the aerospace industry. The moon probes, for example, open out and telescope on contact with the lunar surface. In a recent report on its F-3 jets, General Dynamics explained that ". . . several pilots redesigned this airplane in flight. . . ." The parameters of operation within which this aircraft is effective can be varied in flight in response to specific conditions. An instant "architecture" is now being used by United States forces in Vietnam: "Flying Crane" helicopters carry surgical "pods" on medical missions near the battlefields (Fig. 5); the pod is an emergency clinic, and a cluster of pods can be used as a hospital. Inflated, nylon-vinyl envelopes are in use for lightweight, transportable, instant supply depot architecture.

In painting, sculpture, and theater, the passive spectator is also being transformed into an active participant. In the recent "Theater and Engineering" spectacle at the Armory in New York, Robert Rauschenberg's *Open Score* was so composed as to

Figure 5 A "flying crane" helicopter transporting a mobile "plug-in" hospital pod in Vietnam; from *Life* magazine, February 25, 1966.

be performed by the audience of five hundred; the crowd became a living canvas, so to speak. Art — from ladies' pottery classes to happenings — is, in many ways, returning to a form of communal psychodrama.

What I have tried to point out is that at best the experimental megastructure and the plug-insville architecture are not ready-

Figure 6   *This Must Be the Place*, by Roy Lichtenstein, 1965, lithograph; from collection of Melvin Charney.

325

made environments but simulations of the physical form of new processes of human organization which are evident both in the way people live and in the possibilities of technology. In terms of new technology this work seeks to redefine some of the fundamental values which have marked every form of human settlement.

It has been observed that the form of human settlement has changed and that we are moving into a postindustrial and post-capitalist era.[7] It is this new world in which most of these predictions operate. *They do not "use" technology, but are inherent technological evocations.* They speak of human organization at the nodes of transportation networks — the historic lifelines between settlements, the organization of parasitic microenvironments within servicing infrastructures, of new symbols, and of individual and communal responses that will structure the form of human settlement.

To ask how do we get there from here is unreasonable; it is a product-conditioned question that is seeking another and newer form of product — perhaps an instant futureville full of cosmoshapes (see Roy Lichtenstein's lithograph of 1965, *This Must Be the Place,* Fig. 6). Anonymous architecture has always been "there." Technically most of the visionary projects referred to are "there." They are analogues; and as analogues, they can yield new concepts and be used to isolate some of the new elements which the future will comprehend. They are exciting because they oppose processes that inhibit the full articulation of technology.

[7] For example, Lichtheim, *op. cit.*

Bibliography

A bibliography for the proceedings of a broad and exploratory conference is inevitably rather idiosyncratic. Without making claims for anything more, I hope that the following bibliography will aid the reader in initiating a further study of issues that have been raised. I am indebted to several of the conference participants for suggested titles.

FUTURE-ORIENTED WRITINGS

American Academy of Arts and Sciences. Special issue of *Daedalus*, "Utopia," Vol. XCIV (Spring 1965).

————. Commission on the Year 2000, Daniel Bell, Chairman. *Working Papers.* 5 vols. Privately circulated. Boston: AAAS, 1966–1967.

Baade, Fritz. *The Race to the Year 2000.* London: Cresset Press, 1963.

Barnett, Harold J., and Chandler Morse. *Scarcity and Growth.* Baltimore: Johns Hopkins Press, 1963 (paper, 1965).

Bauer, Hermann. *Kunst and Utopie.* Berlin: de Gruyter, 1965. See review by C. W. Westfall in *Society of Architectural Historians Journal*, Vol. XXVI (May 1967), pp. 155–158.

Bell, Daniel. "Twelve Modes of Prediction — a Preliminary Sorting of Approaches in the Social Sciences," *Daedalus*, Vol. XCIII (Summer 1964), pp. 845–880.

Brown, Harrison Scott. *The Challenge of Man's Future.* New York: Viking Press, 1954.

————, James Bonner, and John Weir. *The Next Hundred Years.* New York: Viking Press, 1957.

Calder, Nigel, ed. *The World in 1984.* 2 vols. London: Penguin, 1965.

Cazes, Bernard. "Group 1985," *The Spectator*, February 26, 1965, p. 259.

————. "French Planning," in Bert G. Hickman, ed., *Quantitative*

Planning of Economic Policy, pp. 179–211. Washington, D.C.: Brookings Institute, 1965.

Cazes, Bernard. "De l'invention de l'avenir," *Critique*, No. 215 (April 1965), pp. 358–371.

———. "Etudes de prospective," *Annales*, Juillet–Août 1966, pp. 947–953.

Center for the Study of Democratic Institutions. A section on "Possible Futures," *Center Diary*, No. 17 (March–April 1967), pp. 15–54.

Clarke, Arthur C. *Profiles of the Future*. New York: Harper and Row, 1963.

Dubos, René. *The Dreams of Reason: Science and Utopias*. New York and London: Columbia University Press, 1961.

Fourastié, J. *Les 40.000 heures*. Collection "Bilan de l'avenir." Paris: Gonthier-Laffont, 1965.

France. Direction de la Documentation. *Réflexions pour 1985*. Collection "Documents pour le Plan." Paris: Direction de la Documentation, 1964.

Fuller, R. Buckminster. *Education Automation*. Carbondale, Ill.: Southern Illinois University Press, 1964.

———, and John McHale, eds. *World Resources Inventory. World Design Science Decade 1965–1975*. (A series with six documents to date.) Carbondale, Ill.: Southern Illinois University, 1963—.

Gabor, Dennis. *Inventing the Future*. London: Secker and Warburg, 1963.

Gans, Herbert D. "Some Proposals for Government Policy in an Automating Society," *The Correspondent* (January–February 1964), pp. 75–82.

Gordon, T. J., and Olaf Helmer. *A Report on a Long-Range Forecasting Study*. Santa Monica, Calif.: Rand Corporation.

Gouschev, Sergei, and Mikhail Vassiliev. *Russian Science in the 21st Century*. New York: McGraw-Hill, 1960.

Jouvenel, Bertrand de, ed. *Futuribles: Studies in Conjecture*. Vol. 1, Geneva: Droz, 1963.

———. *L'Art de la Conjecture*. Monaco: Éditions du Rocher, 1964. See review by M. Cranston: *Encounter*, Vol. XXV (October 1965), pp. 51–52.

———. "Sur la stratégie prospective de l'économie sociale," *Analyse et Prévision*, October 1966, pp. 745–754.

Jungk, Robert. *Tomorrow Is Already Here*. New York: Simon and Schuster, 1954.

———, and H. J. Mundt. *Modelle für eine neue Welt*. 3 vols. Munich: K. Desch, 1964.

328

Kahn, Herman. "Alternative World Futures," Hudson Institute Paper, HI-342-B IV (April 1964).

Landsberg, Hans H. *Natural Resources for U.S. Growth*. Baltimore: Johns Hopkins Press, 1964.

———, Leonard L. Fischman, and Joseph L. Fisher. *Resources in America's Future*. Baltimore: Johns Hopkins Press, 1963.

Lewinsohn, Richard. *Science, Prophecy and Prediction*. Greenwich, Conn.: Fawcett, 1962.

Lilley, S. "Can Prediction Become a Science?" *Discovery*, November 1946, pp. 336–340.

Mannheim, Karl. *Ideology and Utopia*. New York: Harcourt, Brace, 1936.

Massé, P. "Prévision et prospective," *Prospective*, No. 4 (November 1959), pp. 91–120.

———. "L'esprit prospectif et l'application," *Prospective*, No. 10 (December 1962), pp. 17–38.

Medawar, P. B. *The Future of Man*. New York: Basic Books, 1959.

Meier, Richard L. *Science and Economic Development: New Patterns for Living*. 2nd ed. Cambridge, Mass.: M.I.T. Press, 1966.

Mudd, S., ed. *The Population Crisis and the Use of World Resources*. The Hague: Junk, 1964.

Mumford, Lewis. *The Story of Utopias*. New York: Viking Press, 1922.

New Republic, Staff of. *America Tomorrow: Creating the Great Society*. New York: Signet Books, 1965.

Ozbekhan, Hasan. "The Idea of a 'Look-Out' Institution." Mimeographed. Santa Monica, Calif.: System Development Corporation, March 1965.

———. *Technology and Man's Future*. Professional Paper SP-2494. Santa Monica, Calif.: System Development Corporation, May 27, 1966.

Ross, Harry. *Utopias Old and New*. London: Nicholson and Watson, 1938.

Ruyer, Raymond. *L'Utopie et les Utopies*. Paris: Presses Universitaires de France, 1950.

La Table Ronde, Editors of. "La Societé de demain," numéro spécial, *La Table Ronde*, No. 177 (October 1962).

Thomson, Sir George. *The Foreseeable Future*. Cambridge, England: Cambridge University Press, 1955.

Toffler, Alvin. "The Future as a Way of Life," *Horizon*, Vol. 7 (Summer 1965), pp. 108–115.

Vie et Travail en 1985. Colloquium at Château d'Olhain, 7 Juin 1964. Arras: Éditions du Cercle Noroit, 1965.

Wager, W. *The City of Man: Prophecies of a World Civilization in 20th Century Thought*. Boston: Houghton Mifflin, 1963.

Weisskopf, Walter A., and Raghavan N. Iyer. *Looking Forward: the*

Abundant Society. Santa Barbara, Calif.: Center for the Study of Democratic Institutions, 1966.

Wolstenholme, Gordon E. W., ed. *Man and His Future*. Ciba Foundation Symposium. London: J. and A. Churchill Ltd., 1963.

MAN AND MEN

Arendt, Hannah. *The Human Condition*. Chicago: University of Chicago Press, 1958.

Armytage, W. H. G. *The Rise of the Technocrats*. London: Routledge and Kegan Paul, 1965.

Bell, Daniel. *The End of Ideology; On the Exhaustion of Political Ideas in the Fifties*. Glencoe, Ill.: Free Press, 1960.

——. *The Post-Industrial Society*. In press.

Berelson, Bernard, ed. *Family Planning and Population Programs*. Chicago: University of Chicago Press, 1966.

Beshers, James M. *Urban Social Structure*. New York: Free Press of Glencoe, 1962.

Boulding, Kenneth E. *The Meaning of the Twentieth Century; the Great Transition*. 1st ed. New York: Harper and Row, 1964.

Center for the Study of Democratic Institutions. *Technology and Human Values*. Santa Barbara, Calif.: Center for the Study of Democratic Institutions, 1966.

Crozier, Michel. *Bureaucratic Phenomenon*. Chicago: University of Chicago Press, 1964.

Dobzhansky, Theodosius. *Mankind Evolving; the evolution of the human species*. New Haven, Conn.: Yale University Press, 1965.

Dubos, René Jules. *Man Adapting*. New Haven, Conn.: Yale University Press, 1965.

Ellul, Jacques. *The Technological Society*. New York: Knopf, 1964.

Fein, Leonard J., ed. *American Democracy: Essays on Image and Realities*. New York: Holt, Rinehart and Winston, 1964–1965.

Glazer, Nathan, and Daniel Patrick Moynihan. *Beyond the Melting Pot*. Cambridge, Mass.: M.I.T. Press, 1963.

Glazer, Nathan, and Davis McEntire, eds. *Studies in Housing and Minority Groups*. A special research report to the Commission on Race and Housing. Berkeley, Calif.: University of California Press, 1960.

Gotschalk, Dilman Walter. *Art and the Social Order*. 2nd ed., New York: Dover, 1962.

——. *Patterns of Good and Evil*. Urbana, Ill.: University of Illinois Press, 1963.

——. *Human Aims in Modern Perspective*. Yellow Springs, Ohio: Antioch Press, 1966.

Greep, R. O., ed. *Human Fertility and Population Problems.* Cambridge, Mass.: Schenkman, 1963.

Hall, Edward T. *The Hidden Dimension.* Garden City, N.Y.: Doubleday, 1966.

Heilbroner, Robert L. *The Great Ascent; the Struggle for Economic Development in Our Time.* New York and Evanston, Ill.: Harper and Row, 1962.

Hoffer, Erik. *The True Believer; Thoughts on the Nature of Mass Movements.* New York: Harper and Row, 1951.

————. *The Ordeal of Change.* New York: Harper and Row, 1963.

Hoggart, Richard. *The Uses of Literacy.* New York: Oxford University Press, 1957.

Kahler, Erich. *Man the Measure. A New Approach to History.* New York: George Braziller, 1956.

————. *The Tower and the Abyss. An Inquiry into the Transformation of the Individual.* New York: George Braziller, 1957.

————. *The Meaning of History.* New York: George Braziller, 1964.

Lichtman, Richard. *Toward Community: A Criticism of Contemporary Capitalism.* Santa Barbara, Calif.: Center for the Study of Democratic Institutions, 1966.

Lipset, Seymour M., and R. Bendix. *Social Mobility and Industrial Society.* Berkeley, Calif.: University of California Press, 1959.

Lipset, Seymour M., and Leo Lowenthal. *Culture and Social Character.* New York: Free Press of Glencoe, 1961.

McClelland, David C. *The Achieving Society.* Princeton, N.J.: Van Nostrand, 1961.

Marcuse, Herbert. *Eros and Civilization.* Boston: Beacon, 1966.

————. *One Dimensional Man.* Boston: Beacon, 1964.

————. *A Critique of Pure Tolerance.* Boston: Beacon, 1965.

Maslow, Abraham H., ed. *New Knowledge in Human Values.* New York: Harper and Row, 1959.

Michael, Donald H. *Cybernation: The Silent Conquest.* Santa Barbara, Calif.: Center for the Study of Democratic Institutions, 1962.

————. *Proposed Studies on the Implications of Peaceful Space Activities for Human Affairs.* Committee on Long-Range Studies of the National Aeronautics and Space Administration. Washington, D.C.: Brookings, 1961.

————. *The Next Generation.* New York: Random House, 1965.

Morison, Elting. *Men, Machines, and Modern Times.* Cambridge, Mass.: M.I.T. Press, 1966.

Piel, Gerard. *Consumers of Abundance.* Santa Barbara, Calif.: Center for the Study of Democratic Institutions, 1961.

Platt, John Rader, ed. *New Views of the Nature of Man.* Chicago, Ill.: University of Chicago Press, 1965.

————. *The Step to Man.* New York: Wiley, 1966.

President's Research Committee on Social Trends, Wesley Clair Mitchell, Chairman. *Recent Social Trends in the United States.* New York and London: McGraw-Hill, 1933. For summary see Greenan, J. T., *American Civilization Today.* New York: McGraw-Hill, 1934.

Reich, Charles A. "The New Property," *Yale Law Journal,* Vol. LXXIII, No. 5 (April 1964), pp. 733–787.

Riesman, David. *The Lonely Crowd.* New Haven, Conn.: Yale University Press, 1950.

————. *Abundance for What?* New York: Doubleday, 1964.

Simon, Herbert. *The Shape of Automation for Men and Management.* New York: Harper and Row, 1965.

Stover, Carl F., ed. *The Technological Order.* Detroit: Wayne State University, 1964.

Weisskopf, Walter. "Economic Growth and Human Well-Being," *Quarterly Review of Economics and Business,* Vol. IV (Summer 1964), pp. 17–29.

Young, Michael. *The Rise of Meritocracy.* London: Thames and Hudson, 1958.

Zelinsky, Wilbur. *A Prologue to Population Geography.* Englewood Cliffs, N.J.: Prentice-Hall, 1966.

ENVIRONMENT

Darling, F. Fraser, and John P. Milton, eds. *Future Environments of North America.* Garden City, N.Y.: Natural History Press, 1966.

Duhl, Leonard J., ed. *The Urban Condition: People and Policy in the Metropolis.* New York: Basic Books, 1963.

Fein, Leonard J. "Toward the Plural City," *Technology Review,* Vol. 68 (June 1966), pp. 34–41, 57–58.

Goodman, Paul and Percival. *Communitas.* 2nd ed. rev., New York: Vintage Books, 1960.

Gottmann, Jean. *Megalopolis.* New York: The Twentieth Century Fund, 1961.

Herfindahl, Orris Clemens, and Allen V. Kneese. *Quality of the Environment: An Economic Approach to Some Problems in Using Land, Water, and Air.* Baltimore: Johns Hopkins Press for Resources for the Future, 1965.

Jarrett, Henry, ed. *Environmental Quality in a Growing Economy.* Baltimore: Johns Hopkins Press for Resources for the Future, 1966.

Jennings, Burgess E., and John E. Murphy, eds. *Interactions of Man and His Environment.* New York: Plenum Press, 1966.

Jouvenel, Bertrand de. *Efficiency and Amenity* (40th Earl Grey Memorial Lecture). Newcastle upon Tyne, England: King's College, 1960.

——. "A Better Life in an Affluent Society," *Diogenes*, No. 33 (Spring 1961), pp. 50–74.

Kates, R. W., and J. F. Wohlwill, eds. "Man's Response to the Physical Environment," a special number of *Journal of Social Issues*, Vol. XXII, No. 4 (October 1966).

Lee, Reverend Robert, ed. *Cities and Churches: Readings on the Urban Church*. Philadelphia: Westminster Press, 1962.

McHale, John, ed. "2000+," a special issue of *Architectural Design*, Vol. 37, No. 2 (February 1967).

Progressive Architecture, Editors of. A special issue, "Toward the Third Millennium," Vol. XLVII, No. 12 (December 1966).

Ragon, Michel. *Les cités de l'avenir*. Paris: Éditions Planète, 1965.

Reich, Charles A. *Bureaucracy and the Forests*. Santa Barbara, Calif.: Center for the Study of Democratic Institutions, 1962.

Rodwin, Lloyd, and Kevin Lynch, eds. "The Future Metropolis," a special issue of *Daedalus*, Vol. XC, No. 1 (Winter 1961).

Roslansky, John D., ed. *The Control of Environment*. Amsterdam: North Holland, 1967.

Thomas, Jr., William L., ed. *Man's Role in Changing the Face of the Earth*. Chicago: University of Chicago Press, 1956.

Vienna. Klubseminar der Architekturstudenten. "Urban Fiction: Leitbilder für die Stadt der Zukunft," *Klub 6*, 1967.

Weissbourd, Bernard. *Segregation, Subsidies, and Megalopolis*. Santa Barbara, Calif.: Center for the Study of Democratic Institutions, 1964.

Wingo, Jr., Lowdon, ed. *Cities and Space. The Future Use of Urban Land*. Baltimore: Johns Hopkins Press for Resources for the Future, 1963.

Wise, Harold F., ed. *America's Private Construction Industry and the Future American City*. Los Angeles, Calif.: American Cement Corporation, 1966.

Wood, Robert C. "Changes in Living," in *Conference on the Environment of Change*. New York: Time Inc., 1964, pp. 49–56.

PLANNING TECHNIQUES AND THEORY

Adelson, Marvin. "On a Future for Planning." Mimeographed. Santa Monica, Calif.: System Development Corporation (March 1965).

Bauer, Raymond A., ed. *Social Indicators*. Cambridge, Mass.: M.I.T. Press, 1966.

Bennis, Warren G. *Changing Organizations*. New York: McGraw-Hill, 1966.

Boulding, Kenneth E. *The Image; Knowledge in Life and Society.* Ann Arbor, Mich.: University of Michigan Press, 1956.

———. *Conflict and Defense; a General Theory.* New York: Harper, 1962.

———, and W. Allen Spivey. *Linear Programming and Theory of the Firm.* New York: Macmillan, 1960.

Branch, Melville C. *Planning: Aspects and Applications.* New York: Wiley, 1966.

Davidoff, Paul. "Advocacy and Pluralism in Planning," *Journal of the American Institute of Planners,* Vol. XXXI, No. 4 (November 1965), pp. 331–338.

Etzioni, Amitai. *Modern Organizations.* Englewood Cliffs, N.J.: Prentice-Hall, 1964.

———. *Social Change: Sources, Patterns and Consequences.* New York: Basic Books, 1964.

Feyerabend, Paul K. *Knowledge Without Foundations.* Oberlin, Ohio: Oberlin College, 1961.

Kecskemeti, Paul. *Meaning, Communication, and Value.* Chicago: University of Chicago Press, 1952.

Lindblom, Charles. *The Intelligence of Democracy; Decision Making Through Mutual Adjustment.* New York: Free Press, 1965.

Massé, P. *Le plan ou l'anti hasard.* Collection "Idées." Paris: Gallimard, 1965.

Mazlish, Bruce, ed. *The Railroad and the Space Program: An Exploration in Historical Analogy.* Cambridge, Mass.: M.I.T. Press, 1966.

Meier, Richard L. *Communications Theory of Urban Growth.* Cambridge, Mass.: M.I.T. Press, 1962.

———. *Developmental Planning.* New York: McGraw-Hill, 1965.

Miller, George A., Eugene Galanter, and Karl H. Pribram. *Plans and the Structure of Behavior.* New York: Holt, 1960.

Parsons, Talcott. *Structure and Process in Modern Societies.* Glencoe, Ill.: Free Press, 1960.

Skinner, B. F. "The Design of Cultures," *Daedalus,* Vol. XC, No. 3 (Summer 1961), pp. 534–546.

Wartofsky, Marx. *Conceptual Foundations of Scientific Thought.* New York: Macmillan, 1967.

Wheeler, Harvey. *The Restoration of Politics.* Santa Barbara, Calif.: Center for the Study of Democratic Institutions, 1965.

Index